AUTOBIOGRAPHY
&
SURVIVAL
OF A
LOOSE CANNON

JOHN EWING COOK

Published by Honeybee Books
www.honeybeebooks.co.uk

Printed in the UK using paper from sustainable sources

ISBN: 978-1-913675-35-6

DISCLAIMER

The stories in this book reflect the Author's recollection of events. Some names, locations and identifying characters have been changed to protect the privacy of those depicted. Dialogue has been recreated from memory.

FOREWORD

I made my life interesting, partly due to the evil drink
to the people who have been,
who were and still are with me,
which brought out more than one persona

Having said that ......

If you have a strong belief, don't waste your time trying to convince others.
Laugh a lot, find humour in every situation.
Don't worry what others say; even less what they think about you.
Take pride in yourself and what you've achieved.
You have a history, memories and a life lived.
There is still much to do and write.

Remember, life is too short to drink bad wine!

Dedication

*Thanks to my wife for all the hard work and assistance,
long hours by my side to bring this to print.*

*To my publisher Chella at Honeybee Books for her professional
guidance.*

CHAPTER 1

*Born in an area Braveheart frequented, brought up in a village with
records going back to 1220, with Presbyterians and Covenanters,
Weavers, Coal mining, 4000 people, 4 churches,
10 pubs and a close family in the village.*

I was born on the 17th of August 1946 at Lanark Hospital in the county
of Lanarkshire, Scotland and lived in the small village of Stonehouse
until I left for South Africa at the age of 21. I think I must start with
details of my family to get the ball rolling.

My mum was Prudence Hatley Cook (nee Cowper), born 1916. The
only daughter of Janet Williamson Cowper who also had two sons, Gavin
and James Cowper. My gran came from Carlisle, England. I never met
my grandpa. My mum worked at the Stonehouse Hospital in the village
as a telephonist - she mainly worked in the evenings where she was able
to earn double-time and thus more take-home pay.

Prudy was always immaculate, well dressed and a popular figure at the
hospital. She was a happy go lucky person and used to read the teacups
and became resident fortune teller. She was well-liked in the village and
loved a good blether. I take after my mum in that sense.

My mum loved to find bargains in the shops and her cupboards were
jam-packed with handbags, shoes and clothes. Her hair was Jet black
throughout her life, dyed and permed in later life by my dad, who had
the patience of Job.

Prudence was not a great cook but we managed one way or another,
with my dad stepping in on major meals when needed and as kids, we did
breakfasts of toast or boiled eggs which were easy-peasy before school.

My sister and I were cloned accordingly and looked smart, especially
when I went to the Life Boys, Boys' Brigade, Sunday school when the
parting (shed in Scots) in my hair was neat, my shoes and dress belt
polished. Inspections were carried out before I went out the house.

Thanks to my mum's absence due to her working hours, at a young age, I learnt to wash the dishes, hoover the carpets, make the coal fire, iron my shirts, press my suits - using a wet handkerchief, hang the washing, polishing and mending my shoes, adding tacks on the heels to avoid wear and tear taking place, when need be.

My mum's biggest let down was her addiction for cigarettes and she became a chain smoker. In other words, before finishing one cigarette, she had another lit in her other hand. I named her Fag Ash Lil. To be honest she hardly inhaled, was more of a puffer. Green stamps, from the purchase of cigarettes were the order of the day. Once the special books were full, they were used to purchase this and that from the gifts available when one reached a certain limit of stamps collected. With the money spent on fags over the decades she could have really treated herself to other goodies rather than damaging her lungs.

I recall her using protein slimming powders, the in thing in the 50's and 60's, to control her weight. She was slim and trim. Some of these brand names are still around to this day.

I got on well with my mum even although she nagged me from time to time. We disagreed on the great Cassius Clay/Muhammad Ali. She thought he over did his showmanship and she could not stand his antics especially his loud mouth but he kept on winning with a talent second to none. I was a great boxing fan and watched BBC TV Grandstand when boxing was shown, especially the American coverage.

When my parents visited South Africa (SA) to see the grandkids, later on, my mum had dizzy spells and she overcame this by carrying miniature whisky bottles in her large hand bags. Whatever time of the day we would stop at a cafe, order a soda and quietly empty her medicine into her glass. Great move mum and later I also started to get dizzy spells!!! especially on the train journey from Johannesburg to Cape Town and needed medicine.

I recall when I was at a Casino in SA and sat next to a lady, with a large handbag, who had the same problem. I was duly offered a taster as we pulled on the one-armed bandits and a jolly time was had.

When I left for SA in 1967 age 21, I never really questioned whether my parents missed me over the years. We exchanged letters to keep in touch and up to date but it was not the same as being nearby at home to celebrate this and that.

My Mum took out an Endowment Policy for my sister, Janice and myself at 1 penny per week from the date we were born. The man from the Prudential/Council visited every month to collect the rent and mark his collection book. The policy, I think, expired after 30 years and was never cashed in by me. Only on 20 November 2009 did the Prudential contact me from the UK to cash in the policy, it was around £500 pounds. I kept the policy document dated in 1946 and wanted to frame it [note to kids - it's on the memory stick]. That was great foresight on behalf of my Mum.

My dad, Robert James Steel Walker Cook, was born in 1917. His family lived in Millar Street, Larkhall, a twenty-minute journey to Stonehouse. His dad was called John and his dad's dad also John. They both worked in the coal collieries. I remember Sunday visits and the dress code for my dad's parents were Victorian and black. To pass the time, we played Hide the Thimble and I Spy.

My dad eventually worked for the Government in Social Services which I think suited him as a staunch Labour supporter. Keir Hardie, the founder of the Labour Party around 1880, was born half an hour's journey away and Scotland became a Labour stronghold for decades. It is supposed to be a secret when it comes to voting but later on in life, I think my mum was a Conservative. I found out that if my dad received a letter from the Labour party and it did not include his full initials, RJSW, he would write and complain. He was well educated and learned, but very reserved. Sat up late at night to watch the Political Party broadcasts on TV and mumbled away on the views given by all and sundry. There was a violin in the house which he played in his youth, However, I never heard him play the violin.

My dad never swore. He had the patience of Job as he was dedicated in getting me through my early education, he spent hours with me and my homework. I needed picture stories most of the time, but at the end I got my 9 'O' Levels. The 11 Plus was a nightmare but that is another story for later.

Public transport was a way of life but eventually my dad purchased a second-hand car and his brother Jack assisted with the maintenance and servicing. It was an Austin Cambridge. However, he had no patience when it came to me learning to drive. Although we used the country roads, I had a tendency of crunching the gears and keeping a straight line was poor. It was nerve racking so I ended up getting my mate, David Jones, to teach me. I found that voice instruction was best, I just followed my mate's one, two, three etc. Passed my driver's test second time round. I failed the first time by not parking close enough to the kerb when I completed my driving test. My sister passed her test first time.

My dad was a good golfer and played at Strathaven Golf Club, a twenty-minute drive away, eventually ending up as Captain of the club. He taught me the game as a youngster and I have never regretted this gift, which stood me in good stead for the rest of my life. A blessing of note which I will cover later.

My parents were careful with money. We received pocket money and that was that, never any extras but later on they would send money in the post for Christmas gifts/birthdays to SA for the kid's year in year out. On return journeys from SA my dad would quietly place beer/spending money etc in my hand which always came in handy. Something I have inherited and do with my kids.

My dad was involved in a serious car accident and it was touch and go whilst he spent months in the Glasgow Royal Infirmary. Eventually, he came right. However, he was never the same and his golf deteriorated.

The odd time my dad got angry with me was when my sister and I had a tiff and she would turn on the water works. He would chase me round the dining room table with a wet dish towel and try and whip me but I flew upstairs to the bathroom and locked myself in until he cooled off.

My dad never really spoke about WW2 and when I asked him how he avoided being killed, he said he kept his head down. He was based in Egypt and once when he was at a beach with an armoured vehicle, the crew dropped the keys into the sand and seemingly it took hours to find them. I think he was in the Cameronian's Battalion. I should have looked for whatever medals he may have had but maybe my sister has these with all the photos of him in army uniform.

In 1956 he bought, in my name, Ernie Premium Bonds, 25 pounds worth that I still have. Alas not a baw bee won even to this day.

4

I respected my dad but did have the odd differences. My parents loved each other and had the occasional squabble, especially when he went up to the golf club, which was not too often. They used the club for lunches and high tea, which my mum enjoyed.

My parents always told me to stop picking my nose, especially when we visited the Public Park where the Park Keeper had huge nostrils. I was told that when the wind changed, while picking your nose, it could stay like that.

My sister, Janice Williamson Cook, is 2 years younger than me and her husband is Ian. They have two children, Alan and Lauren. They lived in the village all their lives in the council house which they eventually bought. They go to the same hotel in Spain, year in year out, for their summer holidays. I did try and get them to visit SA but their excuse was - the journey is too long. Sad they did not make the effort as a good time would have been had by all. Especially as the exchange rate then, the pound would have bought 10 Rand to 1 Pound. These days its 20+ Rand plus to the pound, a traveller's delight.

Janice was the cleverest of us two and attended Hamilton Academy and obtained a university degree. We did bicker and, later on in years, no speaky. Her daughter got married in America without any reception or photos for the parents at all. I told her that was not normal and she got upset. Anyway, I was always spoilt in her home with great food, chocolate biscuits etc, etc and Ian always had whisky and beers on hand. She did so much for her family making sure food was on the table and home-made lunches to take to work. She even shuffled the cars around every morning, in shit weather, for the men in her life when they could have done that. Guess who had to wash the dishes up every day - I thought that was wrong.

My parents stayed two doors away and Janice looked after them in their later years especially when my dad was on his own and needed home care. She would make meals for him and, when need be, deliver to him. Bought the messages [groceries] and was a god send to our parents. So dedicated and when our parents passed away, she had all the affairs to attend to which she did diligently.

Something has just come to mind. As youngsters we loved Nestle condensed milk and when we were treated, we would open the can, have our spoonful, then store it in the cupboard. The temptation was so great but we managed to control our want for sneaking a hidden spoonful when the other was not around. Somehow, we just knew the fair level and managed to stretch it out over the week.

When Janice started dating, she was asked out by this guy who loaded the crates of cold drinks/iron bru on and off a delivery truck. Don't know how she met him but I think he gave her a dizzy [not turning up for a date] and that was the end of that. She then met Ian, they knew each other from High School and that was forever. On a Saturday night when I returned by bus from the dancing in Hamilton at the Trocadero, I used to see Ian's dad's car parked in the cul de sac where we stayed. They were winching [kanoolding] and the car windows were always steamed up. So, I would bang on the roof of the vehicle disturbing them of course. Tee Hee

Let's talk about my gran - Janet Williamson Cowper originally from Carlisle, England. She ran the village Post Office in Stonehouse, a sweet shop, postal deliveries and telephone exchange. You know the one with the pull-out lines with head and mouth pieces, which had to be wound up before making calls. This was situated right in the middle of the village at the Cross next to the Town Hall. It was an old stone-built building with living quarters at the rear and on the first floor. It was a big place.

In the grounds was a wheel barrow, with big wheels, used to take mail to and from the station. It was stored in the back next to a large hut where the postmen stored their red post office bikes for delivering post in the village. It was a busy place.

With my mum doing lots of nightshift, I stayed on occasions with my gran and slept in an alcove bed. A stone water bottle was provided for my feet and I remember sitting on a potty in front of the coal fire as a bairn. Sometimes I toasted a slice of bread on a wire fork in front of the open coal fire, which was common practice.

My gran was a real lady, Victorian in dress, but had a bad hip and had to hobble around best she could. That bad hip problem was handed down to Karin, my daughter. I have had hip problems as well with lots of chiropractors through the decades. Eventually running the place was too much and she handed over the reins to her one son, my uncle, James Cowper, a dapper man as you could get.

My gran bought a crofter's type cottage in Camnethan Street, the straw roof having been replaced with slate. Then, during school lunch times, I used to go for my soup. She now and again gave me a sixpence. Her garden at the back of the house always needed attention and I helped to pull out the weeds, even although I hated it.

My gran had a visitor, Aunty Jean, who called occasionally and I remember how she drank her tea. The hot tea would be poured into the saucer and she would blow on it then slurp it up. This was common practice in these days and it worked.

My gran told me about her neighbour two doors away who was one of the doctors to the Tsar family in Russia before their demise.

I wish I could remember more of what we talked about. I have a family photo somewhere where she sat proudly in the middle.

On my travels back from SA I used to walk to the old graveyard and find her gravestone after a long search; graveyards are like that. I need to find out the history of her husband whom I can't remember other than from a single photo of him with his Jack Russell called Peter. I think the name Ewing, my middle name, came from him.

My cousin James has produced a detailed family tree that he promised to send me and must chase him for more this, to add as an addendum to this book. A note for my kids - if I get run over by the big red bus please contact James Cowper, get details and update the history of the Cooks etc.

My Uncle James Cowper was a clever man and worked long hours in running the Post Office when he took it over from his mother. He only bought the best in clothing and was always immaculate. He gelled his hair back and washed his eyes out every morning with a special eye glass. He would spend time in his bathroom grooming himself.

I used to help in little ways in the post office, i.e., counting money, licking and sticking stamps on post or sorting mail into their pigeon holes. Helped with the mail bags that had to be sealed with a special clamping device. I loaded mail bags onto a wheel barrow. I hung the mail bags onto rungs ready for sorting. I played hide and seek in the hanging mail bags. I would wander around the shop side and eye the sweets eventually winning my uncle over. "Ok", he said, "have some sweets". Toblerone was a favourite, Frys Cream, Chocolate buttons etc. I was spoiled.

Uncle James used to walk his two dogs, beagles who had a hound dog bark, every evening with his wife Netta with the dogs pulling them along. My uncle and aunt went on a cruise on the Queen Elizabeth as a treat. The minister, Rev Alexander Gemmel, visited now and again and they quietly had stinky drinkies, sherry I should imagine. They updated each other on the village gossip up in the drawing room.

Sadly, when I was in SA my Uncle James died of a heart attack at the age of 54. My Aunt Netta had to take over the reins as best possible and when I visited her, she asked if I would like Uncle Jame's shoes. We wore the same size and the pair offered were special leather ones in a tan colour that I wore for years in SA. Also, I received his nail clippers, open type shaver and hair brushes which I have to this day; they were in a new condition. The clippers/shaver are gold plated and made in America.

Aunt Netta was a cheery person and we got on very well. At the times I stayed at the Post Office I used to go over most mornings to fetch the newly baked bread rolls from the bakers across the road for the postmen and staff. The rolls like those are not made any more and with lashings of pure butter and/or strawberry jam, it just melted in the mouth. Don't forget the egg and bacon rolls she made. Can't beat straight out the oven stuff.

Also, my aunt bought strawberry tarts, pineapple cakes, French cakes, chocolate éclairs, snowballs, jam tarts and all sorts of biscuits. She tried to hide them from me, knowing my sweet tooth had the better of me and I had no control. No wonder Scotland had one of the highest tooth decay records in Britain due to cakes and sweets. I guess it's the sugar. My mouth, at a young age, ended up looking like a lead mine inside from all the dental work which was done by Dr Boyd in Strathaven - Eish.

Aunt Netta's daughter, Catherine Ann, eventually became a post lady and her husband a postie. She took over my gran's home in Camnethan Street and is now retired. Her husband passed away.

On my trips back I visited my Aunt Netta at her new council house. Her legs gave her trouble but got around in her little car and was active in the village plus church work. A sprightly lady who always had cakes and biscuits ready when I called round to see her.

Her son James, my cousin, spent his working days with the Halifax Building Society amongst others and travelled all over Britain with his jobs which involved insurance. He is now retired and lives in South Queensferry near Edinburgh. Aunt Netta sent me a Christmas card every year to SA. I tried to get James to visit but no go. Anyway, I visited him when I moved to the UK in 2017 and hopefully will see more of him as he is an avid golfer and gets involved in a lot of golf matters, teaching, committee work etc. James, like his dad, enjoys the tasty things of life and through the years was referred to as Jim. He has been helpful to me since my return and when I travel, he provides me with information on areas and golf courses. Looking forward to a game of golf with him after recovering from breaking an ankle last year whilst on a golf course. His wife Margaret is not well at the moment and getting various scans etc to trace what is making her feel unwell. Hopefully all will come right. She caught Covid quite seriously but was fortunate to recover after being hospitalised and placed on a ventilator.

My mum's other brother, uncle Gavin Cowper, was a real character. He also stayed round the corner in the housing scheme with his wife Nancy and son Gavin Jnr. Uncle Gavin was a newspaper reporter with the Glasgow Herald all his life besides writing for local village papers in his retirement. Seemingly he was top notch. Took me to an old pub in Glasgow near to where he worked. I remember the art deco interior, especially the green tiles. He also took me to The Burrell Collection in Glasgow. Burrell was a wealthy sea merchant when the port of Glasgow was bustling around 1900. He brought in objects from over the world which eventually ended up in museums. Due to the volume they had to change the valuable items every 3 days. That day we caught a bus to Glasgow and my uncle was chaffing all the ladies. He had a brilliant sense of humour and he was not shy. Enjoyed an occasional whisky.

Every year at his council house home, he bought fireworks for Guy Fox and had a bonfire. He had a corner unit and always varied boxes of fireworks to let off. He was also a very clever man, serious at times with a good soul. Now that I think back, he was a loner and deep. Never owned a car. Nancy his wife was from Leicester and a great baker, so guess who visited her lots of times. She had a great laugh. Had a heart attack and ended up a vegetable so to speak, couldn't communicate. She spent her whole life in Stonehouse Hospital staring at the TV and nodding her head and mainly bedridden. He visited her every day but it was like talking to a brick wall.

At the age of 19 my cousin Gavin Jnr, Uncle Gavin's only child fell ill. For years we kicked ball together and were fairly close. The doctor sent him to Glasgow Royal Infirmary for tests. At one visit he was standing in the waiting room, still unaware of what was wrong with him, when a doctor walked up and said "are you the young man who has leukaemia"? Ignorant that he was Gavin said no, but the penny dropped. What a way to find out about your sickness. Treatment could not save him and he passed away at the age of 23. Maybe this was the cause of his mum's heart attack later.

With these happenings my uncle Gavin changed in his later years and ended up taking trips to Spain/Portugal, meeting people, having a joll [great time]. Decades later he passed away in his home and no Will could be found. Paperwork was discovered showing that he had spent all his money on timeshare resorts in Spain/Portugal. Used these to enjoy life I guess with his fancy ladies as he really was on his own at that stage of his life. Good on him as there was nobody left in his life. I once had to catch a bus on a trip back from SA, from Hamilton to London and I got my times mixed up. The more he asked me to check the more I insisted the bus left at a certain time. I cocked it up and he laughed his head off and would not let me forget. My fault, it was in the days when one changed to so many hundred hours, you know what I mean – the metric system.

Well, that was pretty straightlaced.
Lucky to have a close family, good people.

CHAPTER 2

Wonder what's down the line for me,
as a young lad, in a staid, small village life?

The village of Stonehouse had about 4000 residents living in the old village and the new council houses that were erected around 1930. Four beautiful old churches and seven or eight pubs.

The Town Hall, where I attended the first gathering of the Life Boys, was next to Uncle James' Post Office. There were grocers where the cheese was cut by wire from a huge block 2 feet high, a bakery and a small hotel. In addition, the Black Bull Inn had a little garage. There was a doctor's surgery as well. These were all in an area called the Cross and it was in the middle of the village. Most of the other amenities mentioned above or below were a stone's throw away or a 5-minute walk.

Sweety shops, fish and chip place and betting shop where I placed bets on the Grand National Steeple Chase at Aintree, Liverpool every year. This race gave unbelievable odds even to this day and a sixpence on any outsider was good news.

The Cinema complex was decorated inside from the left overs of a cruise liner. Saturday morning shows consisted of episodes of Superman, Abbot and Costello, The Three Stooges, The Banana Bunch, Cowboy shows galore and biblical epics of note. Search on YouTube for footage of Abbot/Costello, The Three Stooges, Banana Bunch all black and white films, in the fifties. The Primary school would take us to see Treasure Island, Jane Eyre, Hounds of the Baskervilles, Hunchback of Notre Dame, Mutiny on the Bounty, etc. We always stood for the National Anthem, with Mantovani's orchestra playing during the interval when ice creams, sweets and monkey nuts were on sale. Big red curtains would seal off the screen. We would sneak in cinnamon sticks and pretend to smoke these, also packets of barley that we would blow through small glass pipes [like a peashooter] into the audience when the lights were off and main feature showing. Naughty boys.

A main stream bus service, number 54 red double decker that passed through every half hour from Strathaven, Stonehouse, Larkhall, Hamilton and eventually reaching Glasgow Central Bus Station after about 2 hours then returning along the same route. As a lad, no one had a vehicle other than the local doctor and a few business men.

My first primary school was in Camnethan Street; an old stone-built turn of the century, 1900's structure. The Council built a new and larger primary school that managed the flow from the village.

Stonehouse Violet football pitch was established near the Gas Works at the bottom of the village, the ground catered for the annual cattle show and for when the Fair arrived each year.

We had a main hospital where my mum Prudence was on duty as a telephonist doing night shifts, a 2-minute walk from home. I delivered newspapers when I was a paper boy racing through the Hospital corridors which had a maze layout.

Ginestres, an Italian, set up a cafe and also made ice cream and sold in their numerous ice cream vans that toured the village and surrounds. Their product was good and played the usual tunes to let you know when arriving in one's area in the housing schemes.

We had a mobile fish & chip bus with fryers on board that toured around, especially on Fridays.

A rag and bone man came around, with horse and cart, exchanging cups, saucers etc for old clothes plus coal delivery lorries, where men would unload bags of coal from their shoulders into each person's coal bunker at your council house, out the back door. This was ongoing as everyone had coal burning fires for warmth and to heat your boiler/bathwater.

The largest employer of labour was the building contractors called Wilsons that had a very large fleet of old double Decker buses yellow/maroon in colour that took their staff to the various building sites. Most youngsters, when they left school, ended up being brick layers, joiners, plumbers, labourers at Wilsons for life. Maybe I should have gone that route in life and once I had learnt my trade made tax free money for my efforts on the side. Never have I come across a poor plumber. The village centre was smog-like in the mornings, particularly in winter when the buses left at sparrow fart spewing out exhaust fumes.

The Council had a public billiard hall with 6 large Joe Davies slate and green felt tables. I used to collect and set the balls up for the big boys, hard men, teddy boys and do the scoring on the board on the walls. Maybe I should have practiced more at the game and ended up being like Ian Hendry who became very wealthy and World Champion many times at the game.

There was a Police Station and a public bowling green, which the older men used to frequent as a drinking hole but one had to be a member. It was only open during the summer months. It's still there.

In that era, the railway station had one of the highest railway viaducts in Britain, over the local Avon River. Used on occasions to visit Hamilton and get home from the dancing in Glasgow when I was older, 18/19. As a paper boy for many years, I had to collect the newspapers, morning and night, for deliveries from Billy Hunter's Tobacconist shop at the Cross to do my paper round.

Pity that the Beecham/Government closed the line and removed the rails and steel arches from the viaduct over the Avon gorge. What a mistake, as many lines could be opened up today to alleviate the congestions on the roads.

One of the great things the British Empire did was to create Public Parks throughout their Empire, besides the thousands built in most British towns and villages.

Stonehouse had a very large public park with a bandstand where the Salvation Army played now and again, swings/roundabouts/maypole, water fountain/well with drinking facilities from a chained cast iron drinking cup.

It had one of the longest chutes in Britain, but eventually shortened, as it was dangerous. There was a big boating pond, a boat house for the paddle boats for hire and 2 clay tennis courts. There were beautiful gardens, maintained by the council.

Lovely path ways for walks in the summer, the snowy, hilly slopes were used to sledge down during the winter, a large fir tree forest to play hide and seek, was very spooky, at the bottom of the park where the river Avon passed. This was very special and the Council still maintains this but a few things have disappeared as kids today are not appreciative and have found other amenities to keep them occupied. Faces in their phones all day!

Underneath the rail viaduct we also had a scramble car racing and motor bike circuit over the slag remains of an old coal mine. Sadly, all gone now.

There was a newsagent's shop from where I delivered papers from for many years and a Scout and Girl-Guides' hall near the station. A church hall was erected for the Boys Brigade in the church grounds of St Ninians and used for weekly drill, badminton, gym, parades, indoor soccer and had a stage for church concerts.

Stonehouse was in the coal belt that ran west to east across Scotland but all were eventually shut down. Before that the town had many crofters, as seen by the old one storey cottages splattered throughout the village, which all now have been renovated inside and straw roofs replaced with slate.

Let's not forget the surrounding farms where there were traces of a Roman road nearby but, I never got to see it.

The hub of the village was the Cross but through the decades most things change and disappear or get closed down and you are only left with the memories. However, some caring village elders/members/locals/parishioners, produced booklets with old photos of the village and a history which one can Google and read about. Give it a look see and remember there are two Stonehouse places in Britain, it's the Scottish one you are after. Aye

*Just shows how Britain developed with thousands of villages along the
same lines, all at some time self dependant.
What more could a poor boy really ask for, the village had it all.
As we see today most places are in a state of decline and it's sad to see.
Wonder what the outcome will be.*

CHAPTER 3

The good life, la dolce vita, a childhood one cannot replace.

My childhood in 2 Glen View Stonehouse. Well, there was no view of any glen in the housing scheme but we did have a corner unit with a bit more ground to weed, lawn area at rear where washing line was, coal bunker, little hut for bikes, garden stuff and over the wired fence all the other neighbours who would converse for all to hear. There was a wee lawn garden at the front. Not bad at all. Funny most of my homes in SA were on a corner stand.

My parents kept the home in good nick which had 3 bedrooms, bath-room, kitchen, living room, dining room and a sitting room where my mum kept all her nice furniture, a tallboy/glass cabinet where she col-lected all this and that. This room was never used much. My dad would wallpaper every now and then to appease my mum. The bedrooms and bathroom were upstairs.

The rooms were small and the only heating was the coal fire in the living room which heated the boiler. Bathing, in a white enamel bath that did not retain the heat, was on the basis of first come first served. A few inches of water used as the warm water in the boiler would soon go cold. A wooden coal container, outside the back door, was filled up by coal men who delivered sacks on a weekly basis, loaded onto their shoul-ders and emptied into the coal bunker. We were always lazy in keeping the fireplace stoked with coal as we cooried [gathered] around the fire, whose turn it was to fetch some more coal!

There were no telephones in those days. We had a side and back yard with lawn that I mowed with the manual mower and of course the weed-ing, which included turning the clay soil with a shovel, heavy work. My dad grew blackcurrant bushes, strawberries and pea pods. Every year he cooked his harvest and processed his jams and jellies through a cloth strainer in the kitchen which had linoleum floors. He used our pulley clothes line built into the ceiling. Every time it was lowered and raised my mum's black French poodle, Candy, would start yapping as the noise really irritated the dog. My dad would label his jars with the type of jams, jellies and each jar was dated. These were mostly dished out to family and neighbours. Magic stuff, especially when free.

We had a stool in the kitchen where we polished our shoes; fix the worn area on the soles/heels of our shoes with steel tacks, using the shoe anvil. Polished my leather football, team ball, made in Pakistan which eventually split around the stitching. Had to Dubin the ball and my football boots regularly, due to wet weather.

Christmas was special with the usual biscuits and a glass of milk left out for Father Christmas. Our tree was a real one and we enjoyed dressing it up. Our windows would be frosted up with all the various designs. Our presents were simple, long socks full of fruit, Rowntree's selection box of sweets, more sweets and if we were lucky, the present, we had asked Father Christmas for.

Through the years, I received a Meccano set, paint by numbers, Scalextric with figure eight track, train set with track, wind-up Porsche that went back and forth and opened its bonnet, a sailing boat with a tall mast, like a clipper and sailed it in the boating pond at the public park, Triang 3-wheel bicycle, Bagatelle, Compendium games which included snakes and ladders, tiddlywinks, draughts, dominoes, playing cards and of course Monopoly which we played constantly.

My hobbies as a youngster were to build/glue kits of ships and planes, The Mayflower, Golden Hind, Fokker biplane, supersonic jet and a scenic paint by numbers, which was framed.

On holiday collected sea shells, varnished these to bring out the colours, added a bit of colour using my mum's nail varnish. Built little ladies with wide dresses and made flower arrangements. These were put together with glue and all the little shells fitted in to make heads etc. Used to make for the church fete and many sat in my mum's glass cabinets as master pieces. Should have kept some when my parents passed away.

I won a painting competition at school. It showed the burial in Crimea of a British officer with soldiers in uniform of that era in attendance, lanterns showing the shadows etc.

When dinner was served there was no talking at the table nor opening one's mouth when eating food, with no food left, all had to be finished.

When TV arrived, it was switched off whilst eating.

I was not a great reader but enjoyed the Dandy and Beano comics, Kit Carson cowboys and Superman. As kids we collected and exchanged comics with each other. Also had a large collection of marbles and played on a double or quit basis at school and also exchanged these beautiful gems.

At Easter, we would wrap eggs with onion peels and then boil them. The egg shell would come out in all the colours of the rainbow. A tradition was to roll the eggs down the braes at the public park to see which egg rolled further than the others.

On radio I would listen to serials such as Flash Gordon in space and police stories. Later, I got my own transistor radio which I treasured and listened to the pirate radio station "Radio Caroline" broadcast from a ship off the shore of Britain with all the sixties music, which will never be repeated. One can still remember, hum and whistle, not like modern music.

We had a TV and it had a paper type screen, black and white of course. Programmes consisted of Hopalong Cassidy, Pancho and the Cisco Kid, Lone Ranger and Tonto, Sooty, Little Weed and the Flower Pot Men and lots of others I can't recall. It was a great draw card especially Wimbledon, Boxing and England versus Scotland football, Top of the Pops, Six Five Special. I loved seeing all the new groups and songs that came out.

During Wimbledon we would go outside into the street in the cul de sac, chalk out the tram lines, tie string from the lamppost to lamppost in place of a net and tried to imitate famous players such as Ken Rosewall and Manual Santana, who were some of my favourites. The Aussies and Americans dominated in those days but not of late.

In the housing scheme we had a play area with swings and roundabouts and an open field where the council cut the grass for us. Weather permitting, all the kids gathered to play football. Many kids arrived and we picked sides always trying to balance each side so it was evenly matched.

Being a kid has to be some of the greatest days of my life. At the post office, with a large garden and trees at the bottom where we re-enacted cowboys and Indians, plastic bows and arrows were used and we had cap rifles and revolvers that produced the real thing. Famous Indian chiefs such as Cochess, Sitting Bull, Geronimo and the cowboys Wild Bill Hickok, Wyatt Earp, Jesse James. The drama was there, got you! You are dead and the acting was Oscar worthy stuff.

We played war games in the rhubarb jungle down near the Avon River. The wild rhubarb stood head high, easy for hiding from the enemy and we tied grasses together to trip each other up. Those were the days.

In the housing scheme a block of small shops were built that saved us having to walk to the village. Murdoch's the grocers, tobacconist/ newsagent and Bertie the barber. He cut all your hair off, like the youngsters have done today, short back and sides. I hated going to him.

On Sundays my dad took my sister and me on hour long walks past various farms which was a ritual, weather permitting.

Played Peever (i.e. hopscotch - with an old boot polish tin) with the girls and skipping ropes out on the street. The roads were very quiet as there were not many cars around.

Tommy Atkinson, a plumber in the village had his van and a nice deep blue Jaguar. On Saturday mornings, as a lad, I used to accompany him on jobs, carrying and passing tools to him when needed. He would show me how he could drive his van with no hands; eventually I realized he was controlling the steering wheel with his legs/thigh. He was successful and when he built a new home, I helped him move sand, trusses etc on Saturdays. Tommy played golf and I was invited on some weekends to join him, John Wales and Roger Kennedy. We played Lanark Loch and Rosemont where he treated me to an Aberdeen Angus steak which was expensive. He always raced his car to do the ton, 100mph in the country side on route to a golf club, downhill of course. Unfortunately, Tommy was diagnosed with incurable cancer and was in a lot of pain. Eventually he committed suicide by cutting his wrists in his bath.

During the school Summer holidays we collected potatoes raked up by the farmers tractor and piled haystacks. Once after work at a farm, a school friend, Robert Roy had an old army motor bike and offered me a lift. At the bottom of the road, he skidded and I ended up with a bruised and scarred knee. Only once since did I ride on pillion, in Australia, on the back of a Ducati, that never got out of second gear on my instructions. Bass was the boyfriend of my daughter Karin at the time. Still in my bucket list to ride a bike, maybe a Lambretta/Vespa.

Also picked strawberries down on our knees squashing the old fruit in our path as we moved through the lanes. The farmer wanted us to pull weeds out at the same time but we battled with the Thistles. The farmer with his hands of teak would grab the plant at the bottom and extract the whole thing. "That's how it is done", he screeched! When we finished some boys would stuff strawberries up their jukes/jerseys but the farmer caught them every time and shoogled their clothes and the fruit fell out. A good learning curve for us all.

At school the conkers season came around and we all challenged each other with our seasoned chestnuts. We had laid them next to the fire where they dried out, getting as hard as concrete. At some stage your conker would be the champion, until a stronger one came along.

Leap frog was common in the play ground and the train of people got longer, scary but good fun. When winter came, we created long ice slides and had snowball fights not knowing when the next ice ball would hit you. It was very dangerous and we were disciplined by our headmaster.

We also had scarf fights where we would tie a knot in our scarves and went into battle swinging them at each other. If hit, it hurt.

At primary school I ended up being a door boy opening and closing the school doors after pupils had lined up after the bell before entering the school. The kids would come in on line into the cloakrooms and hang their coats on fixed hangers. At that time, I had a leather Biggles pilot helmet with a long strap. I used this to herd the pupils in occasionally whipping their bottoms to hurry them along. One day my strap went too high and hit this well-developed girl, Mary McInnis, across her chest. She reported me and I was called in by the headmaster on my first harassment charge and duly reprimanded.

At school we played lots of football, before school and at the breaks. We also played marbles in the flower beds that had tree in the centre. The ground under and around the tree was very hard and perfect for playing marbles on.

Around this time, I was egged on into a fight with Clive Reeves, a friend, in the flower park. He punched in a repeater mode and I ended up with a black eye, for all to see at the Friday meeting of the Boys Brigade. He was too good for me. Good lesson learnt and I avoided getting into fights in future.

In addition, a bunch of us in a nearby village, saw our art teacher and someone called his nickname out, guess who he saw first - me. At school the following week, he had me out in the classroom and gave me the strap up the wrists, 6 in a row that left my wrists sore and red.

What do you think? It was certainly a free and easy existence. Beats being on cell phones and the like of today's youth.

CHAPTER 4

The growing up years, Eye for the Lassies, Perfect Attendances, Sunday School, Paper Boy, Boys Brigade, Queen's Badge, Trip to Denmark.

Between 12 and 16 years of age I had a job, morning shift before school then four in the afternoon night shift, as a paper boy with Billy Hunter the newsagent/tobacconist in the village, 4 doors away from the Post Office. Sold Woodbine, Players Special, Gold Mild, Mills, pipes, loose tobacco, and Rizzo. Mr. Hunter had one leg, the other lost in a motor bike accident. Got around on his crutches, always well dressed with his bunnet [a hat] and smoked his pipe.

Pay was two and sixpence a week, half a crown, and I used to pile them on top of my wardrobe, eight of these equalled a pound, fairly decent money for a kid in those days.

I did not have a two wheeled bicycle let alone having ridden one. So, my dad must have agreed to purchase one for me and we headed off by train to Glasgow Central Station. From there we walked to The House of Frasers, fifth floor of this renown department store, and there it was, a blue Waverly butterfly handle bar -- was straight across, with 3 speed Sturmy Archer gear change on the handle bar so easy to change while my hands were in grip position---work it out, and well before the introduction of French Gears where you needed a degree to engage. Had to push the bike all the way to the Glasgow station and loaded into the Guard's van. The bike's rims and spokes were chromed and shinny and had a bicycle pump attached.

Later used to polish these wheels till they gleamed. Had to buy a dynamo type light that worked off the turn of the wheel, only problem was when I stopped the light went off. In no time I learned to ride my bike.

They were about 4 paper boys and we had two shifts. Before school and having to rise at 5, a ten-minute ride from the housing scheme to the shop then 5 minutes to the station to collect the papers that arrived in bundles tied together which one had to balance on the handle bars and take to the newsagent's shop for sorting. This was repeated after school at 5 in the afternoon come hell or high water. The dress code was, balaclava, jerseys, long canvas rain coat, warm gloves and wellies. Did not work on the weekend but it was hard work in shitty weather conditions especially in Winter. My route was around some of the old village, up to the 3 posh estate homes with long driveways, and when my light died in reaching their door, I had to rely on the moon many times to find the letter box. Besides that, there was a guy called Manual who had killed 5 people in the county, and every time I saw the headlines always was scared when I cycled to these 3 estate homes that he would jump out the bushes. Eventually he was caught after 6 months. Also delivered to patients at the Hospital and loved running my bike through the various corridors within the complex.

Used to look at the young ladies arriving at the bus stops going to work. The road was always clear but one morning, while I was doing my staring I slowly ran into the back of a parked car to my embarrassment. As they say keep your eyes on the road at all times. When I was 16 years of age, I was already a big boy and the other boys were a lot smaller and younger. Sometimes I felt out of place but I needed the money. It was not long before I started a real job at the age of 17.

In preparing this book many things flash into your mind from time to time. This morning it was some of the people I knew, played with, school mates, neighbours and friends that lived in the village. Merely going to list the names as they come to mind and briefly comment.

There was the man who visited our home to collect the rent, with his account's book that he would update each week. I think he also sold life cover, a man from the Pru---Prudential Assurance Co. Later in life when my Mum passed away out came this Endowment Policy that she paid a penny into every week for me and my sister. It amounted to 500 odd pounds decades later. I kept the policy document for sentimental value. Parents don't do that these days and it was so special to me.

Mrs. Duffy, the next-door neighbour, thought she lost her husband in the WW2 in Asia but he arrived home from a Japanese prison worse for wear years later.

In the cul de sac we had big Bobby Lindsay, a labourer for the village contractors, Wilsons. When I got threatened by the bigger boys, my mum decided to speak to Bobby and offered him a shilling as protection money on me. Bobby was a big brute. I cannot recall any instances but embarrassing for me. Bobby became a preacher, which shocked us all, but you could see the change. Bully for him.

Bert Fleming, also in the cul de sac was a senior leader in the Boys' Brigade which I joined. Around the corner, was Mr. Murdoch, the Captain of the Boys Brigade, but more of the Boys' Brigade later.

Then one particular lady was always looking out from behind her lace curtains to catch us accidentally kicking a ball into her small garden or creating any noise. As a kid she came over as scary and we always dreaded the ball going into her garden, considered the ball lost.

Out the back yard all the houses rear ends faced each other with washing lines for all to see. The mums used to blether when hanging up the washing and Mrs. Margaret McGowan was a loud lady but good soul.

Some neighbours you would not see for months on end and never spoke to anyone.

Across the road was a Catholic lad, George Murray but we never spoke to each other until we were teenagers when I bumped into him in a pub. Sad state of affairs the Protestant/ Catholic scenario.

The village was predominantly Protestant and the Scots had apartheid decades before South Africa but did not put it in writing. One would think with new generations things would change. They have done, but there is still that division with the Catholics and Protestants. Funny how Scotland always pointed fingers at South Africa.

School friend, Tom Smith, became a banker and got killed in a motor accident years later.

The MacGregor brothers played football all over the place in any green patch one could find. We had our field venues, merely put our jackets down as goal posts and would knock on doors to let the guys know there was a game on.

One of the Forsythe brothers who delivered papers with me and Tommy, became right back for Glasgow Rangers for many years until leg troubles brought his career to a halt. I visited his sister Margaret in 2019.

She married Sandy Baxter, a great golfer at their home in Strathaven. Tommy stayed nearby but was not available and recently passed away and Sandy as well.

Then there was the Teddy Boys, the Murdoch Brothers (not related to the Boys' Brigade Captain) and others. Dressed in their drain piped trousers, winkle picker shoes, and long black jackets. Hair Brylcreamed in that Elvis style. When you saw them walking down the street you moved to the other side well in advance and ensured you made no eye contact as the bully boys were always looking for trouble and were a lot older. They smoked and some carried flick knives.

At a young age I had an eye for the lassies although I was seriously shy and never really talked or associated with girls. One girl at Primary school ran around the school yelling out she loved me, what was a poor boy going to do, where to hide, she left for Aussie later in the term.

It was all in the mind of the beholder, Aileen Fleming was the prettiest, Jean Johnston was a chubby girl and cheerful, Rena Tedford, one of the older Wilson sisters had great legs and when I looked at school photos years later always wondered how the class turned out in life. It would be wonderful to have a reunion at the press of a button.

Then there was Gunner, a real head case that lived in Green Street in the old village. Remember going with a bunch of lads on the train to watch a football game. They initiated and picked on the younger boys, by hanging us out by our legs of the train window, which was the shutter type with a leather belt, whilst going over the viaduct. Very scary but it happened, no choice.

Let's move onto Sunday school, Boys' Brigade, Queen's Badge and trip to Denmark. My parents hardly went to church but only recently my cousin James mentioned that my dad had wanted to become a minister. One day I will need to delve into that with James. Something may have happened, causing him to change his mind.

Anyway, I always got perfect attendance certificates year in year out at school, Sunday school, bible class, Life Boys, Boys' Brigade and a library of books with each certificate. This carried on throughout life in my working career, where I never missed a day unless I was seriously ill. I was dedicated and besides, who wants to lie in bed when you have a cold etc, etc - boring.

St Ninian's Scottish Presbyterian Church of Scotland was the Kirk I attended. My Sunday school teacher, and there were many, Mrs Love was pretty and I used to get sweeties. At church the minister preached from the pulpit putting the fear of God into you, Ian Paisley style. Two ministers in my time, the Rev Patterson then Rev Gemmel, both served time in Africa preaching the gospel. After the church service we had bible class either in the church or the church hall. The church was large with beautiful stained-glass windows and with a grand organ. My Uncle Gavin donated a side window of glass in memory of his son Gavin who passed away at 23 with cancer.

My first panic attack happened when I was chosen as one of the wise men and had to recite the bit about baby Jesus being wrapped in swaddling clothes etc at the Christmas Day service. I'm afraid we did not get the exposure of having to stand in front of an audience as a youngster but these days the kids are trained from a young age. This nervousness/shyness/fear followed me all my life. But more about that later.

We had Sunday school bus trips, sometimes to Ayr, Rabbie Burns' country, on the coast where they had lovely large park areas next to the beach for us to play, kick ball, sit and eat our sandwiches. I had a serious problem with motion sickness, it was awful. On the double Decker buses I needed to stand on the bus platform and get exposed to the fresh air. Later on in SA I had the same problem when I ventured onto small boats. Within seconds my stomach heaved repeatedly until nothing was left inside.

Come Christmas we would do carol singing, in the cold or snow, at the large fir tree erected at the Cross in the village. An annual event. Even in these days our church was fairly empty with only the usual faithful attending. Being a small congregation, I suppose meeting afterwards for tea and cake was part of life in the village.

The Life Boys opened up in the Town Hall and was for the youngsters before joining the Boys' Brigade. Dark blue was the dress code with funny flat top hats. We learned various sailing knots and did basic drill work and marching. The usual certificates for this and that awarded.

The upgrade to the Boys Brigade came next and joined the bigger boys at the church hall. One could advance from Privates to Sergeants. I think I eventually became a Lance Corporal with a band on my arm with 2 stripes.

I sat all the various exams and received little medals that you pinned to your jacket. This for first aid, drill work, even visited fire stations and learned fire drill, Indian Bar Bells, Flags/Semaphore. Physical training and marching kept us active especially forming pyramids with us all on top of each other. We had mats below for our falls. Indian bar bells were something different and we had to swing these to routines. Formed teams and did various sprint races against each other. Morse code was taught and signalling with flags/Semaphore. Being au fait with these, counted towards year end awards. Marching in formations with our special flag had to be spot on and inspection of our dress code, polished shoes, our brass belt, and our general appearance. We had a change room to get into our P T outfits, white tops with black drill shorts.

The cream de la cream at the finish of the evening, Friday nights, was to play fitba/small ball in the hall. Jimmy Anderson, a senior, really encouraged us all. He became a legend in the village and did marathon running late into his life and was spotted in the village come rain or shine.

On Remembrance Day every year the Pipe Band would lead a march to the Old Cemetery about 45 minutes away, where the minister held a service in commemoration for the dead in both world wars. The Scouts and Boys' Brigade took turns each year to lead the march behind the Pipers with the Girls Guides, Brownies, public in tow.

The Scouts would wear kilts and marched slowly and when it was our turn we marched briskly like soldiers. In the cold weather marching was much better. As you can imagine the service was very eerie and one could hear a pin drop in the silence. Very gripping.

The Brigade decided to go on a trip to a camp in Denmark financed in the main by our parents. It was not cheap and I'm sure all our parents battled to put money together. However, the Boys decided to collect scrap metal, and this all got stored at old stables at the Minister's Manse. This went on for months but money was raised. It was exciting riding around on the back of trucks loading this and that which had been scouted then storing at the Manse sheds.

We went to a place in Denmark on the coast called Helsingborg. We were in camp huts and one day we were going on a day trip by sea across to Sweden, the port was just half an hour away. I remember we left a large box of sandwiches on the departure quay and decided to return and yes there it was where we had left it. A slight hiccup but honest people in the world.

A day trip was arranged to visit the Carlsberg Brewery and after a walk around were treated to drinks. The older boys got stuck into the beers but we youngsters had to stick to lemonades. How things changed in later life and today a pint of Carlsberg Lager is a favourite. A strong beer especially Carlsberg Special.

Back at base we all went out one day to visit the shops in the local town and came across an ironmonger who had on display a large collection, assortment of hand knives including flick knives. After a look-see some of the bigger boys suggested we go back into the shop and crowd round the display tray, then try and distract the shopkeeper and grab a knife and run like Billy goat. This happened and was so wrong. When we all got back to camp, I had a terrible guilt feeling and approached the staff sergeant and mentioned what I had done and wanted to return the knife. Well to my dismay he said don't worry about it, if you don't want it, I will take it. I could do nothing but the guilt complex stuck to me like shit to a blanket. I had learned a lesson in life and I did go back to the shopkeeper and returned the knife.

We also visited the Gardens of Tivoli and stood on the rock of the little mermaid in the harbour, the famous landmark.

Later at the Boys' Brigade I was awarded the Queen's Badge and still have it. This is similar to the Duke of Edinburgh's award but on a smaller scale. Nice to have accomplished this feat.

My memory at 75 is fairly good - just can't remember the Great War.

CHAPTER 5

With the easy life coming to an end and school exams down the track,
The dreaded the 11 Plus, My Mum/Dad came to the rescue, it was a
battle, I needed picture stories and long hours to get through it all.
I was as shy as can be with no confidence
but managed to change my name!!

Schooling was an uphill battle for me. My first primary school was around the age of 7 at an old school building, circa 1800 in Camnethan Street, Stonehouse. I have the school photo of the class at the time. Then moved to a new school in Sidehead Road, hospital-white in colour, with large grounds, outside toilets, weather shelters, canteen and room for fitba. The classrooms were in single desk formation and the dumbest sat at the front of the class. After tests we were shuffled around accordingly. Subjects were english, maths, algebra, physics, history, geography, technical drawing, woodworking, physical fitness and art. I was above the average of 50 in most subjects but with english I just managed to get over 50 marks, it was always close. My dad sat many nights to assist with my learning. I needed picture stories and repetition of note. It was a slog but I persevered.

Then the Education Dept in Britain decided to introduce the '11 Plus' exam. To pass would mean you went to a Senior Secondary School but to fail, you ended up in a Junior Secondary School which in essence taught you manual jobs, such as woodwork, metalwork and such like. The trouble with the '11 Plus' was it was unrehearsed. The school kids had no exposure or were taught the philosophy behind it. In the test one had 200 odd questions to answer in a limited time period. *If A = Z, X = J what does R = ?* You get my drift, so many equations that made your mind boggle and panic set in. It would have helped if the teachers had given us sample tests before the main exam, but it didn't happen.

I failed and my parents were very disappointed but I got another chance the next year and failed again. My parents were determined that I go to the higher Senior Secondary school and arranged an appointment with the Head of Education in the county of Lanarkshire. Somehow, they managed to get me in but I had to prove myself at the new school and did very well and progressed. However, I lost 2 years as a result of the resits of the '11' plus exams and being placed in a class with pupils who were 2 years younger than me.

This was embarrassing for me but I slogged on and years later when I sat the final 'O' Level exams, which was a must, I passed 9 out of 9 subjects to everyone's delight. It did show some sort of flaw in the '11 Plus' qualification process but dumbo made it. Next stage was to apply for university but I told my parents it would be a mountain too high and after what I had previously gone through, the hours of learning, 2 years lost in transit, it was time to find a job. My sister went through it all with flying colours and got a degree at Strathclyde University. Now that I think back maybe if I had gone the Junior Secondary route, learned a trade working with my hands I would have done alright. These days plumbers and tradesmen make a fortune the world over, so choices in life are so important.

Need to butt in here on something very important. At birth my dad registered me as John Ewing Cook even after my mum had insisted my first name should be Ewing, must have been long standing name somewhere in the family tree. Anyway, I was known as Ewing, pity it was not spelled Euan, Ewan etc as the pronunciation of Ewing is something else. Try it. I have never met anyone in life with first named spelled Ewing, as a surname fine. As a young lad I was called Cookie, no problem, but one day, while I was playing fitba in the park near the housing scheme with the other boys, my mum stood on the back steps and called loudly ---"Ewing, your supper is ready". Well, all the boys stopped in their tracks and looked around with one boy saying quote, "who the fuck is Ewing!!". That was it, and going to the new Secondary school I used my first name John forever and anon as there were a lot of hard boys and I would have been ridiculed and mocked. Guys later used to come to our home, knock on the door and ask for John, and my mum would say "no one by that name stays here". To this day my family still refer to me as Ewing.

Finding a job was not easy with hundreds of people applying say for 10 vacancies or less, most of the applicants with University Degrees to back them up. I wanted to be a draughtsman, and on one occasion the employer's canteen was full 3 days in a row for 13 jobs online.

Everywhere you tried, it was the same story and if you were not highly qualified you stood no chance. Scotland at that time had a shortage of jobs and unemployment was rampant. What comes to mind is ending up being a street cleaner, a coalman etc. Anyway, out of the blue one of my dad's friends, Solly McNiven, there's a good Jewish name, mentioned that there was a clerk's job at the Eagle Star Insurance Co Ltd in Cadzow Street in Hamilton, half an hour's journey by bus. I applied and started work at 17 years of age.

As a very shy person and a country bumpkin, I met my first nemesis - the telephone. 5 people worked in the office with 3 of us in the general office. When the phone rang, I left it but eventually I had to talk to people and build up some sort of confidence. As a youngster when I went to my dad's office Christmas parties, I used to hide under a desk in the nearest dark office until the party was over. I had a serious problem talking to people, looking at them in their face. I was unable to look them in the eye and tended to talk with my head down. That stayed with me for a long time, until the evil drink gave me Dutch courage.

Anyway, as a clerk I had to prepare renewal terms on the various clients when they came up for renewal each month and later prepared quotes for brokers who placed business with us. The boss was Gordon Patterson, whom I admired. He was able to change his voice especially when talking to farmers who had broad accents. Ann Bishop was his secretary and Margaret Ingils controlled the office. Two inspectors, Gordon Clark and Alex MacDonald, also did life assurance quotes.

Now and again, I went out with my boss to visit brokers and learned to carry out surveys. Eagle Star had a Shopkeepers Special policy and as part of my training I ended up catching buses and carrying out these surveys with a plan and report I had to draw up. Burglar Bars, Mortise Deadlocks, good Housekeeping, previous losses and occupation were key elements in accepting the risk or otherwise.

I got used to visiting our key brokers W S Moreland, D W Stedman, Lewis Wotherspoon, a dandy of note. Smooth as butter, dressed to the hilt, with a permanent sun tan from all the trips he made to the Caribbean etc. He was wealthy and his offices were in Strathaven in an old mill and next to the castle.

I had training spells in Eagles head office in St Vincent Street in Glasgow and under the guidance of two senior persons, Mr. Dodd's, head

Motor Underwriter and Mr. Peebles, Fire and Accident. Enjoyed the pub lunches, pie and beans. Also, after work, I attended night classes on my insurance courses before catching the late bus home from Glasgow to Stonehouse.

Started to study for my Insurance Institute Exams and to become a member of the Insurance Institute one needed 10 subjects which entitled you a world recognized certificate showing you were an Associate of the Chartered Insurance Institute of the UK. A must when applying for jobs in one's career path. I eventually managed 6 passes before going to SA at the age of 21.

During lunch times at the Hamilton office, I would walk to the Hamilton Public Baths and at the ripe old age of 18, learned to swim.

The main manager, forget his name, from the head office in Glasgow visited our branch and I was introduced to him. The next day my boss asked me to come to his office. Surprisingly I got a dressing down, in other words my dress attire was not conservative enough and my hair was too long. The one suit I had was dark blue with stripes, cloth buttons with 4 down the front and square cut jacket. The lapels were high up on the jacket and I tended to wear narrow ties, red and black with my winkle picker shoes or Beatle boots. I looked a million dollars but I had to go and buy a new suit as I would be inspected again soon by the boss from head office. I bought 3 button browney suits plus new shoes - that did the trick.

My mum was a great one for sales and came home with this green suit, huge bell bottoms with turn ups. It looked great this bright green for the Mediterranean but in the land of grey skies and a predominantly Protestant housing scheme it went down like a lead balloon. I wore it once and could feel all the people staring at me from behind their lounge curtains - Eish.

On the subject of religion. Ann Bishop in the office was a staunch Roman Catholic and one day we spoke in depth. Their belief was that they would get forgiveness for wrongs when they had mass. I told her I could not grasp that but hey, later on in life one has the right to believe what they want and guess what - I say the Lord's Prayer and asked the same.

This was a difficult time but had to continue. Any failures and not getting to the next stage may have changed my whole direction in life.

CHAPTER 6

Discovered my Willie and found my first love, the Brylcream bottle.
Then girls became the in thing, dance halls especially the Trocadero in
Hamilton. A gang of five was formed, went on holiday,
met at drinking holes every Saturday before the dancing---read on.

Very innocent at the time but did have eyes for my Sunday school teacher trying to look up her skirt when I got a chance as she sat high up on the pew when giving bible class, especially when the sun shone through the church's stain glassed windows.

My parents went on summer holidays mainly in Scotland but we did go to Scarborough and stayed in boarding houses, which was the way to go. I could not stop looking at this English girl, who had a young baby. She had a million-dollar smile and just radiated warmth and always said hello to me, you know, you are so cute little boy. She wore those wide dresses which were the fashion and showed off her legs. In these days the fly on one's shorts had buttons and not zips, a button on my shorts popped off and she noticed this and volunteered to sew it back on. Guess what the next day another button came off, wonder how, and I searched her out. Laugh out loud but was this the start of bigger things to come.

You should remember I am still very young and extremely shy and had not yet been introduced to the evil drink …. as I changed from a young boy, I fell in love with a Brylcream bottle and like all young boys discovered my willie. Most boys must have gone through this moment in their lives, if they had not been circumcised. You actually think the end of the world has come, what I am going to do, when you eventually stretch the foreskin over the head of your willie and then it hits you, how am I going to get it back to where it was. Hope this does not mean my book will be X-rated - tee hee.

At school we were taught how to dance, quick step, waltz and some Scottish reels for annual school dance. I never really had a girlfriend but made our own valentine's cards, you know roses are red violets are blue, and secretly placed them on girls' desks.

When I reached senior secondary school things changed and I was exposed to girls. At school I would pick my favourites but never revealed my feelings. Every morning we had assembly in the main hall of Larkhall Academy with the older girls lining up on the floor above in the corridors. From below we could see the older girls form up and were able to have a look see and pick favourites. The peeping tom returns. I had my eye on one girl, Elizabeth Kirkwood. She lived in Larkhall and it took me ages to getting around to asking her out. I would catch the bus and meet her in her town. She was sophisticated and I was out off my depth, not being a man of the world so to speak. You run out of things to say and she came from a well to do family. Her parents owned a hardware shop. She was tall and slim and really nice but it petered out.

At age of 16 I realised that a long-term relationship was not first choice. Kissing, cuddling, going to parties with the hope of sex, though it never happened with me. Heavy petting would be first prize. Around this time, I dreamt of having a little black diary with the names of girls who were good company, talkative, played golf, neat and tidy. The thought of this diary got more comprehensive as the years passed and as I said, was just a dream. Nice to have diary where I could pick and choose depending on the circumstances. So, I still remained a very shy person.

There was a bunch of us who played football and we all started work around the same time. David Jones, Pep Plenderleith, John Graham, Bruce Bell to name a few. I was eventually lured into going for a drink and remember one time being logged into the back of one of the guy's vans and taken home to the disgust of my dad. That was the start.

Anyway, most weekends we would catch the No 54 bus on a Saturday around 5.30 and head to Hamilton which had dance halls and pubs with ladies' lounges. They were up market and like the girls, we were dressed to the hilt. Money was short and £1.26 had to get you through the evening, pay for the bus return fare, a fish or pudding supper, entrance to the dance hall and drinks beforehand. It was custom to all meet in one particular pub and you could have six to eight guys congregating. Each had to buy a round which could be a beer/pint or Vodka with lime/ orange. Sometimes we would do a pub crawl eying up the girls before hitting the dance parlours.

That was a lot to drink but it gave me the Dutch courage to ask girls to dance and it was no problem if I got a refusal, merely moved onto the next girl for a dance.

My drink of choice was a Carlsberg Special which was potent and my record was 9 of these so I was on cloud nine by the time I got to the dance hall. Before leaving home, it was wise to eat mash potatoes, drink milk or have some oily fish to line the stomach. We would hit the dancing around ten [when the pubs closed] and no alcoholic drink was served in the dance hall. Had to look sober as the bouncers, in uniforms, inspected all and sundry before entering.

The Trocadero was a lovely place with velvet seats where one could sit and talk to the girls. It had low lights with chandeliers, a fountain, a revolving bandstand where the local band, a full band with brass etc played. During the interval a large screen was lowered and the UK Top twenty songs were shown on film with all the latest hits. This was the moment to try your luck for a dance. It was the sixties and it was fabulous. Before entry we queued in line and were frisked by the bouncers. Anyone caught with drink would not get in. Any sign of staggering or drunken behaviour was not tolerated outside or inside the hall. On arrival we would prop each other up and look the part.

Sometimes inside you would feel sick and in emergencies the bouncers would open the fire doors and let you outside for fresh air and we always blamed it on a cigar. Once inside though you would dance the drink off, not really... The girls tended to work in two's and if they wanted to dance would give you 2 dances then sit down. You could always ask for another dance later.

The chat was always, what school you went to or what fitba team do you support. Important to establish if Protestant or Catholic. Sometimes you danced with a girl for more than the regular 2 and this signalled she may like you. If you fancied the girl, you may have taken her to her bus stop after the dance and arrange a date or get together for the following weekend, meeting her at the bus stop or at a pub/ladies' lounge.

Many times you got a dizzy, in other words she would not turn up even although you waited for the next bus. You would then head to the pub where your mates were and got stuck into the drink and head off to the dancing or not. We always had to wear a suit and tie to get entry. To be different we used to trim our hair here and there searching for a certain style.

The last bus was 11.30 and if you conked out the conductress would know your stop and waken you. Some guys would be sick in the upper deck and we had waves of sick rocking back and forth as the bus stopped and started on its route home. Then you had to walk to your home, you know 3 steps forward and 2 back. Young and reckless. Missing the last bus meant a 2 hour walk in dreadful weather but if someone from your village spotted you, it's him again, and gave you a lift home in his car/van.

Sometimes we would venture to the Locarno, Majestic, Barrowland or Denison Palace in Glasgow but always a rush to get the last train home. Don't recall any fights in the dance halls as they were well monitored. However, I had a tiff with David Jones, he was a builder with Wilsons in the village and a friend. Must have been the start of my sarcastic remarks but he poured his beer over me in a ladies' lounge and I did the same back. The game was on and egged on by others went out to the car park. He was strong and I knew he would have the upperhand. We threw fists at each other and I decided to take one on the chin and fall to the ground. I decided not to get up and things cooled down and we returned to the pub. Hated getting my suit messed up. David and I on occasions would pair up and he made lots of back handers by building garage extensions and renovations. Story was he was filtering building materials from Wilson's yard. Tax free money on the side.

David made money and the only one in the gang that could afford a car, a new Triumph Stag in Royal blue.

We would travel to Lanark Loch dance hall and on one occasion after the dance and in the dark, David asked me while reversing his car if there was anything behind. I had a look over my shoulder and saw nothing. He reversed and hit a pole which was only a few feet high and crunched his boot. He was cross and his mother also blamed me later on.

On Saturdays we would pub crawl and eye the girls. Having a car was a winner and I said to David which girl do you fancy, under the influence of course, my Dutch courage. He picked the one on the right or left and I proceeded to go over and do my bit. My punch line was, see that gorgeous guy over there with the car keys, he would like to buy you a drink and may we join you. It worked now and again.

David bought himself a flat overlooking the little burn that ran through Strathaven Park. He is now 77 and never married. It has been 50 odd years since I saw him last.

The gang decided to go to Douglas, on the Isle of Man for a week. Went to a concert and saw Manfred Mann, the organ player was South African with Paul Jones, the lead singer. We had, of course, to cycle round the island and followed the famous Isle of Man motor cycle route which ran around the streets of the island. We never made it and got a lift on the back of a lorry, bicycles and all. We drank as usual and played a prank of one of the guys, John Graham, who was out for the count. Whilst he was lying in bed on his back, we managed to unzip his fly and boot polished some of his willie. Say no more but we were in hysterics and when he woke up and discovered what we had done, he was not a happy chappie.

During this holiday I met a girl from Salford near Manchester. I looked good behind my Roy Orbison sunglasses. Forget her name but it was the days when girls wore beehive hair dos held together with cellotape. Took her contact details and later made the bus journey to Manchester, Piccadilly Square, City Centre. Then onto Salford/Oldham. Her father worked in a nearby aircraft factory. We went dancing to a local Locarno dance hall where one of the top songs was Do the Locomotion by Little Eva. Thought this would be my chance to lose my virginity but it did not happened and never kept in contact.

At the Eagle Star office in Hamilton, which was an old converted tenement building with windows facing a main street and flats across the road. Now and again, I saw this girl with long black hair come out of the building. Imagine a Cher look alike. At lunch times I used to walk to the Hamilton Public Baths. A very Victorian turn of the century pool arrangement with swing doors facing the pool where one changed. At the ripe old age of 18, I decided I must learn to swim. It took a while but gradually persistence won. Back to Cher, her name was Sandra, she seemingly was also noticing me and she said I was an immaculate dresser, always seeing me groomed in a suit. We eventually bumped into each other and without drink in me I managed to ask her out. Besides my suits for work, I did not have casual with-it clothes. On my first date I wore corduroy trousers and borrowed my dad's light brown corduroy jacket and a sort of stripped jersey. She was older and the dress code was not to her liking and the light went out. I was too young but anyway, I had a moment.

Hamilton was the main mecca for dance events and the town hall held Jazz Band sessions and I did see Acker Bilk, Kenny Ball, Dutch Swing College Band and the Pretty Things. The Rolling Stones, just before becoming famous, came to Hamilton. We dressed in those tall chimney hats, which did not stay on for long. The hall was small. standing room only and we were high on drink. So were the Stones as they swigged their bottles of whatever. Brian Jones was my favourite and it was sad when he died in the swimming pool incident later on. Not Fade Away was their current single, a great tune and only later Can't Get No Satisfaction in the summer and that plus Chubby Checkers, Let's Twist Again like we did Last Summer, dominated the charts for almost a year. On the night of the concert, high fencing had been erected around the stage with lots of bouncers present. Unfortunately, the heat, sweat and humidity caused their amplifiers to seize up and there was pandemonium which just added more excitement to the evening.

Back to the Trocadero I met and dated girls. Some turning up at the bus station and others not the following week. One girl I dated for weeks, she was a window dresser in Glasgow and was a good person. We once danced at Denison Palace where the floor was wooden and actually moved up and down as the patrons filled the dance floor. I had keys to the Eagle Star office where I worked. It was on the first floor and tenants stayed in the building. On Saturday nights before taking her to the bus stop to go home I used to lure her up the spiral stairs and open the double mortise deadlock on the front door. This made a racket and trying to get up the spiral staircase was also a problem in the dark and under the influence. The boss had a nice lush Wilton type carpet and we would lie there kissing and cuddling. I tried to take matters further but no way. I always respected girls who said no and it built up a good rapport.

Becoming steady with a girl could last for weeks or less. My mind was getting tuned to the fact that a long relationship heads to the next stage of getting engaged and married. Many of the gang were heading that way and eventually they never turned up for our get together on Saturday evenings, as they were committed elsewhere. There was just no money and to marry at under 20 was not on for me. How did young people manage to support a marriage, home and babies?

I happened to see a scale of basic salaries one would earn when you got to certain ages with Eagle Star Group. I thought there was no incentive. I was having fun, dances, golf, drinking and learning my job. I spent lots of time at the golf club with the young and old members, plenty of stories, jokes and just took it all in and watched with my eyes. Meeting people and reading their characters put me in good stead for my future life. Good manners were very important and stayed with me all my life. These days people do not know how to say good morning, afternoon or evening or how are you. Ladies first, stand up when ladies arrive, pull the chair out for them, open doors for anyone, especially car doors. Excusing oneself, pardon me, when walking on the pavement ladies must always walk on the inside. This was from the gardeloo days, i.e. rubbish being thrown out first floor windows in France and thereby the man being on the receiving end of the rubbish. Help when need be, shaking hands when you meet or having won something----today it's huggy wuggies and kisses on the cheek.

The more people I met the more I learned and to think if I had become a draughtsman or I may have ended up in a cold factory full of lathes and horizontal boring machines, pressing buttons and hardly anyone to speak to.

Right back to the girls. A new girl was employed in the office, Margaret, she was a plain Jane but received lots of calls from guys and this made me a bit jealous and I wanted some of the action. At the Christmas party I was so randy I grabbed her in the office kitchen and gave her a special Christmas kiss and wet my pants, if you get my drift. I later found out in life that many relationships developed in an office environment.

Say no more, a good time it was, lekker.

CHAPTER 7

Fitba & Golf
From a sporting point of view, I watched on TV lots of golf, the big 3 -
Nicklaus, Palmer and Player, football, boxing, especially the Americans.
In Scotland we had a few World Boxing Champions in the straw and
feather weight divisions, Walter Mc Gowan, Ken Buchannan
who eventually got hammered by the great Roberto Duran.

In school I won a medal at athletics and played goalkeeper for Larkhall Academy and at the weekends for Motherwell Bridge Works. I was not bad. A few of the players in the teams I played for, joined Glasgow Rangers, so I was in good company. Went to watch Motherwell at Fir Park where most of the ex-Rangers played and also went to Ibrox once with my Uncle Gavin to a New Year's game between Rangers and Celtic where approx 104.000 fans attended.

Waves of fans went through the streets with their various colours, seas of green for Celtic, Blue for Rangers, chanting away and everyone keeping their distance on the other side of road. It was scary yet exciting to experience. In the ground, it was standing room only and we were all crushed together, many full of booze. I recall the fellow behind me deciding to pee into his empty beer can and could feel the warmth of his pee on the back of my leg. The game was a one/one draw. My dad took me to Easter Road, Edinburgh to watch Hibs play Hearts with some very famous players on display. This was the first professional football match experience for me at a young age.

My Dad taught me how to play golf as a youngster and I joined Strathaven Golf Club where during the school holidays in summer I used to cycle, mostly uphill, an hour's ride away. Returned downhill mostly in the evening during the light nights in summer when it was light till 11.30 at night. Took sandwiches for the day and kept my clubs in my dad's locker. The clubhouse was built of wood, wooden floors and a starting office/hut. These days there were only 9 holes and later farm land was bought and another 9 holes were added. The new layout took decades to become fully established and is a superb course today with the Scottish Open having been played there plus other top tournaments. Dated golfing digests lay on the tables of the old club house and I used to love looking through these and seeing all the winners' names throughout the world, whilst eating my sandwiches.

I played in West of Scotland boy's championship and another tournament at North Berwick which was a favourite holiday destination for the family. North Berwick had many open public putting greens peppered along the esplanade. I played with old putters with wooden shafts. Had many pleasant times on these greens which were very up and down. The Public greens were still in use when I visited in 2019 with the little ticket hut still standing.

When I was between 16-21, I won 3 tournaments at Strathaven Golf club. Killwudie Cup twice and Match Play Champion. Funny that in SA at the Wanderers Golf Club in Johannesburg I won 3 trophies, the Medal Final twice and the Match Play Championship 5 years later in 1972/73 with my name on the board of trophy winners, my glory years.

Also, down the track 4 holes in one at Bryanston, Modderfontein, Amanzimtoti and Kloof all in SA. Unfortunately, at Bryanston, the SA Eagle Insurance Co put up a set of Wilson golf clubs/bag. Someone reported this to the Chairman of SA Eagle as it exceeded the amateur limit of 250 SA Rand. Got invited to the penthouse at SA Eagle house, where I was told they would split nearest the pin/hole in one, so problem solved?

When Strathaven Club issued a Centenary book, my wins were noted as well as my dad as Captain of the club. I played team golf and enjoyed visiting the other clubs in the county. My dad and I played together in foursome games.

I was at drinking age and the business men, farmers and young men drank heavily eventually many dying of liver and heart problems. It was as if there was no tomorrow. There was always a great atmosphere in the bar with a restaurant at Strathaven Golf Course. The old wooden clubhouse was destroyed in a fire and a modern place was erected and extended/revamped later on in years. I could name so many characters of the older generation and of my age that I played with, each with a story to tell. My secret was to try and hit the ball down the middle, get your second on the green and hopefully 2-putt. My lowest handicap was 4.

As you can see golf was in my blood,
could have been better but for the dreaded yips.

CHAPTER 8

*First serious girlfriend, however - SA here I come, moving from
Scotland where religious apartheid was rife, to South Africa where
racial apartheid was law, settling in Hillbrow, Johannesburg,
A new job, new people, whole new environment.*

I met Marilyn McLean, a few years younger than me and she became
my steady. Went to her home and met her mum, dad, two sisters and her
brother, John. The family had an Austin A40 and occasionally got a loan
of the car to take Marilyn to picnics/parks.

Marilyn was very pretty and I felt lucky to have her. I was dropped
three times as a baby and not very handsome.

She got into trouble with her dad when she poured some beer over his
head during a festive period and was sent to her bedroom. Embarrassing
for her but I guess you don't do that to your dad.

We were sports champions at school and exchanged medals which we
wore around our necks.

This could have been the one but the seed had been laid in my mind
that I was heading out into the world and never let on at the time. I was
thinking of Canada and should have thrown in Australia but never came
to mind. I made no enquires but started to hint at work I wanted to leave
Scotland.

Then out of the blue my boss, Gordon Patterson, placed an Eagle Star
circular looking for clerks in Johannesburg, SA which prompted me to
apply and duly did. Went for the interview in London and stayed with
a fellow from our village called Ian. He worked for the Government in
their tax office in London. I slept on the floor of this 1 bedroom digs
and, in my leisure, played and pounded the Beatles Sergeant Peppers
LP which had just been released and was oh so different. Went for my
interview and met the Chief Executive, Fred Haslett, who was in charge
of Eagle Stars South Africa operations.

I had 6 of 11 exam passes for my ACII, Associate of Chartered Insurance Institute, UK, played football, golf and was single. There were other applicants and weeks later I got the nod of approval. Wow, this was exciting and over another hurdle in the passage of life.

I went to a well-known dance hall in London where Joe Loss and his band played. Also toured Soho and Raymond's Revue Bar with the lads. Lots of bright lights and a carnival feeling, full of people.

Slowly I told family and others I was going to South Africa and I don't think they believed me at first. Another Scot leaving the land of his birth. It's a Scottish thing and through the ages and to this day we venture around the world.

I cannot recall a farewell party but I'm sure I said my goodbyes at Eagle Star, the brokers I serviced, my golf mates, my village friends and family. I had this adventure firmly in my mind and it was full steam ahead, with many unknowns for a lad of 21 with the exit flight date approaching.

So, with 1 suitcase my family drove me to Glasgow Central Station and other friends arrived to say their farewells. I'm sure my mum and dad were heart sore and Marilyn my girlfriend. We said our farewells and one of my friends, John Graham, gave me a half jack of whiskey. I boarded the steam train and in 8 hours I would be in London, on my own with a flight to find with South African Airways, a Boeing, from Heathrow.

On the train I sat in a compartment with the manager of Chubb Security from Aberdeen who was going to London for a meeting. I opened my Whiskey for a slug and offered him a drink. He said he was an alcoholic at one stage and did not drink any more.

When in London I phoned Marilyn and she hit me with a ton of bricks. I had not said goodbye to her at the station. I apologized profusely, but the damage done I guess, beginning of the end.

We had a photo shot done at professional photographers, Sharps, in Hamilton which I think I still have to this day in one of my apple boxes. I cut it in two when she sent me a Dear John letter in SA sometime later.

She had met this Member of Parliament and after being apart for a number of years who could blame her. I tried to get her to come to SA but alas...

The paper work for my move to SA was important. I had all these injections for this and that, yellow fever etc and needed the proof for customs. I had an Immigration Permit for South Africa that gave me Permanent Residence. This Permit I have to this day and every time I travelled out of SA, I had to produce the original, in its moth-eaten state. One can hardly read the detail but cannot travel without it. The Department of Home Affairs lapsed my Permanent Residence on 31 December 2021 so maybe I should have taken out South African Citizenship at some stage. At least my British Passport gets me in and out, if need be.

Anyway, got onboard an SAA Boeing 707, which was small compared to modern aircraft. I think it took around 17 hours and I soaked it all in from the window seat I had. There were stopovers, some island where landing rights were granted due to sanctions imposed by countries due to the apartheid policy in SA. When approaching the African continent, the vastness was something to be seen. I remember this fellow I had met saying, have you seen Tarzan yet. This was my first flight and trying to see wild animals but it was impossible from the height we were flying at. When Jan Smuts airport, Johannesburg [Jhb], came into view it was special and vast with all the surrounding African Townships.

Even in those early days free drinks were served on board from the drinks trolley that roamed the passage way, on a fairly regular basis.

We landed safely and I was met by an employee of Eagle Star Ins Co, Hugh White, a Scot. He had played rugby at a fairly high level when back in Scotland. He was an insurance inspector and entitled to a company car, a Ford Cortina 1600. Took me to the home of Brian Wilkinson, a manager in one of the sectors of the company. His home was south of Johannesburg, called Robertsham. Stayed there a few days. My lingo was difficult to follow and speed of speech was a problem for everyone.

Eagle star gave me 3 month's free board and they selected, for the first two weeks, a hotel in the centre of Jhb, near the office, called the New Library Hotel. Very posh and 5 Star. At weekends I used to walk around the city and was intrigued with the African township music that came from the radios of the security guards, who were based at the entrances to most of the corporate buildings.

I later moved to the Rondebosh Boarding house in an area called Hillbrow. It was clean with a 3-course meal at night, plus breakfast. Before every meal one was alerted with the playing of an African musical instrument, called a Kalimba All the employees were dressed in white with a fez on their heads.

It took me half an hour to walk to the office in Fox Street, centre of the city and a little longer after work as it was all uphill and with a few drinks under one's belt. It was a great walk, the mornings were bright, blue skies and sunny. Paradise compared with drab Scotland. When the sun shone in Scotland I used to race to the park, strip my shirt off to catch a tan. After a few days you had a sun tan that screamed you had just been on holiday to Spain. I went a nice brown. The weather in SA was a big plus.

Johannesburg was a young city built on a river of gold from the late 1800, not like all other major cities where an actual river flowed nearby. It had lots of tall buildings and the streets were in a diagonal format, criss/cross. Hillbrow was the in place and sat high up on a koppie/hill. Pubs, Hotels, Steak Houses, German Beer Halls with Eisbein served with sauer kraut and eateries galore.

Fontana was a small super market that was open 24 hours and renowned for its readymade cooked chicken, blotting paper of note after a heavy drinking session. Most restaurants provided free salads with your meals. Huge Texan steaks, beer was 20 cents a bottle and Castle draft on tap.

The intersections had "robots" aka traffic lights, bioscopes aka cinemas. I remember being driven through many suburbs surrounding Jhb for a look see. Tosee the likes of Houghton was mind boggling. I wrote to my parents describing it as fairy land. Remember, I spent my life in a little village where the weather was grey, dull and wet. I did not feel lonely, everything was a new to me. To get up each day with blue skies and sun was bliss, which definitely put a spring in my step.

The Eagle Star building was in the centre of the Jhb financial hub with banking halls and corporate head offices. It was around 12 floors high and Eagle Star occupied many of the floors. I worked in the motor dept and learned a lot under the head, Mr. Dey, and a fellow called Les Page-Shippe. Ladies such as Mrs. Wigsal and others added a homely atmosphere, really very pleasant and helpful. English was the minority language and Afrikaans dominated but changing as most of the policy documents were required in English. Most people were bilingual and friendly.

There were a few immigrants from the UK and an Insurance football league, where most of the guys were from the UK. Around 10 teams, with league and cup knockouts. Although I moved jobs later on, I played for at least 10 years as mainly goal keeper with Eagle Star, visiting various football grounds in the suburbs surrounding Jhb. We would congregate after the games and carried beers in the boot of cars or went to nearby pubs with mates, families and girlfriends. Eagle won on a fairly regular basis and I still have team photos. Only one coloured in the team, Errol Stein, great guy and worked in the life department of Eagle Star. Made lots of friends and it was a good time in life, free and easy, wish I could have a replay.

The office had one of those telephone exchanges, plug in plug out with head gear and a large reception area and a sick room. We had a tea/ coffee trolley manned by African tea ladies/men who wheeled them around to our desks, tea/coffee served in white wally cups. They had a huge mail room where the African men looked after the incoming and outgoing mail. I built up a rapport with many and they were big football enthusiasts supporting mainly Kaiser Chiefs, Orlando Pirates and Morocco Swallows. Got on with the main man Agrippa and others. There was a defining line with apartheid, them and us but no threat of violence felt and feelings withheld.

After work the Africans went their way home mainly in taxi type buses or trains to their homes in what were called locations built for the masses.

I got on with most people, I enjoyed people and loved to blether away, tks Mum. Getting the usual letters, every fortnight from my parents and Marilyn my girlfriend. She knitted me a giant jersey done with those big knitting needles. It arrived at the office in the middle of summer and when I tried it on it almost hit my knees and we all had a good chuckle to say the least.

The 2 reception ladies dressed in company's uniform were typical Barbie doll look a likes, with bee hive hair styles. I eventually persuaded them that I was missing my girlfriend and needed some kissing practice. They were gullible and I did get a few practice kisses in the sick room, done in a nice manner, as we had all got to know each other on a daily basis.

Bearing in mind I had come from a small office of 5 persons to a company with hundreds of employees, I felt it was time for a move from the Motor dept to the Fire & Accident dept to gain more experience and this eventually happened. After 2 years and mixing with the business fraternity and noting the opportunities in the insurance world my feet got itchy. Read on.

Well, now in the land of milk and honey,
the weather and life style are a big plus.

CHAPTER 9

Moved abode, bought a car with my Barclaycard, part time job at a Road House, met more brothers from Scotland, went down deepest gold mine in the world, visited Mozambique.

At this point I had moved on from the Rondebosh Residential Hotel to the Casa Mia Hotel still in the Hillbrow area and stayed there for a few months. In the office I met Gordon Farleigh, ex policeman from Somerset, UK. Typical pommies' humour and he mentioned that the boarding house he stayed in had a vacant room and included meals.

Went off to 60 Geranium St, Rosettenville, a suburb south of the city where most of the mine dumps were, half an hour from the Johannesburg [Jhb] City Centre and a bus service from outside the home to Von Wielligh Bus Station with 5 minute walk to Eagle Star's building.

I met the owners, a Mr. Carr-Smith and his wife. He had retired from the mines. They had an in-house coloured lady who lived on the property in a room on the side and was the all-inclusive domestic. A great person and always seemed to be on a high. Her cooking was great. I got the nod and moved in.

Gordon Farleigh was their favourite and later on they debated whether I stayed or not. I remained, just. Gordon was more talkative, syrupy and knew how to appease the old couple.

On the side of the house a guy called Dirk lived in his caravan and paid rental. Dirk was a poor man's James Dean, blond, white tee shirt, jeans. He had his own business and kept to himself. Mrs. Carr-Smith was a Queen Victoria look alike.

A relative/daughter/married woman aged around 40 used to visit on occasions and played the house piano. On one occasion while I was watching her play piano, I got aroused. I had shorts on and she noticed I had a tilt in my kilt. Old man Carr-Smith was having a bath and timing was important. She fondled me and as I was so randy it just all exploded and that was the end of that, never had the opportunity again.

Rosettenville, was an old mining town. A clean suburb with shops, eateries, building society, Adelphi Cinema and a few pubs. It was within walking distance of a popular race course called Turfontein, founded in 1887 and home to the South African Derby.

This was to the south of the city and many Portuguese people resided in an area called La Rochelle which had magic Portuguese beer halls and was very popular for business lunches, cheap and good food. I frequented La Parriena often and for years to come. Still in existence to this day. Prawns, steak or chicken with chips were the in meals with rocket fuelled hot sauce served only in used whiskey bottles. They also had a collection of customer's business ties hanging all over and from the grape vines in the veranda area.

Mine dumps surrounded Jhb especially south of the city where the gold reefs lay underground. One area called Wemmer Pan had a popular lake, with parks, rowing, boating and a number of soccer grounds where we played some of our insurance league/cup games. Festivals with music, food stalls, selling of clothes took place on a big scale every now and then. I bought a leather jacket which I must have worn 3 time and is still in my cupboard brand new. Funny how you want something and it's put away in your cupboard forever.

A major soccer ground called the Rand Stadium was nearby where the Southern Suburbs team played. Many well-known UK players, nearing the end of their careers, played in the South African League. I attended a few games.

The Wemmer Pan lake manmade from water pumped out of nearby mines. When the wind blew, we got our share of dust from the mine dumps. Today 90% of the mine dumps are gone having been reprocessed for any remaining gold content. Johannesburg, in certain areas, had limited building heights due to the many underground tunnels throughout the city from mining gold. I remember a few minor quakes whilst working in the office buildings. It was rumoured that the government flooded these tunnels with crude oil for the rainy day when the world would isolate SA. In the land of vast mineral wealth, one would think oil was around but alas none was found after decades of drilling on land and offshore.

I played a lot of golf at mine courses, which were immaculate and visitors got the benefits of the mines in house prices for drinks and food. On Sundays I played with a troop of guys meeting every week and giving me a lift. The beers flowed at the 19th hole. The courses were pretty straight up and down with slight dog legs right and left, lined with blue gum trees imported from Aussie. Blue gum trees were used in mines to support the tunnels. I wish I could flash back to these wonderful days, a great era for me. The weather in Joburg was always sunny with late afternoon downpours to cool things down.

I decided to take on a part time job at Wembly Road House and which had an Ice Rink. When I got home from work, I then walked for half an hour all the way to the Road house and at closing time - 11 pm/1 am on weekends. I walked, sorry ran home in the dark, in the middle of the road where the tram lines were. Why? the guys at the Road House said that at night Africans may jump out of the trees and get me. Never happened but did scare me in the beginning.

My job at the drive-thru Road house was to place food on plates per the orders that came in via waiters. What would happen is that vehicles would arrive in the parking areas provided, waiters would take their orders to the serving hatches and the inside staff would then provide the readymade food from the kitchen. A special tray would hook onto the side door of cars and the drivers would lower their windows and get stuck into their hamburgers, milkshakes, coffee etc. When finished, flick their lights for collection of the tray and be ready to go.

Most of the guys spoke in Afrikaans and many times I was getting talked about and on one occasion, when I was in the giant fridge, they closed the door on me for a good 5 minutes. Not a nice experience at all.

One plus was that we served the spectators at the adjoining Wembly ice rink where ice hockey was played by professional teams. Swiss Bears, Edelweiss etc. Exciting to watch when you had a break.

I stopped the Road House job as the late hours were exhausting and knackering me.

I was then promised a job as a barman at one of the golf clubs but I needed transport. I found a charcoal grey 1960 Morris Minor going for R350. I needed to get the cash to the owner by lunch time on one particular day but did not have all the cash. I had a Barclaycard with a

R50 withdrawal limit and duly went to 5 branches in the morning and drew cash to pay for the balance of the car.

Got the car and was then told the job had fallen through. Barclays were looking for their R350 and I said I could only pay off on a monthly basis, which they agreed to. This paying off on a monthly basis became a habit that lasted all my life, like most people. It was the way we lived, revolving credit. Today in the UK I bank with Barclays.

The Morris got stolen, I went to the police station and insisted they take me for a drive into Soweto. The largest African township in Johannesburg to look for it. An experience, scary, but never traced the vehicle. A few days later the car was found parked in a nearby street, out of petrol and not damaged. Lucky me.

I was introduced to rugby by going to big matches. I remember going to Ellis Park in Jhb and saw the All Blacks versus the Springboks. Colin Meads, Bryan Wilson - the Maori winger and other Kiwi's. For the Springboks - Gysie Pienaar, Sid Nomis, a Jewish winger who was the Springboks' lucky mascot and other great players of that era. This was the old Ellis Park and we sat on railway sleepers in those days.

Most of these guys were from farming stock and the Hulk did not have a look in - they were massive. Also saw the Qwaggas play a touring Lion's team who were lucky to get a draw. Andy Irvine, Gavin Hastings and Mighty Mouse Mc Laughlin, to name a few who were in the famous Lion's team - they won the series against the Springboks.

For soccer I went to Balfour Park where Highlands Park played. Many Scots played. I visited a well-known road house called the Doll's House. Watched at the Rand Stadium Durban City play Southern Suburbs in a cup game. Durban also had a Durban United team.

Decided to move home again from Rosettenville. Gordon Farleigh, my house mate and I fell out. We both worked at SA Eagle and they held a function at a sports club. A fun game of rugby was arranged against Trust Bank employees. It was my first game of rugby where I ran all over the place, lost in space, but managed to touch the ball once as it flew through the air. Never played rugby again. Decided one needed to be seven feet tall and built like a battleship. It definitely was a game of who could nail who first and put them out of action.

After the game there were cocktails, drinks and braai. Gordon made a few remarks at me and I lost it. With a few drinks in me I let him have it with a right cross and then a scuffle happened, but was broken up. Thank goodness as he was a lot taller than me and had been a policeman in the UK. Next morning got reprimanded by management at the office. Gordon had a black eye, yeah!

I found a rent controlled flat halfway down the hill in Hillbrow with 2 bedrooms, plenty of space and well priced. Out of the blue I met up with a fellow golfer from Strathaven Golf Club, where I played my golf in Scotland. John Aitkin was a qualified accountant working on a contract in Jhb and we decided to share the flat.

He drove this white Valiant with red seats and column gear change. We were on the 7th floor of this block and in the mornings whilst brushing our teeth we looked out the bathroom window and spotted naked girls opening their curtains in the block next to us as well as a swimming pool to gauke at. A freebie of note.

Eventually John met his future wife Mary and they found their own flat, got married and I think ended up with three or four kids. A good Catholic girl.

My monthly salary was R145 and the buying power of the Rand in these days, was unbelievable. Bought a whole sheep cut up by the butcher, groceries, drink money, petrol and jolling [partying] money. Everything was cheap and the Pound to Rand exchange was on a level. These days it's 20+-1, how the Rand has depreciated.

With the insurance football league, I met many guys. Two Scotsmen come to mind, Joe Hanlon, a red head with a barrel belly and ardent Celtic supporter. He captained the Eagle team and enjoyed his pints of Castle draught and met many times at the German Beer Hall in Hillbrow. Most of the lads stayed in this area. Joe was mainly selling Life Assurance products and decades later him, his wife Ann and family moved with Eagle to East London, on the east coast of South Africa. I visited once and it was sad to see him having a few whiskeys during his breakfast before work. He would drink at lunch time and at his club at the end of the day. He thought he could handle it but he eventually died of a heart attack in his fifties.

Billy Macintosh, our centre forward, another Celtic supporter who got hooked as well on the evil drink. On travels back to Scotland, we met in Glasgow at the restaurant inside Parkhead, Celtic's famous ground. This was special as a Protestant and Glasgow Rangers supporter and remember taking away the menu, serviette and a drink stick. When we were back in SA, Billy was told by his wife to give up the drink or else. He stopped drinking forever.

Wee Jimmy Murray, another Scot, worked in the office and met an English girl also in the office. She had jet black hair, a peaches and cream completion and was around 3 feet taller than him and was very elegant. They looked the odd couple as they walked hand in hand when they went out at lunch times and all eyes seemed to be on them. Anyway, I do believe they married, had children but it was a turbulent marriage and eventually separated.

There was a divorced lady from Rhodesia, Morag Brewer who strutted along in our open plan offices. She was years older than me but I got brave and asked her out, ended having a meal at her flat. She knew what I was after but no go. Still greeted each other in the office afterwards.

At this point I must say that large corporate offices and the like were ideal for meeting the opposite sex. One was seeing ladies dressed to the hilt so to speak, pretty and easy to chat to when appropriate. This scenario continued throughout my life as I moved jobs, the office environment, cocktail parties and golf days. Friday night drinks in the office pub and getting back to the office after lunch loaded with chaff and Dutch courage. Coincidentally a young lady, a stunner, came to Eagle reception to see someone, gave me the eye and chatted briefly.

At this stage I had tried to encourage my girlfriend, Marilyn, to come out from Scotland. I mentioned that many young girls occupied commune houses if that would help. However, you could tell from the tone of her letters that she had found someone else and I got the inevitable "Dear John" letter. Seemingly she married an MP. The photo we had taken in Scotland of us together, I cut in half. Nothing much I could do and was not going back to Scotland. I have her photo amongst others, in the bottom of an apple box.

While I was at Eagle, I walked to the Chamber of Commerce in Jhb and organized a free trip to a gold mine at Welkom in the Free State.

This was the deepest mine in the world. We had to cover up so got the gear on and had an incredible experience. We were taken to one of the tunnel faces and had to crawl on our hands and knees at one stage. I was claustrophobic big time, especially when enclosed in small places. We flew in a Douglas DC 10 and funnily enough the 75th D Day celebrations are on TV at the moment 6 May 2019 with lots of DC 10 planes in a fly past.

Whilst flying to the Free State the guests received free sandwiches, smokes and drinks on board and the same on the homeward journey. After going down the mine we were spoilt with an unbelievable lunch consisting of the best food. The wine, beers and best whisky flowed with every kind of fish, meat, desert, coffee, liquors and all on the mine. I stuffed myself.

The mine also had their African miners doing traditional dances, i.e. a gum boot dance with drums, whistles and song. It was a great day.

Also remember going on a bus trip with SAH&R, South African Harbours and Railways, in a dark maroon bus and headed to Lorenco Marques now Maputo, a port in Mozambique. Stayed for a few days, enjoyed the Laurentino Beer and free prawns that were placed on the outside cafe tables. Visited the harbour and walked around the city to up market 5 Star Polano Hotel which is still tops to this day.

A choice of a meal or a visit to a strip club was on the agenda. I went to the strip club and the one stripper beckoned me to pour beer over her breasts which I did perfectly and immediately ordered another beer. It was a fun time and everyone enjoyed the performances, music. It was very tasty.

Well as you could see I was spreading wings,
getting exposed to the world and
letting life take me forward.

CHAPTER 10

Time to move jobs and ride the learning curve,
Thrown out of prestigious Golf Club, Marriage in Scotland,
Nearly cancelled on night before wedding.

The Eagle Star was good to me and my next step would to become an Inspector, visiting various brokers and plying for business. I would have been entitled to a company car, expense account, golf days etc. The guys in these positions were a few years older than me and their next step would to become Branch Managers, like Bill Ferguson, Brian Wilkinson, Wooliscroft, and Le Cordia.

I decided however to send my CV to various insurance broking houses. I received replies but did not have broking experience. A broker basically placed their business, private companies, public companies, personal insurances and insured their clients' Assets, Liability, Vehicle, Personal Accident etc with insurers like Eagle, Protea Ass, Royal Ins Co, Mutual & Federal, Commercial Union, American International etc.

The insurance market industry was very professional and strong competition abounded. Brokers received an average commission from insurers of around 16 to 20% on the overall premium paid.

The broker, C T Bowring, said I did not have sufficient broking experience but out of the blue I got an interview from Stenhouse Ins Brokers, an International Broking House, founded by a Scot Hugh Stenhouse, whom I actually met later, on a visit to SA. I got the job. From working with insurers to insurance brokers, another learning curve.

Their offices were in Mobil House, near Braamfontein Station, central Johannesburg which had a famous restaurant. The interior was Art Deco style, with black and white checkered floors. Silver cutlery, immaculate young blond waiters in white uniforms with great food at very reasonable prices. One had to book in advance. It was recognized as a gay meeting place.

The manager of Stenhouse SA was an elderly Jewish gentleman called Adolph James, believe it or not. His son Bernie, was a friend of mine. Two Directors were Scottish, Angus Georgeson and Jim Cumming. Later on in my insurance career I worked with his son Ian Georgeson. Before leaving SA in 2017, I bumped into Bernie at the Wanderers Golf Club, forty odd years later.

I was under the umbrella of a very clever fellow called Dave Bezer, an aloof person but who knew his insurance. I was his back up as such on the accounts he looked after. This of course was a learning curve. In any career, the more you learn and get exposed for the better.

Jim Cumming assisted me in writing minor reports. He said just put something down as a starter, a first sentence and then things would follow. A beginning, middle and a conclusion. Use the KISS principle - keep it simple, stupid. Used this principle throughout my career.

Service was of utmost importance - return the telephone call, confirm everything in writing and if you cannot make it happen on that particular day, tell the client accordingly. These important basics stuck with me. I met many people who did not abide with these principals and it let them down but was part of their makeup.

I made lots of friends in the Stenhouse office. The claims lady, Maureen was from Glasgow and later on a new MD, Mc Donald plus a new accountant arrived - 3 Scots. Got on with the ladies in the accounts dept and I mean that in a nice way. Another lady employee, Mrs. Preller was a looker and a Barbie Doll. I cannot remember her first name and she was very pretty, married with kids. As a young man one can look and fantasize. She was a right wee stoater, Scots for something which is an outstanding or exceptional example of its kind, often used for an attractive person.

Also, an Aussie guy, a French Mauritian, Trevor Rochat and Trevor Dissel. Later in my career worked for Trevor Dissel at Enthoven's Insurance brokers.

The offices were near plenty of restaurants and one in particular, called the Phoenix, served German beer and Eisbein to go with it. We were in the centre of Joburg city. There was a tailor just outside Mobile House and I decided to have a chocolate brown suit, wool mohair mix, herring bone style with single button and turn ups made. To match, I bought brown suede shoes, which I passed onto my son Gordon in Jhb before leaving to come back to UK and are still in immaculate condition. A few years later that suit was stolen in a burglary, but must say I looked like almost a million dollars in that outfit.

Mr. Hugh Stenhouse visited the Jhb office and he asked me how the market was (referring to the insurance market of course) but I said, it depends on what shares one bought. There was a silent moment but staff saw the funny side as the Jhb Stock Market was booming at the time. In later years heard that Mr. Stenhouse was killed in an accident when a truck hit his vehicle.

A famous Springbok cricketer, Roy McLean worked on the marketing side at Stenhouse and he managed to assist me in joining the famous Wanderers Golf Club where I spent most of my weekends. The club had many other sports facilities on hand. I was a member for around 20 years before moving to Durban. In the years 1972/73 I won the Match Play Championship and twice the 36 Hole Medal Final in the 2 years. My name is there to this day on the Winners' Board.

Then I got the dreaded yips/hands twitched on short putts of around 1 foot, and my 4 handicap drifted. I was still a competitor and always seemed to win prizes at the various corporate and insurance golf days in the 4 ball teams I played.

At my golfing weekends at the Wanderers I met, played golf with Beverly McLean and we went to the driving range for practice. Always said hello, then one day at the bar whilst having a drink with her, 2 members approached me and I was accused of flirting with Beverly, which was not the case, purely friends having a drink. These members physically threw me out of the club. I refused to go and kept returning and burst into a committee meeting and told them what happened and that I had not misbehaved. They would not listen and I told them that my dad was Captain of a club and I knew my manners, etiquette etc.

I phoned Beverly that evening and she was shocked as to what happened. I don't think they knew I was friends with Beverly. This really caused trouble and I wrote to the uppity committee explaining my innocence and requested a written apology.

I stayed away for weeks and Roy McLean said on a number of occasions that the club asked for me to return but I refused until I got a letter of apology. This eventually happened and I returned and was water under the bridge as they say.

I met my wife, Merle, from the office, when escorting her to the nearby car park. After a time, I was invited to her home to meet the family who of Afrikaans origin but English speaking.

Eventually I met my future brothers-in-law, the rest of the family and was introduced to braais [barbeque] and lots of drinking. I enjoyed the company and family socialising. I noticed that everyone had nice clean homes.

I decided to get married in the village church in Stonehouse with prior travelling through Europe. It would be different and we could see other parts of the world. I don't think her nearest family members were happy with this situation but we headed off through Spain. We saw a Toledo bull fight which I did not enjoy. Madrid was a beautiful city. From there we travelled to Rome, Italy and Lisbon, Portugal. We bought souvenirs plus some clothes and these plus all the wedding presents were packed into umpteen suitcases for our return journey. After the wedding we flew back to Jhb and the airlines were more lenient in those days with luggage volume. Only one case was opened which did not have wedding presents packed in it and thus we avoided custom's duty.

Merle was very, I will call it temperamental, and I could not help looking at the dark headed Spanish girls dressed in their red Flamenco dresses. Got blasted on a number of occasions. Took lots of photos and had slides made of this trip and I think that these are still in one of the apple boxes.

We made our way to Scotland by train, were picked up at Glasgow Central Station and home to my parent's home. Merle picked her wedding dress which was special, plus the head gear and veil. Wedding gifts began arriving and were kept in the drawing room at 2 Glen View, Stonehouse. My family was introduced to my future wife over the next few days, plus visits to the golf club for tea and meals.

My Dad organized the wedding reception hall at the Maltings in Larkhall and paid for it all. He was disappointed that her father in SA had not made an effort to contribute to the cost. The local church, St Ninian's Scottish Presbyterian was the venue as this is where I had spent my youth at Sunday school, Bible class, Life Boys and Boys Brigade. The

Reverend Alexander Gemmel would officiate in the beautiful church with stained glass windows and large organ. A piper had been arranged and a photographer from Sharps of Hamilton.

All the photos in the wedding book which again is in an apple box and some film footage (kids have a look see the footage). Funny that people look at these initially and then one's album is put away in a drawer for decades, me with my long hair and pork chop side burns, a real laugh. Must say the photos in black and white were grand.

The week before the wedding was traumatic and Merle was causing friction by saying things and blaming others for this and that. While touching up her wedding dress, she dropped the iron and it broke. I cannot be specific but she was always ridiculing people. This led to us having a tiff and a wrestling match and scarred my face with her engagement ring. I had to go to the chemist to add make up over the scar for the day of the wedding. The friction was so intense that my dad came to me the night before the wedding and suggested It be cancelled. However, I had made a commitment and we were married the next day 13 May 1972.

The day of the wedding went well and I went to the pub in the morning for a few drinks and was a happy chappie for the rest of the day at the reception where the drink flowed. Left the church in usual taxi to the reception and had a scramble where one throws small coinage out the taxi window to all the wee wains waiting to gather a few bob from the shower of coins.

Travelled around Scotland on honeymoon for a few days in a little Mini. Returned to my parent's home and packed many suitcases with wedding presents and headed back to SA.

We stayed in a rented flat just below Hillbrow, Mariston Heights, and to pass time we would go window shopping in the middle of Jhb during the evenings and weekends. Edgars, John Orr's, Stuttafords, OK Bazaars, Dions, etc.

Kagan and Sharp was a specialised shop of beautifully made oak furniture in the Spanish design. We visited this shop and admired the handmade furniture for years. We viewed a lounge suite consisting of a 3-seater couch plus 2 armchairs, an extending dining room table with 6 padded chairs and a sideboard. An oak study desk with 6 drawers and a green velvet chair caught my eye . A king size ski bed with sliding drawers beneath for linen storage and a padded headboard plus a dressing table with 3 swing type mirrors with a piano type padded seat. Add on a circular coffee table with mini me side tables and a leather studded lounger chair. Although it was very expensive, when we moved into our first house, we bought this lot for an arm and a leg. To me it was a one-off investment, not mass produced per se. I was not a spend thrift but I liked good things.

With Merle, I always thought things would come right long term but it never did and it worsened. I thought it was caused through that time of the month for women but it was more serious. Today people take medication for bipolar disorders and maybe back then that would have helped. It was a Jekyll & Hyde scenario and ended up in battles of words, moods and physical confrontation. This lasted until we parted 17 years later and finally divorced on 13 April 1989.

Well, that was a little different but on we go.

CHAPTER 11

Another job-move to Robert Enthoven Insurance Brokers with 8 wild
years, Ferrying public to vote at election, Bomb threat at Christmas
Party, Drunken fights and walkabouts, Missing air tickets,
Breaking into board meeting, Luncheons,
Stealing a police car, Drakensberg Pump Station!

Job wise was fine and I stayed with Stenhouse Brokers for around 4 years and then an offer came up at another broker called Robert Enthoven Brokers based in Jhb city centre. They had modern offices at Unicorn House, with a huge Unicorn statue and water feature at street level.

The job was as back up to senior brokers and I learnt a lot placing small and large accounts with local insurers, many of which were UK and American based. This market was well respected and a highly professional industry.

Mr. Enthoven was a Hollander Jew and came to SA, I guess in the war years in Europe. He would meet other immigrants at the Jhb train station. He assisted with insurance especially building contractors by providing his own personal guarantees to insurers so they could build, construct complexes of all sorts and get insurance cover. Bob Enthoven was a chain smoker and drove/parked his gun metal, 2-seater Chev Comaro in the basement parking. Hair swept back and always dressed immaculately in silver grey suits.

He had 2 sons, Dick Enthoven who now owns the Spier Wine farm in the Cape and Patrick Enthoven who worked in the business and also has been very successful forming and still involved in the Hollard Ins Co, the second largest in SA.

Dick was a MP for Randburg, in Johannesburg, with the United Party led by Sir De Villiers Graaff. At election times I used to drive around and fetch and return voters for the polling stations on Dick's behalf.

Patrick, decades later, arranged a gathering of past Enthoven employees every 2 years or so. It was always great to see each other and reminisce and

Patrick paid for everything. I kept in contact with Patrick and he visited London in Nov 2018 and my new wife and I met him at Hammersmith at a pub next to the bus station. He now lives in California and holds an American citizenship as well as his SA one. Will contact him if we visit America sometime over the next 5 years I hope as part of a first trip to USA. Patrick gave us an invite.

At Enthoven's, I worked for 2 Directors, Paul Fouche and Trevor Dissel on mainly corporate type accounts, getting renewal terms from the insurers, processing endorsements, raising premiums. To name a few accounts, Plascon Evans-paint manufacturers, Diesel Electric/ Bosch-electrical, Federated Timbers - building suppliers.

I also looked after what they called Motor Floor Insurance Schemes. Insurance was sold on new vehicles at General Motors and Cargo Motors/M Benz outlets throughout the province of Transvaal, Jhb and surrounds. Every month I visited these outlets, which numbered around 20, to collect the coupons that were issued plus payment cheque. These all had to be checked back at the office then submitted to insurers. Easy money for the dealers, broker and insurers. Travelled to Van Der Bijl Park and Vereeniging, a couple of hours outside Johannesburg. Started very early in the morning to 5 in the evening as one always had to have a chit chat with the salesmen and sometimes a coffee.

Enthoven's were brilliant and introduced cost centres, in that we all had codes to enter when premium debits/credits were raised against your team per se. This was a first. The accounts dept and Mr. Enthoven could see on a monthly basis the income generated in each team. Clever. Budgets were well managed. Mr Enthoven would call into everyone's office daily and asked what's going on so always had to be prepared. He opened every single piece of mail and was on you like a house on fire for answers and progress. It worked.

I gained a lot of experience and eventually looked after about 120 small commercial accounts. Did not lose many due to professional service and client contact. At Renewal a detailed letter/6 pages covering all aspects of the covers that were in place or not. A letter was posted to the client as pigeon mail had gone out of fashion. Most important as a referral in event of claims. In these days the letters were posted by mail, no email or computers/lap tops.

One had to dictate all correspondence on a dictaphone that was fed into a central typing pool, an original with 2 copies, one for the file, a reminder in the diary system. The typing girls made mistakes and also sometimes did not pick up my accent and had to be returned for alterations. Frustrating at times but eventually slowed down. The girls in the typing pool were a good bunch and we played darts at lunch time and sneaked in a drink or 2.

The girls were pretty and Mercia from Alberton, a secretary, thought she was the bee's knees. She was model stuff and could wiggle her bum. Afrikaans speaking and very uppity but still had a good look when she walked down the passage in slinky slonky fashion.

Lots of characters, Jack Selby, was a director and Marine manager. He and Paul Fouche bought land out near Halfway House, between Jhb/Pretoria and built mansions. I visited a few times during construction. Jack's house was in the shape of a cross, not my cup of tea, and Paul's a thatched home. Owner builds, so took a few years to complete.

I can see a picture of some of the staff. Don Stanger a huge fellow with a deep voice and bellowing laugh, Pip Lorentz on contracting insurance, who decades later I heard he was sailing pleasure voyages from Durban to Mauritius, Pierre Steiner a marine specialist, Jan De Jong a Dutchman, with beard and all and this Irish guy who found out I hated snakes and one day bought me a Chelsea bun in a brown paper bag with a snake inside. Everyone was waiting and as soon as I ripped the bag open and saw the snake, my office chair, with wheels took off backwards at the speed of sound in the open office with me screaming with fright. Everyone was in hysterics. Eish!

I looked after some clients in the construction industry, Jan Fokkens and S M Goldstein, and remember taking the financial director of Goldstein's to lunch and he tasted and turned away 3 bottles of red wine in a very up market restaurant. I was gob smacked.

Also visited a contract site in the Drakensberg Mountain range in Kwa-Zulu-Natal where a European consortium called Batignolles/Cogefar was erecting a huge pump station, drawing water from the Tugela River. It was pumped up the mountain and sending it down again through turbines to generate electricity. This was an Italian/French consortium. I was looking after the French side and had to visit to arrange insurance covers on the vehicle fleet, offices and temporary village/school erected nearby, a huge site. I decided to take a bottle of French wine for the company secretary and the only place to get this was Benny Goldberg's bottle store in Wynberg, north of Jhb, near Alexandra Township. A specialist bottle store and known as the biggest in Africa in those days. I stayed 2 days on site, did my surveys, gathered all the details and had my breakfast/lunches in their temporary canteen. All prefab style. The French brought their own chefs and the village was quite a complex.

Mr. Enthoven always had a Christmas lunch in the office and one year, believe it or not, we got a bomb threat over the phone. The staff was alerted but by that time we were all full of hooligan juice and nobody budged but instead started a bun fight at the tables to ease any tension. Mr. Enthoven always gave us a bonus, never guaranteed but rose by R250 every year. Could have been more but at least we all got something.

Alan Thomas, an accounts' executive, was one of my drinking mates and Fridays were always all fall down days in the insurance industry. On occasions we walked past a Mercedes Benz outlet and there was always this second hand 6 door black limousine that we were going to buy and take turns to being chauffeurs in a taxi service.

Alan, who looked like Burt Reynolds and I used to belt it at the York Hotel which was only a short distance from the office, so easy to get out and in. He sometimes got so drunk that he went on walk about. Search parties were sent out to find him and that sometimes took a couple of days. Was once traced miles outside Johannesburg. He had a chip on his shoulder, "disinherited" he said.

One year at one of the posh clubs in Jhb, Enthoven's held a special get together and we were all in dressed in black tie. Alan got involved in a punch up and shirt ripping scene with a fellow employee, Richard Tot Babberich the 3rd, and was asked to leave and both duly reprimanded the next day, black eyes and all. At the time it was fun, but a few drinks followed by a few wrong comments and we had a war.

Another fellow Terry Dooley, a Maori from New Zealand, aviation insurance specialist, got caught with another employee under the influence while driving and were taken to the police station to be charged. They were standing around and decided to slip out the side door. They then duly got into a police car, drove it through a fence and ran it through an open field causing lots of damage to the vehicle. The next day Mr. Enthoven had to rescue them from the police cells. We had a good laugh.

In my time at Enthoven's I got involved with Terry Dooley in a pub crawl of note right through the evening into the early hours. I was flying overseas the next day and mislaid my air tickets. This was panic stations and we had to back track all the places we had been. Luckily, we got into a closed restaurant and found my tickets on the table where we had something to eat. That was a close shave. Terry died of a heart attack many years later and I think the evil drink had something to do with it.

I met my good, great friend Kingsley Fourie at Enthoven's.

I now headed up a Profit Centre, responsible for retaining/servicing commercial accounts and learning all the time. This involved socialising a lot within the insurance market, trying to get deals/placements done, being with clients and getting them to support you while other brokers were quoting on their business. Golf days, there were many, cocktail parties, always out to lunch with your buddies almost on a daily basis, especially Fridays for all fall down sessions and bonding, tee hee. I had become a professional drinker.

Drinking in the insurance industry had become second only to a sales-men of SA Breweries. It's difficult for the ordinary individual to imagine the pounding one endured, the drinking went on for hours sometimes and recovery the next day was of course another visit to the pub to top up. This went on for decades, and nowadays can hardly manage a couple of pints if that and into tap water these days, nobody to drink with.

Let's not spoil the history. Luncheons, these were lavish in the early days when things were cheap as chips and someone else was paying for them on their expense accounts. We all had expense accounts and revolved them with each other, using ghost names, but mainly phoning your mates and telling them they had been taken to lunch, in case they got a call from the accountant in your firm. Why not as we put our bodies on the line and sometimes took lots of beers to get a deal, a pounding.

I remember the inspector Ian Redman from the Standard General Ins. Co taking me to the New Library Hotel Jhb, 3 course meal of the best, beers, wine, deserts of crêpe suzettes followed by liqueurs cognacs, cigar of choice. That day he said you can have as many Drambuies as you like - I had 12.

Dave Pickford from IGI would say to me, would you like to go for a lunch or a massage, well all I could say was, if you don't mind, I will have both. These types of lunches were common; the only thing missing was a yacht and a Lamborghini.

Getting home was always dangerous but somehow managed without any GPS, the difficulty was always trying to find where the car had been parked. When pissed the mistake is going back to the office, but I always wanted to check on any outstanding calls. Don't worry one always sobered up when returning calls to clients.

This is a great story. I returned to Enthoven's office after a heavy lunch. At some stage everyone wants to say their bit in life and I heard a board meeting taking place. I barged in and demanded a drink from the board-room bar as well as one of Mr. Enthoven's special Habana cigars. I duly sat on the corner of the boardroom table. Went round the board members telling them this and that, their good and bad points and what the staff thought of them. Knowing the state I was in, hopefully they took matters with a pinch/bag of salt but then, in a moment Mr. Enthoven walked in and as fast as a speeding bullet I left the board room. The next day I passed Mr. Enthoven in the passageway and I apologized. All he said was, "John hope you enjoyed yourself yesterday but don't ever let it happen again.

It was fast and furious,
Lewis Hamilton does not have a look in on being in the fast lane
and there are many circuits still to be completed.
Geronimo!!!

CHAPTER 12

Marriage counselling, First home built, Second hand trailer that I moved heaven and earth with over 35 years, Brick driveway, Morris Minor to VW Beetle, TV introduced 1976, Other odds and ends done around the new house, Karin pool drama, Man on the Moon, Bruce, the Doberman.

I was with Enthoven/Willis brokers between 1971-1979. Anthea Duigan was Mr. Enthoven's secretary and believe it or not met up with her 30 years later in a little village called Beauly near Inverness. I will write about this later on.

My kids were born during this period, Karin - 30 May 1974, Robert Ewing - 21 September 1976, Gordon Andrew - 10 March 1980. Our marriage was rocky, always arguing and my drinking did not help. We went for counselling which did not assist. Should not say this but the lady counsellor seemed to sway to my side.

During my Enthoven years they merged with Nebicon, the broking arm of Nedbank Ltd, a national bank which opened up leads on the new business side. Some of the fringe benefits were the use of Nedbank canteen facilities which I used for lunches and occasional breakfast. The canteen was just around the corner from Enthoven's offices in the city centre. I grew a beard around this time and needed a fresh identity card for entry to canteen.

Nedbank in Johannesburg held an annual review during lunch time at Her Majesty's cinema, Eloff Street. These were commercial/comical adverts that appeared in the advertising world and lasted for a week.

The bank provided housing loans for employees at a rate of 2.5% which was next to nothing. Time to buy or build a house. The northern suburbs were popular and the place to go but prices were very much more than south of the city. I was a south of the railway line Johnnie. Found a piece of ground near Uncle Charlie's Interchange and made a purchase, R2.500, through Corlett Drive Estates, in the koppies/rocky hills. However, ground was never proclaimed and managed to get my money back. Found another piece of ground, corner stand, high on the koppies/hills, in a suburb called Glenvista, south of Johannesburg and was very picturesque. The roads and infrastructure were all in place.

Approached several builders and ended up with a Portuguese fellow called Paul Areggo. We drew up a plan for a small house which consisted of 2 bedrooms, study, 2 bathrooms/shower, open plan lounge/dining room, kitchen, double garage, utility room. Got hold of house design books from the library and was keen on Spanish style. The square metre allowance was low so choice of tiles/carpets/kitchen units was limited. We managed Spanish arches to entrance area, with bagged washed plastering, all painted white. All this for R21.500, with no garden, driveway, nor surrounding walls.

I had to apply to the bank and my go between was a fellow called Val Bruno, a flash Harry of note. He declined my application as the property was south of the city and everyone in the office stayed north of the railway line. The southern suburbs, a part of the old mining fraternity with mine dumps, with mines surrounding the suburbs of Rosettenville, Turfontein Race course, La Rochelle the Portuguese community, Regents Park, Forrest Hill, Ridgeway, Mondeor etc. All pleasant places with shops, cinemas, good schools and infrastructure. Glenvista was the new south and further suburbs being developed with new homes. I would not give up and eventually approval was granted.

My first home and what a step up from the council house I was brought up in. Funny how one goes through the full circle, now live in a fairly modern rental apartment, a la council house in the UK. Nothing wrong with my parent's council house but you know what I mean. Blue skies, braaivleis and Chevrolet.

The build started and it was very, very exciting, checking almost every night after work how things were developing and seeing the bigger picture. As I said I wanted Spanish theme and had a picture of a fire place. My wife and I argued big time on the design during one of her bad days which happened on a regular basis. You had to be in the middle of one of these fights to understand. On one occasion on a visit to the site I took along a pocket tape recorder and secretly recorded the argy bargy that took place so people might believe me of these fits of rage that went on.

Eventually we moved in and I bought a second-hand trailer from a guy in the office. This trailer lasted till I left SA in 2017 and my son Gordon is now enjoying its worth. It was used for everything under the sun, moving homes, sand, building materials, dumping waste, garden refuse, mining sand for driveway etc. It had a metal cover which took 2 people to fit over the trailer to keep things dry. Once or twice, I overloaded with building sand or garden soil and had punctures. Had to unload at side of road, jack up, get tyre fixed and reload. Not an easy job, back breaking. The trailer had mini type tyres but it was a saviour.

I decided to construct the driveway myself and ordered the bricks which were piled up on corner of the ground. I duly visited a mine dump and collected mine sand with my trailer. I did all the shovelling/loading/unloading. I had a straight edged piece of wood and a spirit level. Wheel barrowed the sand to edge of garage, levelled it out bit by bit and checked with my spirit level. I decided on a herring bone design which locked in the bricks nicely. There was a slope down from the garage to the future entrance gate to driveway, from street. I was working to the centre of the driveway. By the way, this was done piecemeal, after work and on weekends. As I neared completion, I ended up with a circle in the middle and a no fit as per my design. I had to lift my brick work and start again and try and judge getting a seamless finish. It took a third go and eventually it looked good. I brushed in mine sand between the joints and voila. Should have mixed in cement, watered, but cement tends to mark the bricks, then it's messy. It was ok other than from weeds which appeared later and a curse. Not many, but a bugger trying to get them out from between the bricks.

I wanted a perimeter wall with a side gate entrance and driveway. Rather than paying over the top for a builder to complete I took the task on myself. I found over the decades that if I could manage any job then I gave it a go, which always saved costs. A winner was the fact that being in a new suburb the roads and sewer/storm water systems had been blasted and laid down. There were loads of beautiful natural rock lying all over the place on vacant ground where future houses were to be built. Materials free and just had to find labour, cement and sand. My trailer was now in full use.

I found 2 Africans, Wilson and Paul and picked them up every weekend, gave them breakfast/lunch and paid them in cash. There were master builders. We would go out and collect rocks especially with flat surfaced sides, load the trailer and unload at the site. The rocks were large and heavy and it took 2 of us sometimes 3 to lift them onto the trailer. Foundations had to be dug and levels done. The wall was 6 feet high and 1.5 feet wide. It took 6 months to complete and the back troubles I had later on in life I'm sure came from the rock lifting. I sold my 1960 Morris Minor and bought a second-hand V/W Beetle 1300 which had been imported from Germany and attached a tow bar. A low revving vehicle but did the job with lots of slipping and sliding as the area we stayed in was hilly and had many one in eight slopes to contend with, besides the weight being pulled. The wall turned out magnificently. A real beauty and admired by all and sundry. Only achievable with Wilson and Paul's input.

SA never had TV until around 1976 and one Sunday the newspapers had a picture of one of the moon ventures and I showed it to Wilson and Paul. They just could not believe what they saw nor how it happened no matter how I explained it to them, pointing to the moon. Back to the house additions - at the back of the house outside the kitchen I added and mixed concrete for a small area and erected a 2-pole washing line.

Next on the agenda was the garden and again I used the trailer to fetch soil fill and created a garden. At the same time brought in rolls of lawn which I laid down and what a difference this made. Planted those straight up and down, cemetery type conifer trees. During the build of the house, a huge boulder that we were unable to move, ended up a feature.

Next to that I had to dig out a large trench for a Septic tank. I had to brick and cement the walls as well as concrete the floors. It had to be water tight. Within 6 months we had a full sewer system connected and operational.

Next was a small swimming pool, kidney shape. It was erected in an area where we had beautiful views of the escarpment as we were right on top of the koppie with uninterrupted views.

Had metal gates made for entrance to driveway and side gate in Spanish style. As they say a home is a man's castle. Later on in years I added a family room, flat roof and a bar with my Guinness, Whisky etc coloured glass hangings that I had collected through the years. When I visited Scotland, I collected bar mats, bottle holders with a tot measure attached, water jugs, anything I could lay my hands on to give an authentic look. The brick bar top was finished off in tiles. There were wooden stools and even a little bar fridge tucked under the bar counter. Tenants Lager, McEwan Export come to mind. I was not a drinker at home except when family and friends came round for barbeques. Most of my drinking was done during business and after golf, which I played most weekends.

The kids enjoyed this house as the driveway was say 40 yards long and they could ride, with their feet, their little plastic bikes by pushing along. All the petrol stations sold these in various colours and the kids had years of enjoyment. The bikes always went on holiday with us. It was safe and secure and kept them off the street.

I bought them a big asbestos sand pit to enjoy and eventually when they could swim, the pool was used a lot. There was a permanent safety net stretched over the pool, a real nuisance but served its purpose. One day when family was around, we were sitting round the pool, next thing Lance a youngster, tugged my arm as Karin was battling in the deep end, managed to rescue her before it got serious.

I decided to buy a pedigree Doberman, black and tan, with ears cut back. Called it Bruce, he was a beauty. However, one day he was next to Karin and his mouth was level with her face. I had a vision that if she pulled his face or ears - you know small kids do this unknowingly – and Bruce may have snapped at her with his huge mouth and teeth. I decided he may be dangerous being a young dog so I sold him to Don Stange, a dog lover in the office. Thereafter, it was little Maltese poodles, Muffy and Sooty.

I did a bit of jogging around the Glenvista suburb and also attended lessons at a nearby home/garage and did some form of karate, white gown and belt. Training was hard with skipping on the spot for 10 minutes plus exercises. We would then put on soft boxing gloves and do 5 minutes of hitting the hell out of each other. This was physically exhausting. Other than keeping fit it did nothing for me in life and my Bruce Lee dream never happened.

We were in this home for about 12 years. Across the road were the Meikles and a Scotsman on the other corner. When I visited London once on business the Meikles asked me to buy them specialist ballet shoes for their daughter which I duly did.

Next to the pool I decided we needed a pergola/gazebo/lapa and saw a thatched one advertised in nearby Mondeor. So my trailer to the rescue again, collected with help from casual labour and all I needed to do was concrete in 4 large gum poles, and secure on the thatched roof. Duly done and it worked well but was close to the neighbour's garden wall. Not long after the authorities told me to take it down as the thatch was a fire hazard. Did sell on to someone and then put up some cross beams and laid roof tiles to replace.

Talking about the neighbours, they had a dog that barked at the moon and used to wake us up most nights. I asked them to keep dog inside but to no avail. I traced their phone number and every time I was wakened in the early hours while sleeping, I would phone their number barking into their phone. They got the message loud and clear.

Very special times, got motivated and worked my backside off
which stood me in good stead for the future to come.
Hard labour very satisfying especially when one does it themselves
and accomplishes set goals. All my own work so to say.

CHAPTER 13

First born named Karin on fairway of Wanderers Golf Club Jhb,
Karin's dislocated hip, Football Coach at Mondeor Meteors,
Domestic unrest continues, Drive Ins, My ghost heart attack,
SA Grand Prix, John's HiFi equipment, My 4 Major Golf wins 1972/73.
3 Timeshare Units, Entry to the first Sun City Million Dollar
Amateur Golf Tournament, First car crash.

Our 3 kids were born between 1974 and 1980 and I attended their births at the General Hospital in Jhb. Karin our first born had a club foot/hip dysplasia problem and for a girl that would have been a nightmare throughout her life. This was not picked up at birth by the paediatrician.

We spent long hours listening to Karin crying and having to lift her out of her cot and hold her in our arms. This seemed to help and the crying stopped but as soon as we laid her down again the crying and pain started up. It took us a few months to realize there was a serious problem and went back to the specialist. They discovered she had a hip problem that was not picked up at birth but should have been. Of course, lifting her eased the pain on her hip. The doctors devised a hip harness made out of metal with padding. It pushed her legs against her chest so the hip bones would knit/bind and she had to wear this for the next 6 months. This did help and we were grateful that all came right. We kept the contraption and showed it to her in later years. She just ran the Comrades Marathon in SA 2019 successfully and through the years has done a lot of running, so all well. I chose Karin's name on the first fairway at the Wanderers Golf Club in Jhb. Walking down the fairway I decided that Karin could not easily be abbreviated, however, it could be spelt in many ways as I found out later. I wanted to name her after my mum Prudence but at the time there were not many Prudence's around and it may have embarrassed her later on in life. My mistake Karin, at least I could have given you a Prudence middle name but alas.

Robert Ewing was born in 1976 and Robert was my dad's first name and Ewing my middle name. My dad was Robert, James, Steel, Walker

Cook so I had choices. Robert was healthy and a strapping lad, we had the pigeon pair. Four years later whilst in Scotland and visiting Balmoral we stayed in a boarding house full of people from all over the world. Can't remember reason for trip? That evening Gordon was conceived, made in Scotland. I remember later that my Uncle James said we should have called him Balmoral or was it Braemar.

Down the track back in SA when my wife discovered she was pregnant, it was a problem. She was stressed already with the 2 kids, me and life in general. She wanted an abortion which was illegal in SA. We decided to go to the UK and went to book tickets in Jhb, just off Von Wielligh Bus Station. Went in and priced the tickets but we could not afford the trip and thank God this happened.

Gordon Andrew was born 1980. Gordon after my boss at Eagle Star in Hamilton whom I had admired and Andrew after my wife's dad Andries. At the time of birth, we called for the matron as Gordon was going slightly blue and in my panic, hastily placed the oxygen mask on him as he needed air otherwise he may have had brain damage. He is not quite right today and maybe he suffered slightly – kidding Gordon.

The kids all went to a Nursery School named Tambooti [an SA hardwood tree] and got good reports. Then onto Glenanda Primary which was just down the hill from where we stayed at 80 Vista Drive, Glenvista, Jhb. I attended all their sports days and year end events. Somewhere in them apple boxes are school reports but I think most of these were dished out to them to look after. They will now create their own paper trail etc etc. Eventually one keeps everything under the sun.

Karin did ballet I think and took the boys to Mondeor Meteors where under 10s were taught the basics of football. I became a coach and was in charge of Arsenal. About 10 teams were formed all under English strips and we used half the field for the youngsters. Trained on Wednesdays and games/league/cup on Saturdays. The parents turned up to support their kids and they were very involved screaming and shouting on the side lines. There was a little club house that sold beers/hot dogs. I spent many enjoyable years being coach and the mums showered me with Christmas presents/whisky as they could not believe the change in their kid's attitudes, etc.

At home we were still in a bad place and arguing most of the time. Just noticed in a Sunday Times supplement that 46% of couples argue once a week or more. I should have walked away more often but continually got the mutters/degrading stuff from her and she would not stop as I added fuel to the fire. At that stage, I used to head to the kitchen and start breaking plates on the kitchen floor one by one until she stopped. This and the screaming and shouting were upsetting for the kids and all had to be brushed up afterwards with lots of guilt feelings that it had to go to such lengths. I used to go to the OK Bazaars to replace the crockery and the guys in the office would chirp, another fight John. At one stage she cut up her wedding dress. In retaliation to my crockery smashing?

On the other side of the coin, she was a good cook and the family always had breakfast, lunch and dinner. Even when I came home late my supper was in the oven. She baked as well. The house was always immaculate but it got to a stage where no one was invited round to our home unless days of cleaning took place. Clean and tidy and due to her upbringing where her mother was a fanatic for cleanliness. The kid's clothes were always clean and ironed, however, when she employed a maid, and that was seldom, it lasted only a few days. In her eyes the kids had to have the best quality in clothing and toys, no matter if I found say bicycles etc at better prices. I gave in most times. Nothing wrong with that and I did my share of assisting as well as looking after the garden, cutting the lawn, cleaning the pool, bringing in a salary, providing holidays each year, etc.

By the way I laid the lawn, Kikuyu a hardy grass by sticking in off cuts which eventually spread and knitted together. I bought an electric Flymo grass cutter which worked on hovercraft principles and was great on sloping areas. Only problem there was no grass catcher and had to rake up afterwards. Years later I bought the real McCoy. A drum type of lawn mower with 18 blades used in the main on bowling greens that had fine grass. Cut the edges with large hand cutters which I used for decades until I bought a Weedeater which really made life easier. Almost forgot my heavy metal stomper, used on driveway to compress the mine sand and always came in useful when levelling areas. All this gardening created many black, plastic bin bags that had to be taken in my trailer to the municipal dump on a fairly regular basis. Went off track a little.

Our family had a good life with annual holidays to the coast every year. We used to go to movies at "Drive In" at Mulbarton, just 5 minutes away and, Top Star, was on top of a mine dump near Jhb city centre - these were our favourite. We watched films from the comfort of our car that would be parked on an upward angle next to a speaker that you would attach to your car side window by sliding it down a little. One could buy cold drinks, crisps, hot dogs, curries, etc. It was a cheap night out. The family hated me as I would like to drive to the exit just as the film was finishing to get the car out before the rush into the bottle necked exit.

We used to shop in the early days at Southdale shopping complex and used the Wimpy for ice creams, hamburgers and waffles with cream. Gordon was known as the Old Man by the friendly waiters, he was still little. A Doctors' surgery was in this complex and never forgot the day I thought I was having a major heart attack whilst driving. I raced to the surgery, burst into the waiting rooms, ran up to the reception in front of many waiting patients and demanded to see the doctor as I was convinced I was having a heart attack. He took me in and I still had these excruciating pains in my left arm. He did the usual tests and I was fine, the pain was caused by a pinched nerve in my shoulder. When I came out of the doctor's room, I apologized to everyone sitting around who had seen my Oscar winning performance and we all had a good chuckle.

One day while driving along Booysens four-lane road into Jhb city centre, this young guy whizzes next to me as I was about to turn right causing him to break hard and for my car to skid sideways towards the robot/traffic pole. Everyone came to a standstill and the guy's car was behind me. My wife and Karin were in the car and she was pregnant with Robert. I completely lost it in a moment. I put the car in reverse gear then slammed my foot down on the accelerator and drove my tow bar into the side door of his car pushing his car back into the kerb. I then raced off down the right hand turning and before the guy knew what hit him, I was gone. Realised later I was wrong but he could have injured or killed one of us with his careless driving. I was sober as a judge when this happened, the trip switch just went.

On the subject of cars, I did go to watch the SA Grand Prix at Kyalami, just north of Jhb, in the days when the sponsors could afford the event. It was a long struggle getting into the parking which was in open veldt and in these days the public could wander through the pits before the race. I had a decent seat in the stand and it was noisy from start to finish. Jim Clark, the Scot won the race. Never been to another Grand Prix due to the noise and the fact the cars just went round and round. Not a turn on for me but a great experience at the time. The South African, Jody Schechter, came of age later winning the World Championship for Ferrari.

I also took family almost every year to the Rand Easter show at Milner Park in Jhb. Lots to see and choc a block with people. Fair grounds, candy floss, all sorts of exhibits, you name it and it was on display. In and out of caravans for sale, Jurgens, Gypsy but never got round to buying one. Would have been the answer for a family of 5.

Now and again, we travelled to an animal park, which the kids loved, in Alberton, on Sundays. At the same time went to the tile place called Italtile and admired all the imported Italian tiles for kitchen/bathroom floor, walls, eventually using these in a new home at 6 Kurt Ave, Glenvista Ext 3, years later.

At home I had my Kef Speakers (made in the UK), Pioneer Turntable, Kenwood Amplifier and a large Sony tape recorder. I spent hours tracking and recording music from the radio. This became dated after a while but I had recorded tons of songs from Woodstock, Tamla Motown, American Black artists and Sixties music from the UK. Bought this equipment around 1970 and sold it when we left SA in 2017 for tuppence and it was all in pristine and working condition.

Used to visit Mulbarton driving range where the owners lived in prefab Rondavel type homes. One day I must have dropped my Girard Perregaux Swiss watch and later that day went back and spoke with the owner. My alarm went off at 6.30 in the morning so we rendezvoused the next day. Yes, we heard the alarm which did not ring long and could not be traced, so we did the same the next day. Hit the jackpot and traced the sound coming from a nearby hedge where someone had hung the watch. I assume someone must have found it and decided to hide it in the hedge for the time being. Lucky me.

As I mentioned earlier TV arrived around 1976 and in a way, it was a pity. When one had get-togethers, we all chatted round the braai fires and at dinner tables without the TV grabbing attention. In actual fact I felt SA was more like the fifties, dated in many ways but oh so pleasant and life moved at a slower pace. When TV finally began broadcasting, people were gob- smacked. We had mainly Afrikaans programmes, then English and Zulu. A soap called Dallas with JR Ewing etc brought everywhere on a Tuesday night to a standstill. The streets and roads were deserted as this programme gripped everyone.

Golf wise 1972/73 were good years and I won the 36-hole Medal Final 2 years in a row and the Match Play Championship at Wanderers Golf Club in Jhb, no mean feat. Around this time the club house burned down and we had a prefabricated drinking hole for many months. Our barman was called Churchill. Decades later the new clubhouse also burned to the ground. Golf clubs tend to have a habit of this, I guess when they are losing money.

I'm trying to get things down on paper in order from what I remember but there may be a lot of jumping about as my memory is not that great. I have letters between my dad and me which will account for the history I have forgotten. However, in June 2021, I used a memory stick to record all the exchange of letters, birthday, Christmas cards, all my father's day photos and lots of history. I have done a memory stick for each of the kids and will eventually add my diary which is over 400 pages and rising.

My parents, Robert and Prudence (Prudy - I called her Fag Ash Lill because she was a chronic chain smoker), visited SA early 1980. I remember this Toyota, with long snout, it was a secondhand vehicle I had as my company car. We crammed 7 persons into this car and went on holiday. The kids were small so had to sit on laps. No restriction in these days. By the way I had a Morris Minor 1960 model when I stayed in Rosettenville, went to Uncle Charlie's Road House for drive in eats and had 7 adults on board on that occasion. Another record.

We visited Swaziland and stayed at the Holiday Inn with beautiful mountain views surrounding us.

We visited the Cape – a train journey from Johannesburg and stayed in a boarding house at Muizenberg with beautiful views over the bay. Went up Table Mountain via cable car and also visited the wine areas. It was special for my parents and all of us as it was one of the most beautiful areas of South Africa.

My parents loved their food and went for Sunday lunches to the Carlton Hotel in the centre of Jhb. It was one of the highest buildings in the city with a viewing platform. It had an eat as much as you want buffet with the best food on display. It was good value for money in those days.

The 3 Ships Inn, within the Carlton Hotel, was a renowned 5 Star restaurant, with event facilities and included insurance year end Christmas parties and conferences. The Carlton Hotel and office block - 30 stories, decades later were closed as decay and lack of support caused the complex to be closed, which was a shock. Today I still think it is a ghost building which opened in 1972 closed 1998. Now derelict like many areas of Jhb inner city (a la Gotham City). This was my parents first visit.

The family went on holiday to the Blue Marlin hotel catering for parents with small children. They had lots of nannies and separate eating periods and a dining room for the children which was a noisy event each time. Based in Scottburgh south of Durban, it had a kiddies' pools and a larger pool for the grownups. Full board with 3 courses in the evening, eat as much as you wanted attitude, which suited everbody. We had a short walk to the beach and had to cross a railway line. Kids will have lots of photos to bring back memories. We went there for a number of years.

Further down the South coast was the Marina Beach Hotel, which also had Rondavels surrounding the family run Hotel. A great pool, bar and dining area. Went over the Christmas period and the owners the Chamberlin family from Wales made this place a gem. The beach was a stone's throw away and had a Blue Flag rating with a tidal pool on hand. Peter Chamberlain, the son, was a hit with everyone having previously worked at Walt Disney Studious as a Compare. He showed off his album of photos when working at Disney. He had that wit, organized all the entertainment for grownups and especially the kids, dressing up as Santa.

On the agenda was a trip to the Wild Coast Casino for meals and cabaret shows. He taught the guests how to play the cards and roulette and had wine tasting evenings. Golf was nearby at a number of courses such as San Lameer, Wild Coast, Port Shepstone etc and I played as much golf as possible with guests with beers afterwards plus happy hour at the hotel, and all the chat that went on.

Peter had this large white Jaguar which he treasured. It had 2 petrol tanks to fill. Peter was bubbly all the time and previously married. However, he found out he was gay and lived his life accordingly.

Decades later when his parents died and no one wanted to buy this gem of a hotel, it just went derelict, got ransacked and stripped to its core. I visited the site a on number of occasions and the last time it had been bulldozed. Yep, you can't bring it back but I had super times.

Peter became the announcer of the Lotto results on Natal Radio in Durban and I bumped into him years later, Had a few beers and he told me about his young army partner.

More memories coming back, the Hotel had this huge Fir tree at the entrance and the Hotel dog Bear, looked like the Dulux dog. Fancy dress competitions were held for kids and grownups and our kids won. I remember Gordon being stung by a bee and his eye swelled up. My wife made me a Scots kilt out of crepe paper and I also won the drag queen competition, curlers, makeup and baby doll nighty.

The dining room at breakfast was where we had a scene around the table and the wife would not stop arguing so I said if you don't shut up I will throw this orange juice at you. I did but missed her. Peter saw the funny side of the incident, immediately came over, said "bad aim" and you have marked my curtains.

Peter also embarrassed me by announcing at one lunch time in front of all and sundry that my payment cheque for the holiday board had bounced. It had only bounced because my employers had not deposited my salary in time. We had a good laugh. These days you depended on your double cheque at year end to pay towards credit card debt and your Christmas holidays. I'm afraid I never came right with money until well into my sixties.

My parents came to SA a second time and they stayed in a Rondaval at Blue Marlin hotel and enjoyed their stay. However, they did not like little beasties, especially those in SA. On one occasion a gecko crawled, as they do, up the wall to the ceiling and my mum got such a fright. My dad grabbed his wallet and threw it at the gecko. His throw was on the high side and wallet went down a hole between the thatched roof and ceiling. Gone, with his money in and panic set in. We called Peter and we tried to trace the route of the wallet. Eventually it appeared on the outside of the Rondaval in a little nookie and by using a tree branch hooked it out.

One evening my dad joined the throng and after a few drinks the guys questioned his list of names, Robert James Steel Walker Cook. We never really got the whole story but they appeared to be names of family lost in the Great War. Really need to lay my hands on a family tree. My kids must follow this up with James Cowper and Alan Brownlie. This would be of some interest as they have already established the family tree.

Peter used to throw small coinage into the swimming pool and all the kids would to dive and recover them. They loved that and had money for ice creams. The guests were served tea and scones at around 4 in the afternoon, under the palm trees.

Holidays were great especially treating one's parents to the glorious sunshine and life style. My dad did not agree with the SA policies and that police had guns. However, dad when you travelled many times to Spain the police had guns in full view of visitors, no comments. That's the way it was and the Natal South Coast was special, again south of the railway line, far better beaches than the rocky ones on the North Coast.

CHAPTER 14

Sold my 3 Blue Chip Timeshare units, Sun City Rod Stewart/Elton
John, First Million Dollar prize money at Nedbank Sun City,
also played in first Million Dollar Amateur at Sun City,
Morris motor accident, Gifts for employees, Blue Film, visit to London,
IRA Bombs, The show Let Thy People Come, Resigned from Robert
Einthoven, Go broking on my own and/or move to another broker.

I bought timeshare in 3 resorts for a selected week's stay each year from property developers Stocks and Stocks. La Cote d'Azur was situated on a hill side next to the beach with beautiful sea views in the popular beach town of Margate on the South Coast of Natal. Self catering units with in-house restaurants, swimming pool, gym, and daily entertainment if need be. Margate had all the amenities and great beaches, a busy place during school holidays and all the year round.

Another resort, picked at a different time of the season was called Bakubung, right next to Sun City, a Sol Kezner creation. You could walk to the Sun City complex from the unit if need be. It was African styled, thatched roof, nearby hippo pool with resident hippos, braai, outdoor veranda where one could sit and listen to Africa as we were right next to the very popular Pilanesberg Game Park with the Big Five. The game drives in the park were regular and we did the usual game drive every time we visited. Sun City had an internal bus service, casino, restaurants galore, live shows starring Rod Stewart live and Elton John. Water world, with giant manmade waves appeared every 10 minutes plus manmade beaches. It was very realistic and it was a pleasure dome/resort. Another complex was erected right next to Sun City called Lost City, with another golf course. Sol Kezner created some wonders around the world. One of the holes had a water feature full of crocodiles suitably designed so one could view from the tee.

I used to visit the Nedbank Million Dollar golf tournament many times with all the top golfers in the world attending, limited to 20 of the world's best golf professionals. A great day out for the lads.

My friend, Kingsley Fourie, and I played in the very first amateur Million Dollar event and got our certificates, signed by Gary Player to prove it. It was played during the winter and laid out as per the big event. Played 4 rounds over a 4 day stay that was a drunken orgy and we both got alcohol poisoning, sick as dogs which did not help the golf. Scores all in the upper nineties and over 100. The trouble was the hard ground during winter and the balls kept running down into the bush, little ravines and made scoring very difficult.

At the beginning of the Nedbank Million Dollar golf event a bunch of us regularly did a day visit each year mainly on a Thursday the starting day when not as busy as the weekend. Watching the Pro's practice was exciting. Johnny Millar from the USA tied with Spain's Seve Ballesteros after the four rounds and had a sudden death playoff that ended on the nineth extra hole. That was a first ever, additional nine holes, and Johnny Miller won the Million Dollars. This was the first tournament in the world with a first prize of a million dollars.

At home life was good and family/friends took turns in having get togethers around the swimming pools, all fall down sessions. Don't know how one got home sometimes, no road blocks those days.

Once, I was on my way to a braai after golf, out south and belting along in my Morris Minor when it took off, skidded, and went down backwards on the other side of the road. I had no control and pulled on the steering wheel which took me off the road and through some blue gum trees onto a road next to the main road. I pulled the steering wheel again, went through a garden fence, ended up almost at the owner's front door and came to rest next to, believe it or not the guy's new car he had just bought days before, a Peugeot I think. I got out, quickly sobered up. As people gathered, I slipped away and went to George my brother-in-law who stayed nearby. George, I said "I need your help" and we need a pick as the hub over the wheel of the Morris had jammed the wheel and the vehicle would not budge. The Morris was solid steel and we had to use the pick to free the wheel/tyre. George did all the talking and we eventually drove away with no real harm done, but I was oh so lucky.

While at Robert Einthoven's I ran a Profit Centre with about 5 people in my team. In my own personal way, I used to buy a small gift for each person at Christmas, duly wrapped. I would look around the shops, sales and normally bought ornaments as it was mainly women in the team. This was something I carried out for the rest of my career. It gave me great pleasure to acknowledge the team members' hard work. It was a winner, so easy, but worthwhile.

This was the blue film era, which was a no go in SA. However Deep Throat was doing the rounds. A bunch of us decided to show the film in Enthoven's office and cover ourselves by inviting a number of directors. We decided to show the film in the main office and sorted out the seating arrangements for a large gathering. At the same time used black bin bags to cover the windows facing the main street for fear of the cops passing outside.

This was real cloak and dagger stuff and we had arranged to meet the contact in Hillbrow, Jhb and were to park behind him at a certain time. He was paid the money and we moved the video from his boot to the boot of our car. A scary moment as we had to check all was clear for the ten second transfer. All such films/magazines were banned in South Africa at the time.

The opening night, the only one, was a success. We had lots of drink on hand and the place was mobbed with insurance guys. May I say we had a "STANDING" ovation. Fortunately, there were no reprisals but a talking point for weeks in the insurance industry.

Enthoven's used to send, every year, 2 well deserved employees over to London to visit Lloyds and meet our London broker connections. Enthoven's had branches country wide and it was great honour to be chosen.

One year I got the nod with the branch manager of our Pretoria office, Jake Jacobson, a true-blue Afrikaner who had never been overseas before. He took his wife and they enjoyed the sights of London. It was during the IRA friction in London when hotels etc were cordoned off. It was frightening with lots of police car alarms around the city centre. The Hotel we were in had their own detectives.

We were shown around Lloyds of London, the heart of the insurance world where many corporate risks were placed. Also met other representatives of worldwide corporates that we handled in SA one being the Burma Oil Group that I serviced in SA.

Everyone dressed in pin stripped suits and business was conducted and accepted by a mere signature on their share of the risk on a placing slip once the broker had discussed the risk with you. Very unique and went back to the coffee house days where Marine insurance was arranged on the imported goods from around the world. One had to queue in line at the box where the underwriters did their business, fill the slip to 100% and then the goods were fully insured. Of course, later supported with closing instructions.

Jake was very naive and when we were entertained by the local insurance toffs who spoke the Queen's English oh so awfully well. Jake got grilled on the apartheid policies in SA and his beliefs. There was no hiding place to lots of questions and I felt embarrassed for him.

A few days later his wife returned to SA and I get this knock on my hotel room door. Jake was standing outside with this pile of Playboys, Hustler etc and said "John, I've finished with these and need to throw them away. I decided to grab a few which I stuffed into my case for the trip back. A dangerous move as books of this nature were banned in SA. Went through customs however, without a hitch.

Jake asked if we could go and see a naughty show called Let Thy People Come, a live show, playing nearby. I won't go into details but lots of nude scenes with music playing. In one scene this coloured guy with his raincoat on was dancing/singing then suddenly opened his raincoat. Well, this shocked Jake and at the top of his voice yelled— "John did you see the size of that guy's cock?". He was completely oblivious to the audience surrounding him and he got a lot of looks. Hope you see the funny side of this.

Back in SA I worked with many guys in the insurance industry and at golf days, Insurance Institute dinners, pubs and insurance football games kept us networking well.

I got promotion at Enthoven's and took over a Director's job that involved Contract Works insurance and guarantees. All new to me but once again on a learning curve, becoming jack of all trades. I still ran my team and this was an add-on and I read all the files to get familiar with the clients' insurance portfolios.

One had to be introduced to all the clients and read the characters followed in most cases with a bite to eat and drinks, That's when one got to know clients better as they dropped their guard.

The Hollander whose position I took over, Richard Tot Babberich the 3rd, was returning to Holland. He was a jolly fellow, a Billy Bunter look alike and he enjoyed his lunches and drinks.

We visited various contract sites, read the risk. One day on our travels in the countryside he stopped, took out a gun to fire into the open veldt, open land, just for the sake of it. He asked me if I wanted to fire the gun which I duly did. That was the first and last time I fired or handled a gun, except my stubbed nose 45.

The insurance of Contract Works was specialized. I had to meet a new group of underwriters with more socializing which I wallowed in. Months passed and I was managing the work load however, I did not receive any pay increase for the extra duties.

Richard was still around and one day while chatting to him over his desk I happened to see his pay slip glaring at me. Funny how you can read upside down when need be and I duly noted his earnings. When increase time came around, I received a pittance of a R100 more per month.

I complained but one of the main directors, David Way, declined my request which was R25 more a month. I would have been happy with that but still less than what Richard was earning. David was a pompous fart, facially looked like Mick Jagger, it was the lips. He was a blue-eyed boy at Enthoven's and deservedly so, a technically good broker.

One year, Enthoven's organised a year end dinner, black tie affair at a posh venue. Drink was flowing and words were exchanged between employees, with the Hollander, Richard and Alan Thomas a fellow employee landed up fighting with shirt ripping and a bit of drunken boxing. This was not acceptable and the guys were thrown out. The next day black eyes and scars were there for all to see. Great stuff.

Maybe at this stage I should have gone on my own and opened up as an independent broker. I looked after and serviced around 120 small commercial accounts and larger corporate ones. I was on very good terms with my clients and never dropped the ball. I guess if I could have persuaded say 30% of the small commercial clients to move with me that would have been my bread and butter income and build from there. The timing was appropriate but I looked at the pros and cons.

Life was good, I had a secure job, company car, petrol paid, expense account, housing loan at an interest rate of 2.5%, what more could a poor boy want. Through the rest of my career, I thought back to this moment and should have made the effort. I would have made it and been successful plus well off monetary-wise. Water under the bridge.

The next thing that happened was I received a call from another blue-chip broking house, in Jhb city centre called, J H Minet & associates, with J H Minet of London their head office. Also represented elsewhere in Africa.

They had an office called Minet House and was right next to the Von Wielligh bus station in the centre of Jhb. About 30 handpicked employees worked there and the Chief Executive was a gentleman called Christopher Keey [Kit]. As part of the interviews, I had to go to Kit's home in Bryanston for tea and scones, very relax-a-vous, but one was scrutinized to the nth degree. I could only be myself, no private schooling like many that worked there, but an honest and willing horse. I had gained comprehensive knowledge whilst at Enthoven which put me in good stead. More interviews with other senior members took place.

In the end I got the job, handed in my resignation to Enthoven's and was immediately summonsed to Mr. Robert Enthoven's office. I explained my predicament and said that for another R25 a month I would have still been on board as I had a happy 8 years with the group. Well, he was not pleased and as usual under these circumstances was offering me the earth to stay on board. On principal, I had made my mind up to move and that was that. However, whilst in Mr. Enthoven's office he phoned David Way, the guy who turned down my request for a R25 increase. He stood outside Mr. Enthoven's office when I left. Well, I'm sure Mr. Enthoven blasted him over the matter after losing a long standing and dedicated employee for the sake of a mere R25 a month, which in those days was mickey mouse money. Had a farewell but my memory bank is failing to register.

Yeah, sad to leave Enthoven's, should have opened up my own business, knew I would have made a success of it, the moment and opportunity never raised its head again. Decisions, decisions.

CHAPTER 15

*Minet's Brokers, Servicing of blue-chip companies such as Dorbyl,
International Harvester, J I Case, Revlon, EMI etc, Paul Travers aka
Shakin' Stevens, Skinny Dipping at Chief Executive's home,
Cops stop me in ballistic condition, Guardian Angel, Dance routines to
We Will Rock You and Simply the Best, Trip to Kariba,
Tiger Fish, Cornered by a Hippo.*

Joined Minets in 1979 and received a second-hand car from an existing employee, David Martin, who was getting a new one. Did not bother me, it was a blue automatic Chevair.

Minets was very highly respected in the insurance market and made new business gains with their innovative proposals to large corporate accounts many quoted on the Jhb Stock Exchange and with overseas connections such as Unilever, Dunlop, Stewarts & Lloyds, Edgars, Cullinan, International Harvester, J I Case, Revlon, EMI, Thorn Lighting, etc etc.

A great innovation was to charge fees for work done as opposed to taking full commission which could average around 16% on the premium paid. A sort of cafeteria approach. The client would select how many times they wanted to see us, claims' volume, risk management work etc and the fee worked out accordingly. This could change on the time management involved.

Some of these accounts I took over and serviced later on in my 13-year career when I was responsible as a Profit Centre Head with 10 support staff. This involved retaining/servicing/ new business of blue chip/public companies, commercial accounts ongoing supervision/training of staff/ account executives and personal accounts.

Initially I joined to assist a director, Paul Travers, in looking after the Dorbyl Group. They had factories all over SA involved in locomotives, buses, ship building and repair, oil rigs, civil engineering, armaments for SA Government, heavy engineering. Years later I put together this collage of Dorbyl combining all the divisions of this group, a sort of picture story in a booklet. A huge and time consuming effort. Kit Keey, the Chief Executive, took copies with him to London and I received lots of praise. I wish I had kept a copy for myself.

Paul was a great guy, about 12 years older than me, a main Board Director. A jolly fellow and a drinker of note aka Shakin' Stevens. Just down my alley. We got on well and toured the various branches of Dorbyl on a regular basis, entertaining the client's branch and financial managers.

On one of my first visits to Dorbyl, Vecor - a branch of Dorbyl, a heavy engineering works, in Vanderbijl Park - 2 hours south of Jhb, I got lost. I could see the huge plant from a nearby roadside and was running short of time for the meeting. I decided to park the car and I made my way over the surrounding fields and fences. Got there dressed in my suit but soaking with sweat as you can imagine with the sun blazing down. I was late but we all had a chuckle.

Besides that, we flew into Port Elizabeth, East London and Cape Town as part of our annual renewal visit. This went on for over 10 years - a "joll" on every trip. Once when in East London, a touring bus arrived at our hotel full of tourists. They had dancing so we joined in and had a party with them. There was a work hard play hard ethic at Minets, as long as you did not drop the ball and kept your work up to date, then all was well.

I used to go into the office on Saturday mornings before heading off to golf and Sundays as well. Secretly some of the bosses would check through your client files to judge how things were going.

Minutes were always prepared after meetings with corporate clients and sent to the appropriate parties.

Some stories. I remember that somebody put a fish into Paul Travers air conditioning. His office ponged for days. Word got around and it was removed, but was hilarious at the time. Paul was a member of a snooty club called the Science Club. I was invited now and again. However, after a heavy lunch a number of us hit the Science Club, where I signed everyone in and we were pretty noisy. Of course, it got back to Paul and I was blasted for using and signing his name to gain entry.

I remember being in Doug Giles' office, the director responsible for Marine business. Whilst he was on the phone, I doodled on a calendar on his wall, by drawing little droppings under the seagull's legs while I waited. He did not immediately notice but later he did and threw a fit. He wrote and insisted that I replace the whole calendar which came from Denmark as all the monthly pictures were hand painted. This went on for months and every time I bumped into him, he reminded me. He was a pompous chap, pipe in mouth and spoke very larney. Much later I remember going to the top of the Carlton Hotel for drinks and had cheese and biscuits with him. First time I was introduced to lots of salt on the cheese. Years later he left, disappeared and joined the faith. I never replaced the calendar.

I remember attending a function at Kit Keeys' home in Bryanston, Jhb Northern suburbs where the top executives from most of the insurance companies had been invited. It was humming and the drink flowed. Yours truly decided to strip naked and jumped into the swimming pool. However, when I wanted to get out with all eyes on me no one would give me a towel until much later. Got my second breath but when I left later in the afternoon, I was ballistic.

I got a bit lost a bit trying to get out of the suburb and ran into a crash barrier damaging the front of the vehicle. Reversed out and headed home. Just 5 minutes from home this cop car pulled me over. The traffic officer said he had been trying to catch me for some time and wrote out a speeding ticket. Now, I am still sitting in the driving seat, drunk as a skunk, and he asks me for my registration number? I left the car and stumbled to the front to read the number but the front had been caved in and my plate was crushed underneath the engine. I went down on my knees, put my arm under the vehicle, pulled the twisted number plate into my hand. "Sir", I said, "here is my number!"

I was still in my swimming gear and it had to come, "have you been drinking Sir?" How I mumbled through that and managed to say I just stay round the corner, was a miracle. He let me go. I will admit now and you will see as my life goes on that somehow or other, I had a Guardian Angel. Judge for yourselves.

This stripping down, after drink, happened a few times. I remember at a Christmas lunch at the Holiday Inn in Jhb city centre. With the place full of party goers, I climbed onto the tables and started dancing. Then stripped down to my underpants, ran across the table tops and jumped into the swimming pool.

Once I took my wife to a party and as I entered the home, a voice rang out saying, John nice to see you with your clothes on - well that stuffed the evening up. At a Wedding I joined into a game of strip pontoon in a side room and ended up in my underpants.

Me and 3 other members of my team decided to do a Minets Christmas Party skit. We dressed up as the village people, got a hold of a dancer on one of the Pleasure Cruise ships. He gave some practice sessions and helped us with our dance moves on Queens' We Will Rock You. Simple steps but effective.

The day arrived and we were in some room nervous but drinking wine as if there was no tomorrow. The Minets' staff were oblivious to the cabaret show and, the music was switched on, pounding as it does. We appeared from nowhere onto this makeshift stage. It was sensational, we got a rousing applause and the atmosphere was electric. They scream for an encore.

At this point John did his solo, jumped on a table with Tina Turner's Simply the Best blaring out at full volume. Yours truly was gyrating to the music and the clothes started to come off in rhythm to the music. The women were really going wild, screaming more, more, off, off, as I removed my underpants. Old shrewdy that I was, I had put on 3 pairs of in preparation of this. The women surged forward craving my bod. I ripped off my second pair and just before I was about to be devoured, I jumped off the table and ran for the hills so to speak. What it feels like to be a Rock Singer, but alas no groupies came to my dressing room. It was a party of note. Enough of that for the time being.

Minets had an in-house pub that ticked like a bomb and was used every evening at around 4.30 till late. It was a watering hole for everyone to congregate and get up the arses of the bosses and report back on the events of the day, such as renewal meetings, winning the renewals for another year and new business gains.

Guests were always there, from clients to all and sundry from the insurance industry. Deals and issues discussed including problematic claims that were sorted out. We had a dart board and competition was fierce. Visitors from our branch offices visited from time to time and you received free invites for a meal in the evening. The drinking continued into the wee hours. Occasionally peed in the flower boxes. Nothing like burning the candle at both ends, no wonder my marriage fell apart. Could not avoid the treadmill scenario and this was just the tip of the iceberg.

At one of these get together evenings we had visitors from our Salis-bury/Harare office in Rhodesia. John Anderson looked after the Edgars Retail Clothing Shops and offered the guy who looked after the Edgars portfolio in SA to come visit and spend a week at the Minet Lodge on Lake Kariba for some fishing. Tim Tucker, the silly little f-----, refused the invite saying his wife would not let him go-----so faster than a speed-ing bullet I put my hand up, I can manage!

Three others got the nod as well, Tony Bedford, Geoff Kaufmann, and ??? forgotten his name. We flew into Harare and stayed at the Hilton Hotel for one night. It was very English with a fellow playing on a grand piano in the lounge dressed in tails. We had these large steaks; Rhodesian beef was renowned for their size, quality and with lots of wine to wash them down.

Next morning, we were taken to an airfield and crammed into a light aircraft that took us to an island on Lake Kariba where we caught a small boat to the lodge. We carried a few ammunition crates that were full of earth and worms to use as bait for the Bream we hoped to catch.

The only fishing I had done was when my dad took me in a rowing boat in a harbour in Scotland and dropped a line with a lead weight on the end into the dark waters.

We arrived at the Lodge and that evening had fish pate and whiskey with ice. We had decided not to drink the local water, but forgot about the ice in the whiskey. The next morning, I had an upset stomach and the runs which stayed with me for days. Either the water or the fish pate was shitty.

The first morning out we tried to catch Bream with our worms, but were not successful. Decided to use bait called Capenta, like a little sar-dine, and fish for the famous Tiger fish, hoping for more success. These fish gave us a real fight of it and it was exciting trying to land one. One guy hooked a huge Cat fish, whose head, was the size of a football. He cut it loose. It was too big and would have sunk the boat.

There were lots of inlets with the tops of bare trees still above the water line after the valley had been flooded when the dam was built. We saw a rogue hippo and ventured into the inlet for a better look and all of a sudden he disappeared below the water. The guide said to be careful as hippos drop to the bottom then run along and resurface. This is exactly what happened and the hippo blocked our exit from the inlet. I guess we were being eyed up for diner.

We all panicked and moved the boat closer to the bank. Our intention was to get out and drag the boat along the bank edge and eventually escape the inlet, away from the hippo. Little did we realize that this dam was infested with crocs but took our chances and waded next to the water bank round the side past where the hippo was monitoring us . It was very frightening but the hippo did not move from his central spot.

Back on the boat we carried on and just before reaching the Lodge there was a tug on my line and was in a gruelling fish fight. The Tiger raced all over the place, under the boat, around the trees and I needed help from the guys to eventually land my first Tiger, tooth missing and all.

Like all the fish, they got weighed on land and appropriate photos taken to see if any past records had been broken. I had a fairly large fish and decided to freeze it.

That night over drinks and a fish braai, a suggestion was for me to have the fish stuffed by a taxidermist. This I duly did onto some nice wood and had the 3 guys who assisted me, names mentioned on the plaque. I paid my dues but could only get my trophy out by getting in touch with someone who was emigrating from Rhodesia to SA.

I eventually managed this and it was received TWO years down the track. Had it on the wall of my home for decades but then the scales started to flake so I dumped it, fond memories though.

The subject of crocs came up one evening and the fact that I had not seen one. One of the staff said come with me and with torch in hand, headed for the banks of the dam. He shone the torch at the water's edge and all one could see were rows and rows of red eyes staring at us. To see it was to believe, pretty awesome.

We did some touring in a larger boat used for tourists and saw the magnitude of the dam and reclaimed land. We went near the dam wall where divers got sent down in cages to carry out maintenance work. Cages are used as at depth, the Cat fish are ginormous and could cause harm. We got treated to lunch on board and near the banks saw elephants, hippos, and fishermen using their scooping nets to catch capenta which is sold to all and sundry and part of the staple diet for the many.

The short stay was over and, on our way home we stopped at a resort called Boomie Hills with beautiful views of Lake Kariba with small islands peppered here and there. Then a sight not to be forgotten was a troup of elephants crossing the lake from one island to another. All in tandem and eventually only seeing the trunks sticking up above the water as they hit the deeper water with all appearing and reaching the other side. Quite something.

Fun fun fun, some dancing, seeing beautiful parts of Rhodesia with a bit of adventure thrown in.

CHAPTER 16

Sales, Kids. Locked in Supermarket, Flew back to Scotland for Uncle Jame's funeral, Love bite to a lady's bum, 52 Investments, Champagne extinguisher at Minets, Golf Day, Opel Kadet stolen, Portable flame thrower at up market dinner, World Title fight at Loftus Rugby Stadium in Pretoria, Scene with SA Heavy weight champion.

For many years I used to love the clothing sales at all the big stores, Edgars, John Orr's, Greatermans, Truworths, Woolworths and other retailers, especially after Christmas. Besides buying suits and shirts for myself I bought Christmas presents to send overseas for the following year. It's a Scottish thing. Kept these and sent to family in the UK. It worked well and was affordable but eventually the postage became expensive and some parcels did not arrive.

My parents, when they wrote to me, always included spending money for the kids and this went on for years and years. I still have all my dad's letters in an apple box, over 50 years with lots of history. I have just loaded these onto a memory stick for each of my kids including photos and other memorabilia. Strangely, all letters from my parents with money inside arrived safely.

In the mid eighties, Karin was 10, Robert 8 and Gordon 4 and I was hitting 40. After preschool, Glenvista High school was the next step. All the kids did exceptionally well and always had good reports. Home life was up and down and I was still living the life of Reilly. My wife and I did not see eye to eye but were still together and tried to enjoy our family holidays.

I do recall that when we went shopping Robert would run all over the place hiding in the clothes racks and giving us hassle in that he would not listen to our calls. The kids were all looked after and for example when I wanted to buy bikes, I would search for the cheapest deals but their mother insisted on the best of the best and this applied to clothes etc., all costing more. It was not easy financially and my wife stayed at home and looked after the kids, house, cooking, cleaning etc. for a good 15 years.

Most people relied on their credit cards year in year out and thank goodness I received a double cheque at Christmas which helped to pay off my credit card as the spending snowballed and of course it built up again in the new year. Living above our means, as a matter of course, but that was the way of life then and I guess it is to this day.

Robert and Gordon were into the BMX era and had the best bikes and would take them to nearby tracks. They looked the part with the tops, gloves and crash helmets. I think Karin was doing ballet etc.

Another John classic - remember racing home after work, with a few drinks in me, but had to stop at the Pick & Pay Steeldale to do monthly shopping. It was late and near closing so I was running around and, in these days a full trolley was the order of the day. Up and down the aisles I went in this huge store with list in hand throwing this and that into the trolley. I was in a corner of the shop and things went quiet and all of a sudden there were no shoppers.

My trolley was full to the brim and I eventually found the exit tills but no one was there. I raced to the exit sliding doors but which were closed. I started banging on the glass doors and luckily some staff members, who were getting into their cars to go home, heard and saw me. They came to my rescue and said "Did you not hear the announcements of closing over the intercom?" - and as Homer would say Doh!!. Can you please put the shopping through the tills I said and the reply was that all the systems were on a timer and automatically shut down.

I ranted and raved and one kind staff member said she would process using a small calculator. It took ages but that's what I call service and I was fortunate as I could have spent the whole night inside the store eating all their chocolate cakes. I really got my shopping mixed up, had too much of this and not enough of that. Piled it all into the boot/back of the car and days later I was still finding packets of Tennis biscuits under the seats.

My Uncle James passed away from a heart attack in the village back home and I flew over to his funeral. Someone had got hold of Minets' office while I was out entertaining a new employee, Jeff Jones at the Gresham Hotel. Any excuse for a piss up but that was the usual thing. I arrived back at the office around 4.30 and when I heard the sad news decided on the spot, I was flying out that night. My colleagues assisted me to book the flight and Tim Tucker took me home. I packed a bag and went off to Jan Smuts Airport, Jhb. I am now ticking and every air hostess and booking-in ladies, got the sweet talk from me.

Eventually sat down in my seat and ordered the usual free drinks from the booze trolley - Castle beer, whiskey in the miniature bottles, small bottle of red wine for starters. I was in seventh heaven from there on. Even managed a little sleep.

Family collected me at Glasgow Airport. My Uncle James ran the Post Office in the village that was left to him by my Gran, Janet Cowper. I stayed at the post office when young and he and his wife Netta always looked after me. Sweets on many occasions from the sweet counter, Fry's creams and Toblerone and always spoilt with cakes of all sorts.

Aunt Netta offered me his shaving set which was gold plated, made in the USA and his set of 2 hair brushes, plus nail clippers which I still have and use to this day. We both had the same shoe size [10] and I was offered a lovely leather pair in a tanned colour which I wore for years in SA. They loved their dogs and walked them most evenings to the station and back. The dogs were 2 Beagles - one was called Bobby Beagle. I remember then treating themselves to a trip on Cunard's Queen Elizabeth.

Back to Minets. Barry Jenkins was the Chief Executive and Nedbank Group had a share in the Minet operation. Barry was a quiet spoken person from Natal but not supported by all of the decision makers. He was uppity and a bit of the old school tie.

I remember we had a crisis with an account under attack - Arenstein Motors - a large motor dealer for General Motor products. The owner was a scrooge of note and would challenge every cent they paid, even for an amount of 10 cents. Unbelievable but true. The owners were difficult to look after as everything was always under scrutiny. Barry's visit to Mr. Arenstein saved the day for the time being.

Barry was eventually ousted, but stayed, his position replaced by a young buck called David Harper whom the shareholders supported. David looked after Stewarts & Lloyds Group and managed the Group as MD in the Transvaal. I was under David's umbrella till the day I left 13 years later and felt we had a good rapport but, when I needed him later on in my career, I was dropped like a hot potato.

I was invited to a dinner party at David's home with others from the Minet stable and a guest from Minets' London office called George Dures, who eventually worked in the Jhb office. As usual, John was into the hooligan juice and got carried away in the usual clowning way. As the evening continued the party got a bit raucous and I lifted a lady over my shoulder and gave her a love bite on her bottom that pierced her jeans. Never thought anything about it at the time as the party was in full swing.

Next day David came to my office and asked me if I remembered what I did the night before. I said to David it was a great party. He said he had to take a lady for a rabies check after I bit her on the bum. I did not get reprimanded and it was taken in good spirit, I think. This was the start of things to come.

In between the usual business, David had formed a small investment Closed Corporation society, with friends outside Minets, who were all up and coming clever dicks, financial directors and owners of businesses. They met at David's home every month and investment opportunities were discussed, especially the Jhb Stock Market and purchase of land. The club was called 52 Investments. We all put in R100 each month. This was a learning curve for me and in the main I sat back and took it all in.

A piece of ground, with the possibility of business rights was purchased, named the Clay Oven, in the Bryanston business area. We held on to this for 3-4 years and made a good return, probably R2000 each in the group of seven. Years later this patch of land became very valuable and if we had held onto it longer, we would have made a bundle of money. We should have put the land rights in a bottom drawer and forgotten about it. Eventually the society was dissolved and each took our share thereof which was minimal. But that's life. Water under the bridge.

When I joined Minets there was a respected gentleman called Rolly Hayhurst, an in- house surveyor. He died of a heart attack at a young age and Kit Keey, our Chief Executive created the Rolly Hayhurst Memorial Golf trophy that was played annually for invited golfers in the Jhb insurance fraternity. This became an auspicious event with insurers, reinsurers, brokers and the top brass from Minets clients and market supporters.

All costs were for Minets account including a sit-down meal at the end of the event with great prizes being dished out. It was all fall down but great fun and the event ran for decades until Minets were bought out way down the line.

One year, being suitably attired in evening wear after the Minet's annual golf day at Randpark Golf Club the following happened. There were tall cylindrical tubes with flower arrangements, full of water, standing 4 feet high as centre pieces. I jumped onto the rectangular table and grabbed a glass tube, added some bubbly, put my hand over the top and shook it with all my might. Voila, I had a portable water canon that I sprayed on all and sundry, reloading as I went up and down the table soaking everyone in sight. The guys thought this was the greatest thing ever and one fellow, Eric Oxford was so drenched he went to his home nearby and changed.

That evening when we left the Randburg Golf Club Jhb for Vic Field's home, a Peter Ustinov double, for more drinks but we were very much aware of road blocks. The cars got into tandem mode as they left the club and sure enough Vic's car was pulled over by the cops. I had immediately pulled of the road and was peering from behind a bush at what was happening. Eventually the cop car, lights swirling moved on. Jumped into my car and caught up with Vic and just then the cop car was behind me. He must have seen me earlier and circled round behind me from another road. We all pulled over to the side of the road and Vic got out and spoke to the cops and gave then a cock and bull story that I was his friend and I agreed to follow him to his home. Whatever he said I avoided any sort of questioning and we all managed to get to Vic's place where we spent the night. By the way, you can drink yourself sober!!

I reduced my vehicle allowance and used the saving towards air tickets to the UK for one occasion when I took the family. The sacrifices I made! I had an Opel Kadet 1300 which was a great little car and used to put our holiday luggage on a roof rack. Once, returning from Natal, a case came off going up a very steep hill just outside Pietermaritzburg. Being on the inside lane of a 3-lane highway, there was no accident and the traffic was quiet.

Around this time, I took the family to Alberton, near where we stayed, to see Superman, at the cinema inside the main shopping area. Parked where everyone else did but when time to go home the Opel had been stolen. I do not recall how we got home as there were no cell phones in those days.

At that time, while I remember, we had snow in Jhb and everyone was delirious throwing snow balls even from the balcony of our offices. Some were building snowmen in the centre of Johannesburg. This was in September 1981 and maybe happened twice in the last few decades.

Back at Minets. I was going to all functions on my own without the wife. David Harper held a Christmas function every year at his home. A black tie affair and very grand with many of the branch managers and their wives attending.

We all sat at different tables and changed around with each new course of food. I sat with Bill Cousins and his wife from our East London branch. He had a stutter and at the time I did not know he was a religious fellow. I am, by now, cracking some jokes, in full swing. I told the following joke which I thought was pretty harmless. Many around were listening.

This huge bear and rabbit met at the river after hibernating throughout the Winter and were having their first crap of the year. The bear turns to the rabbit and says do you have a problem with it sticking to your hair? The rabbit said no problem and in a moment the bear grab the rabbit and wiped his bottom. I went through the antics. Ha Ha It didn't go down well at the table so I moved on and told my x rated jokes elsewhere.

It was winter and David had portable gas heaters with a jet type warming mechanism that blew out fire, almost like a flame thrower. I grabbed one of these and went from table to table asking the ladies if they would like their what's it warmed up - not really. I was staggering around with a handheld heater and the flame was sort of melting nylons and taking out the Skiers/etc from the ladies' Winter mohair jerseys. Nobody was burnt but use your imagination, I was in full control. All of a sudden, the directors told me to cool it. They backed me into a corner and I was swishing my flame thrower from side to side defending my position. Eventually I surrendered and no one got third degree burns. The night went on but this went down as one of my fun moments and the story got told for decades to come.

Once at a cocktail party, sober as a judge, I moved backward and fell through this 6-foot glass reception table where reading material was placed. I was lucky and pulled up with only a few tears in my suit but it could have been a lot worse. The moral of these stories – sober I could have been injured. Drunk – with far worse antics – nothing happened. Angel at work.

A tradition I had, after drinks in the Minet pub was to pee in the basement parking before going home. A piss artist of note as I used my willie as a paint brush and created/conducted beautiful wall drawings of the Black Forrest on the concrete walls. Anyone with a new car got his wheels christened as well.

I was always interested in boxing and before leaving for SA I used to watch BBC's Grandstand on TV with commentators Raymond Glendenning and David Coleman. Many American fights were shown including the great Cassius Clay/Muhammad Ali bouts. SA had some good boxers and world title fights were held in Joburg. Victor Galindaz etc.

A world heavy weight title was won by Gerrie Coetzee when he knocked out Spinks in the USA, a shock result. Later Gerrie had to defend his title against Big John Tate from America.

Gerrie was from Boksburg near Jhb and had a high pitched, squeaky voice and he carried his Cocker Spaniel around. Gerrie's voice was something to be heard. The defence of his title was to be held in Pretoria, at the rugby ground of Northern Transvaal, the hallowed team at the time.

Some of us decided to attend, a first live boxing event for many of us. We had taken braai meat and beers etc for the after match get together in the car park. However, we wanted to take some hooch into the ground. I decided to take a half jack of Captain Morgan rum which I stuck down my sock as the police were nabbing everyone at the gate using hand held detectors and disposing and pouring the booze away, even the little sachets of spirits that one could hide on a body. I was searched but they did not use their device near my ankle. People were injecting oranges and naartjies with spirits as a guise.

We got in and celebrated but that was short lived as when we sat down in our seats this police officer decided to sit in the same row next to me. We waited for ages for him to move on and at last the large Coke bottles the guys brought in could be loaded from my spirit bottle. All was well.

The atmosphere was great but Gerrie got well beaten. He had bionic hands and busted one early in the fight which did not help him. At the braai later the police wandered around had the cheek to ask for beers. Bloody hell – the cheek - no way Hosea.

Some years later the then fight of the century was on TV just after midnight. A bunch of us went to the Carlton hotel to watch Marvin Hagler/ Sugar Ray Leonard fight. I think Hagler won but sometimes as a viewer they seem to get it wrong.

My all time favourite, besides Ali, was Roberta Duran, with hands of stone. Unfortunately, money dragged great fighters into higher weight divisions. Eventually they got nailed and Tommy Hearns, another great, got the better of Duran, longer reach, taller, heavier. Iit was sad to watch.

At Minets after drinks in their pub we used to go to a steak house in Braamfontein owned by a Rhodesian. It was north of the city centre, 5 minutes away. Always around 10 guys came along and Minets would pay the bill.

I had just been sick in my wine bucket but was in my element and out the corner of my eye I saw Pierre Kotze with his huge handle bar moustache - the new heavy weight champion of SA. He was actually a light heavyweight fighting in a higher division. He was sitting with 2 blond haired Afrikaans minders. I had been following his progress and he was about to fly to America for a big fight.

I jump out my seat against everyone's advice and headed to his table. His minders jump up as I pulled out a chair opposite him. The dust settled and I chatted to him about his upcoming fight, that he was not really a heavyweight, and then asked him to measure his fist against mind to prove my point. In the background everyone in the restaurant was watching and listening to me going on. When I asked him to stand up to see how tall he was 2 of my friends dashed to my rescue, lifted me by the arms out of the seat and whisked me away. I guess to safety. There you are, my first world title-fight over in round one. Tee hee.

I always thought I could handle the drinking problem. Next day was a new day and if I went out for lunch or whatever I would try and restrict my habit to 2 drinks. This never seemed to work and it was like - light the fuse and stand back.

I decided to phone Alcohol Anon and did this twice in my life. On both occasions, years apart, I ended up talking to a Scotsman on both occasions. We blethered about the home country, football, this and that. Never actually discussed my problem and after 10 minutes it was cheerio.

The solid drinking never left and I always felt I had it under control. I never really drank at home and was more of a social drinker. Enjoyed family braais, golf days, business lunches, get togethers with business associates and the lads. Always managed to drive home and thank goodness was never got caught for drunk driving until I moved down to Natal.

On some occasions when caught by traffic officers, one said he would drive me home and on others, I managed to walk the straight line, one foot after another etc to indicate I was ok.

One evening, coming out of a pub, I collapsed and lay in the kerb. When I woke up, I had been sick and luckily my head was turned to the side otherwise I could have choked on all the diced carrots that came up.

Yes, the demons played their part and I always promised myself it would not happen again. I prayed hard and the only way out was to stop drinking. Alas, I was my own worst enemy and continued to rock and roll. I do believe I had a guardian angel looking after me to an extent but never relied on that as my saving grace.

On one evening after lots of drink, I contemplated crashing my car at high speed, near my home into a concrete pillar on the motor way and put my foot down. It did not happen, thank God. Too yellow.

As you can imagine life at home remained on thin ice and I was oblivious to how my family really felt. Will need to ask my kids to give me feedback on the good, the bad and the ugly at some stage.

Riding the wave, hoping the drinking would go away,
but still going off the rails. They say only the good die young.
I guess there was and is a Guardian Angel.

CHAPTER 17

*Bosses M Benz replaced with VW Kombi holiday transporter
had for decades, Wrestling match on busy highway,
EMI and Pink Cadillac, MD of EMI thrown out Wild Coast Casino,
Sequins, Oil Rigs and ship that would not launch until third attempt,
Dorbyl picture book-a winner, Promotion to Director,
Sent my nude calendars to the Chief Executive,
'Shy' Lad to runner up in debating competition, Leo awesome and adorable,
A Willie and Titty competition in Chief Executive's Penthouse.*

Around this time, I had R2.500 which I invested in a single premium Prudential Endowment assurance policy and left for decades in my bottom drawer. In 2016 or thereabouts it was worth R230.000. Just shows the power of compounded interest over a long period of time.

At work most of the guys would buy new cars after every 3 years and I decided I would ask my boss, Paul Travers, if I could buy his Mercedes Benz when it came up for renewal. He had already bought his previous Benz for his wife. Anyway, time would tell. Paul cared for his Mercedes 230 blue/silver colour and the best looked after Mercedes south of the Limpopo. It was immaculate and always nice and shinny. It had 100.000kms on the clock and was four years old.

A story that one has to laugh at. Paul took his M Benz on a holiday to a game park. Near the rondavels he was staying in, the owners decided to re-tarmac some of the internal roads. This spraying machine quietly did its business and slowly moved around the complex and I guess it was windy and a multitude of fine tar spray covered his Mercedes in tiny tar spots that of course hardened.

He was as mad as a hatter and spent days rubbing off the damage with a tar removing solvent. We pissed ourselves with laughter in the Minet's pub as he was so meticulous on the condition of his vehicle but all came right with no damage but lots of elbow grease.

I eventually got the vehicle and it felt grand looking at the Mercedes star on the bonnet. The star lost its shine when one day I had to drive some insurers to survey the Letaba Citrus Boards farms in the Northern Transvaal which was a good 3 hour drive from Jhb. When it was time to leave Letaba, one of the guys all of a sudden had an appointment he had to be at and asked if I could hurry along. The roads in general in SA are long and straight, with the highways in good condition.

Paul never really drove his car above 100kms per hour and as time was of the essence I push the vehicle to around 130 kms an hour. Eventually we heard this clonking noise, slowed down and managed to get back to Jhb.

I took the vehicle to a garage and the drive shaft etc had broken, the driving speed went into unknown territory, which a Mercedes should have managed. I was so disappointed and when I got the R7.000 bill I had hissy fits. So much for Mercedes reliability.

A few months later the MD of one of the smaller accounts I looked after mentioned that his wife did not enjoy the VW Kombi Bus she was driving and I decided to buy it. Gun metal grey, 3 rows of seating with tons of packing space at the rear, plus a tow bar and cost R36.000. I drove this vehicle to 432.000kms before selling decades later. If this vehicle could talk of all the adventures it went through, it would be special.

Besides using it daily for work, the vehicle was great for family holidays and was used every year to travel the 7-hour journey from Jhb to the south coast of Natal on the Indian ocean. It was always packed with 5 of us on board and full of suitcases, bikes, golf clubs, etc. The Michelin tires lasted for 80.000kms. On the way there we would stop halfway at Harrismith in the Free State for lunch at the Wimpy and also fill up with petrol. The journey was approx 750kms in total.

Great travelling on the main freeway at an average speed of 120kms per hour and the kids slept most the way. During holiday times the roads were busy especially when one hit the coastal road from Durban to Marina Beach. When congested with traffic it was slower moving, with stops and starts. It was tiring and sleep was a danger, however, thank goodness I got fed sweets, coke etc, to keep awake and alert. There were always spells when I wanted to nod off and in split seconds this did happen. The Beach Boys Greatest hits were played plus Moby and many others so it was a real festive mode as we drove along next to the Indian Ocean.

The Kombi had 5 gears and about face to normal. I always had trouble getting into reverse and in its life time I had many visits to the garage to fix the gears. My son Robert once tried to take the vehicle for a joll (without my permission) but had so much difficulty in finding reverse gear he gave up.

I had a secret press button switch installed at the rear where the boot lid was raised. I needed this as many attempts were made to steal the vehicle as it was ideal for the taxi industry. On many occasions they could not start so ripped into the wiring on the steering column and under the dash board. A lot of damage was caused but it was never actually stolen.

Several attempts – once outside Amanzimtoti Rugby grounds, parking when visiting someone in Toti, at the Pavilion Shopping Centre when I returned to see the vehicle rocking with someone trying to engage the engine. The police were called but it was too late to catch them. They broke the power steering lock with a hammer, which they left in the vehicle, making it very difficult to drive home at slow speed with the steering buggered.

The battery sat under the driver's seat and on one occasion the family, Robert and Gordon's girlfriends went for dinner to the revolving Roma restaurant overlooking the Durban Harbour. On the way there someone had rested their heels on the lid of the battery case which caused the battery to go flat. Eventually on the way home we came to a standstill, on the motorway at around 11 at night with the highway still busy. We stopped and got out and all of a sudden, tempers flared and blame was being dished out. Always happens when drink has been consumed. A wrestling match began, which was dangerous with all the vehicles flying past and the women became hysterical. You can imagine the scene.

The boys stopped their tiff and I seemed to be blamed for driving this piece of "shit" and someone decided to punch the armour-plated side window - to no avail other than badly bruised knuckles and hand. We can now laugh out loud. Sylvia, Gordon's girlfriend and now wife managed to get hold of her dad Steve who rescued and towed us to safety.

The Kombi had arm rests, great for long journeys. One sat up high, especially good when visiting game parks and had a large sliding door on the side. I installed a dash board fan which was small and did a great job in conjunction with the many windows on hand. The Kombi was part of my life well into my retirement.

As part of my duties at Minets I was the servicing broker for EMI Music based in Steeldale, south of Jhb. They had their annual golf day every year at Houghton Golf Club and I was always invited. It was a party of note after golf and I really wanted to buy the pink Cadillac convertible they had on display every year. I got a deal of R10.000 from the financial director Jannie De Beer, but had not a penny with which to scratch my bum. Dream on John.

However, EMI had just built the first CD factory in SA and I was sitting with the Marketing Manager at the dinner table chatting away. I mentioned that I enjoyed Boere music. A few minutes later he presented me with the first Afrikaans Folk Music CD off the production line.

I treasured this for decades and when in the mood belted it out at home and in my Kombi especially when staying in camping parks. Really got the patrons going with great sakkie, sakkie. dance music.

The EMI guys decided that they wanted to go on a golfing trip and stay at the Wild Coast Hotel Golf resort on the border of SA and Transkei, facing the sea. The course was designed by Bobby Jones Jnr, a natural links course of much beauty with a club house giving 360-degree views. A difficult course due to the wind coming from the ocean but a pleasure to play on.

On the road down from Jhb we were going to stay at Jannie's holiday home in Umkomas for one night and have a braai. The next day the vehicle train, 2 Kombis set of for the Wild Coast when all of a sudden, I lost first and second gears. Our plan was to try and time the traffic lights as and when to catch green to keep going. This was not a joke but I managed to judge the vehicle's momentum, the robot/traffic lights and got through 12 sets of lights to our destination. A feat of note and the roars of approval every time we got through a set of lights was awesome. I was the best thing since sliced bread. We stayed in Margate, a holiday resort on the coast, while the vehicle was in for repair at a local garage.

After our game of golf at the Wild Coast we headed for supper and the Casino where we formed syndicates and hit the one-armed bandits. There was also a blue movie cinema which we all piled into and a senior employee at EMI wanted to attend but had left it too late as he was addicted to the one-armed bandits. He tried to gain access to the blue movie but security was called and he was not allowed to enter the cinema. This really caused a commotion and the incident ended up on the back pages of a Sunday paper which as you could imagine did not go down well with the powers that be.

At Minets I was progressing nicely and looking after the Dorbyl Group with my boss, Paul Travers. We were a good team and when we felt like a drink, he would tell his secretary that we had gone to Nissho Awai and off we went to a drinking hole nearby. This was a ghost place, supposed to be the Japanese loco engine supplier's office for the trains that Dorbyl built. It worked well as our secretive hiding place.

Nearby was the Gresham Hotel and occasionally some of us went to lunch on the third floor where they had cabaret and tasty strip shows, which was a bonus. Bars with strip shows in Jhb and Hillbrow were the in thing.

I remember once lining up a guy I named Robert Redford. Eric was always immaculately dressed in pin stripe suits. On occasions guys were asked to go on stage by the dancer and yes he got the nod. Nothing to do with me earlier speaking to the dancer to line him up. All he had to do was stand still against a wall and the dancer would do a hand stand and wrap her legs around his neck.

A good laugh and when he returned to the table, he discovered he was covered in sequins and panic set in. I spend hours in the toilet, well a long time, trying to remove all the evidence. However, every time he moved another sequin would pop out from his hair or suit. Anyway, we did the best we could to save his marriage amid much laughter.

I also remember going to the pub at the Gresham with a guy called Chris Step who asked a few guys to celebrate his birthday. I returned to work around three 3:30 to find notes on my desk from Paul stating "Need to speak to you urgently", then every 15 minutes further notes in red, where are you, now urgent please see me, etc. When I returned, I told him where I had been and believe it or not, he said, well, let's go and join Chris and we did.

A few days later when Paul was at lunch, I did the same to him and pinned notes all over his cloth office seat. Picture it.

While servicing Dorbyl, I visited the launching of vessels at Durban harbour. Dorbyl also fabricated steel structured Oil Rigs that were towed across the seas to customers in Europe for final fitting out.

Minets received a claim for a new tug boat that refused to launch even with the breaking of the champagne bottle on it. All dignitaries had to return for another try but eventually it only launched on a third attempt after importing a special grease from Germany that finally did the trick to the embarrassment of all and sundry. I think it was Brylcream. The insurance claim amounted to R120.000.

Dorbyl also built rolling stock, carriages and imported electric engines from Nissho Awai in Japan for the trains. Buses were also built and at Broderick Engineering in Vanderbijl Park. I needed a special pass to enter their fabrication shop where canons/shells, military equipment, etc were being made for the SA Defence force.

Dorbyl, in the ports of East London and Cape Town, did mainly ship repair. Other branches fabricated huge boilers for the power stations and I had the chance to climb to the top of one of the new power stations being erected called Matuba. The government built 4 at that time, all coal fired. They still running but are continually breaking down with load shedding of note.

The Dorbyl workshops had to be seen to be believed with giant cranes moving steel around. I always wondered how lonely the machinists were pushing buttons on giant vertical and horizontal boring machines, no one to talk to, roasting in Summer, freezing in Winter.

The annual insurance renewal of Dorbyl was a mammoth task due to its diversity. The local SA market, Lloyds of London and reinsurance markets participated. The account was always being attacked by other brokers and it was a feather in the cap for the Minet team that were involved and retained this prestigious account for decades.

I had created a collage with pictures/art work of all the Dorbyl divisions and activities they carried out. It was a work of art, even if I say so, and created for a renewal exercise, a first ever. A picture book with all the relevant info. Kit Keey, our chief executive took this to London with him and it was a winner. Everyone congratulated me for this unique booklet. I wish I had kept a copy as a keepsake for later years.

Minets were growing with board of directors being appointed for the various provinces, Transvaal, Cape, Eastern Province and the Free State. Eventually I was appointed as an Alternate Director in the Transvaal. Received lots of congratulatory letters from my peers. I kept a few and are in my apple box/on a memory stick.

A few years later I was made a full Director of the Transvaal region. It did not really mean much financially, just more responsibility. Prior to this I had kept calendars, the ones with naked breasts, etc behind my office door. After the promotion, I was instructed by the Chief Executive, Kit Keey, to get rid of these. I duly rolled them up and placed them on his desk with a note to say as I no longer had any use for them, maybe he had. It went down well, but another Braveheart moment.

I had to attend board meetings and prepare accordingly. Nervous as can be, sweaty hands, a voice that could go squeaky when my turn came to speak, with no drink in me. You may not understand but for me the pressure was great. I have carried this nervousness and shyness throughout my life since boyhood. Maybe a beer before each meeting would have done the trick.

I decided to do something about it and out of the blue the Insurance Institute were running courses on public speaking. Minet's decided to do an in-house course for staff with a pucker professional running the course. It had many sessions, teaching and one-on-one guidance. I had to give it a try. Went through a lot of attempts, read the literature they handed out and studied the lecturer as he went through the motions. This was done on a weekly basis. We were all subject to having to stand at the podium and read/present something which was marked by the lecturer giving pluses and minus, all constructive. This included use of the eyes, body and hand actions to express things. It happened over a number of weeks and was torture for me.

At the end of the course everyone had to do their own presentation and a knockout tournament and was to be judged by the lecturer A different talk each time and marked accordingly with explanations. All the staff who volunteered for the course, included directors and the managing director, David Harper. This went on over a few days and videos were taken of each one's effort.

To cut this story short and believe it or not I made the final, beating the MD enroute. The fellow I had to take on in the final was Trevor Daniels, a claims' manager. Each one had to prepare a talk of no more than 5 minutes. I was first up and my subject was The Golf Ball. Briefly, I described the history of the golf ball, The Feathery, a ball made from hide and stuffed with goose feathers, the Gutta Percha stuffed with wood chips then onto the Rubber Wound ball, and then liquid centres, synthetic and dimpled covered. Today the advances are astounding.

I took a new wrapped gowf/golf ball from my pocket and held it in front of me unwrapping this virgin golf ball. I described the intake of the view that the ball would experience once hit, as it flew through the air taking in all the sights, trees, sky on its maiden flight. You get the gist, just cannot remember how I finished off.

The other guy talked about a sneeze, Attishoo, which won the day with all the antics. I felt much chuffed after weeks of torture.

All supposed to be your own original story but months later I was at the dentist and lifted a Reader's Digest in the waiting area and paged through. There it was - the whole article on Attishoo, word for word. Sneaky bugger, but I guess that is how some people roll through life.

For me I did exceptionally well and kept the video of my speech. I think it is still in one of the apple boxes. Kids hunt it down as it's the only video of your dad live on stage, in my 40's.

I do not normally blow my own trumpet so let the Stars column in the Daily Mail Wednesday 9/10/2019 do it for me. I never study the stars but my wife, Bernice saw this and passed it on.

"You're are a Leo, born under the majestic symbol of the lion. Awesome and adorable, fierce and cuddly, you can inspire love and fear. So why do you so seldom capitalize on your awe-inspiring charismatic strengths. It's as if you sometimes forget your persuasive powers and your ability to charm. Yet even when you're not aiming for maximum impact, you remain a tour de force. You've earned your right to be centre-stage today. Don't let anyone tell you differently and enjoy the well-deserved acclaim". I wish I knew had all these attributes earlier in my life.

You may wonder why I came off the rails and flirted with the girls and I thought it was all to do with my drinking habit. Should have read my stars more often. Never a good-looker, as I was dropped as a baby 3 times. Miserable face but had a nice smile and dressed smartly. Just could not smile 24 hours a day and people on occasion would say "why are you looking so dour Cook" - Eish! Anyway, the girls still loved me and that reminds me of a girl in the office who gave me her home number. I had a casual chit chat with her and decided to ring her at home. Got through and was as smooth as butter. After a few minutes the voice said "I think you want to speak to my daughter". Nice one John, can you believe it, they had identical voices. That was that.

The Minet pub evenings were never ending and late one evening, a decision was made, when the pub closed, to venture up to Kit Keey's executive suite where more booze was on hand. Lettie Coetzee was his secretary and as he was out of town, she had the keys. About 10 of us, male and female, went up to the penthouse suite and more drink flowed. From somewhere a Big Titties and Willy competition was going to be held with prize money thrown in.

Tiens Smit, was going to give a blank cheque to the girl winner, which happened to be Lettie - both since passed. The cheque was handed over but I never found out the amount that was filled in. The guys cheered this on but now it was the guys turn to do their bit. I crawled under the coffee table and was caught cheating in some form or manor and was disqualified, so that avoided me having to expose myself, great move John. The other guys fell into the trap and I cannot remember who won. Another day in Africa.

I used to visit Swaziland with a Scottish/Irish golf group and stayed at the Holiday Inn with a golf course on hand. It as another boozy weekend. Also Federated Ins Co had a golf day every year and I remember racing down the hotel passages against Steve De Boer trying to set world records. A sight to be seen.

What more can I say, it's was all happening, one could not dream this up if one tried, Perhaps a film in the pipeline? Perhaps, so read on.

CHAPTER 18

My wife's dad passes away, A new home after 10 years, Guinness record as Kombi beats parking car barrier, Glenvista Ext 1 a 360degree view site. I become Designer and Project Manager, A man's home is his castle even for a short time, Parents visit but short stay in a toxic environment, 10 credit cards, Night shift job with Fidelity Guards, Laid low with 2 serious Cancer operations, Testicle in a bottle.

Merle's dad, Andries/Andy passed away in December 1980 from cancer aged 63. We had been in our home for just over 10 years and probably should have remained there. I found out in life that moving homes is not always the better route financially etc. Rather pay one's home off, stay there, save and have a less pressured life.

My son Gordon was born earlier in the year and for some reason Andy did not visit to see him so I never visited his home. This lasted for months but eventually when one of my brothers-in-law George was at my home, he persuaded me after a few drinks to smoke the peace pipe. A cake was bought and I accidentally sat on it in the car on the way there. Hey this Scotsman can be stubborn when he gets a bee in his bonnet.

Merle received R6.000 from his Will, £285 in today's money.

Anyway, I moved homes and addresses around 14 times in life and never used a removal company. Why stay in one place or move and see the world? Just think, one village and one home for life.

My VW Kombi and my trailer that I used for over 40 years, was a big part of my life, where I went, they followed. If it could only talk. Gave my trailer to my son Gordon, in Joburg, when I left SA in 2017.

I was a packer of note through the years whether in the garage, moving homes, going on holiday, packing the Kombi and trailer.

To this day I still have limited clothes when travelling, hate having to wait for suit cases at the airport as just delays things.

Always cleaned our cars, needed a step ladder for the Kombi to get to the roof.

While I remember, only person ever to do this, after drinks of course. One evening while leaving Minets underground parking I decided to put down my foot on the accelerator of the Kombi and try and beat the up/down arm used on the exit of the parking. I managed but just caught the beam arm and snapped it off as I whizzed through at a speed of knots. Jackie Stewart never had a look in. No one saw me as I raced up the exit ramp but the next morning the hunt was on for the culprit.

Days later they pin pointed me as they had found paint marks on the window column of the driver's side. No escape. I think I had to pay up, another black cross but recorded in Guinness Book of records, only person to beat the boom, so to speak. Give it a try sometime, once the foot is down no turning back. Geronimo!!!!

Right, back to houses and Merle's R6.000 received. We used to drive around the koppies/hills where we stayed and a new extension Glenvista 3 had been added with all the infrastructure, roads, storm water drains and street lighting having been installed. These building sites were being developed where there were some beautiful view sites from the koppie/hill.

One in particular was in a cul de sac, number 8 Kurt Ave, Glenvista, Extension 1. It was very rocky on top but had 360-degree views. We looked around and around but this was the one and with the R6.000 and my savings we bought the land as an investment and possibly build upon.

There was a guy around the corner who dabbled in everything, held karate classes which I attended and later on in life he was a wrestling referee on TV. He had a licence to draw up housing plans. I took him to the site and he came up with some draft drawings which provided basic houses, and he did a build cost which was very expensive.

I had other ideas and fiddled faddled with designs. Eventually came up with a unique, Castle looking style, fitting into the rocky piece of ground, 330 square foot, one off design, never seen again in my life. A one and only, may I say gob smacking. See appendix for photo.

The building contractors were too expensive so decided to build on a sub contracting basis which was really the way to go if one had the time and selected reliable sub-contractors.

I visited lots of contract sites with new build homes. Quietly checked out workmanship, if good, had a chat with the individual builders, many who were on contract work and asked if and when they were available to work for me. The most important guy was the brick layer.

They of course had their buddies and eventually I had contacts for plastering, plumbing, roofing and electrical. Plumbers were very expensive, never understood why. Boet Botha was my bricky and he ended up helping and guiding me on all aspects.

On top of this I had to source suppliers, the main being Cullinan bricks and Federated Timbers who supplied a good variety of hardware. I sourced a cement supplier and used my trailer to fetch and deliver bags to the site to save a few bob. Hundreds of bags of cement were used on this home. Later giant cement trucks with telescope extension arms were used to pump in cement for foundations and upper slabs for flooring.

I arranged an extension to my mortgage facility but found out when it hit the ceiling, I had to take out credit cards and revolve money as I had hit dire straits, monetary wise. Had about ten cards on the go. In the end it became a financial nightmare on top of all the other delays, hiccups, redo's and fuck ups. No choice, had to finish the job come what may.

Most people are under budget when it comes to building, as you always want something more special when it comes to finishing like tiles, kitchen, bathroom units, etc.

I've set myself up as the Project Manager and it was a nightmare as I had to juggle, run around to the builders' yards, order this and that, ensure the sizes/quantities were correct, be on site every evening to check things out with Boet. Pay for goods, in and out of the office and stretched my lunch hours. Of course, management noticed this, but kept my job up to date, however, was treading on thin ice. There were always problems.

The house was going to be built with face brick, a burnt brown effect. The loads of bricks could be slightly different as they were coming from different manufacturing/kiln days. On site these had to be mixed as colouring difference could be seen on the wall structures.

The foundations were a problem as the site was not just a flat piece of earthed ground. It was filled with jutting rocks and boulders which had to be built into and around so this took a lot of complicated brick/concrete foundation laying. Boet was a super star and made it happen.

The windows and sliding doors were made of aluminium; rust free, with one way glass vision in all the rooms and the lounge area had sliding doors onto outside patios.

A mistake or not, but I decided to use quality internal fittings and once started, the flow had to continue throughout the home. Italian tiles, toilets, basins from Italtile, some even had signatures to make them extra special. Exclusive taps. The floors and walls were tiled to the ceiling using imported tiles from Italy.

Carpeting in the bedrooms, kitchen and scullery tiled, with beautiful oak cupboards and imported kitchen accessories, Blauenecht etc from Germany, dishwasher, fridge, chip maker, hidden lighting, and breakfast nook with sliding door onto garden area.

There were sliding doors going out into garden areas everywhere. Cannot remember the light fittings but again they were quality.

I had a built-in bar of brick with wooden top and my drink mirrors etc I had collected on my travels, Gin, Castle Lager, Guinness, to name a few. I had collected a Tenant's water jug, cloths from bars in Scotland, tot pouring units for bottles, ash trays, all the real McCoy, and 4 bar seats.

The ceilings in the dining, lounge area were in knotty pine, 6 inch wide, tongue and grooved and in between huge laminated beams, and I mean huge, to see them was to believe.

Very open plan with levels that added uniqueness to the layout.

The entrance from the outside had at least 20 steps leading to 2 large wooden double doors. Once through the doors, one faced an atrium with a water feature and flower arrangement.

Above the entrance doors was a sort of turret effect with 3 large stain glass windows a foot wide and 10 feet tall where the sun blazed through the coloured glass into the entrance hall/atrium.

Next to the atrium was a winding staircase to a study, my man cave as they say today. This is where after a few drinks, I would retire to and play my vinyl records etc on my Pioneer turntable, Kef speakers and Kenwood amplifier. I gave it a blast, loud as can be, eventually got ear phones but not the same. The view from there was grand.

All the wooded balustrades throughout the house were done by an Irish fellow whom I tracked down. His work was special and all stained in a dark finish to match the heavy dark wooden doors with quality brass handles throughout the house.

The French cathedral glass windows above the entrance door were made by my lady glass teacher, she used all her broken bits and put together 3 abstract windows and with all the colour glass, the effect was beautiful.

Next to our ensuite bathroom there was another sort of walk out area and I made a cockerel leaded glass window, all my own work.

The double garage, automatic single door, was really big with a concrete ceiling and a walk out above from 2 of the bedrooms, with beautiful viewing area.

There were sliding doors from the lounge/dining area out to a shaded patio overlooking the pool area surrounded by large pavers, which the kids loved.

A surrounding wall was built and provided great security.

As usual I evolved the garden, which had some lawn and rocks by creating magical areas for planting. I laid out the new garden which took time and months to develop. Rock plants such as the Cabbage Tree, Red Hot Pokers, etc. This all took time - I guess approx 2 years of hard work, stress and financial trauma. I think it triggered my cancer which was around the corner.

We had sold our home in 80 Vista Drive and had temporary accommodation where we had to move twice due to the delay in completing the home.

In actual fact I stayed in a caravan parked at the new home's building site. It was a nightmare but eventually came to finality.

For me it was a Mission Impossible but finished up Mission Accomplished. It took its toll on the family and put me in dire straits financially, paying off credit cards gradually as best possible. I think in these days about R230.000 rand was spent and worth I guess R3+ million today.

It was a part of life I will not forget and shows what one can do if you put your mind to it. The place was admired by all and sundry.

Pity I did not take more photos. Not too many visitors as my wife was very house proud and the home had to be spotless for visits and put a damper on socializing.

I was burning the candle at both ends and our marriage was deteriorating with lots of verbal, screaming bouts that must have affected the kids but they seemed to manage and do well at school with good results, all done by themselves. Well done guys you did great and got to University and managed your degrees.

When it came to discipline, I remember wanting to shut them in their bedrooms if naughty. I remember trying to do this with Karin but her mother thought otherwise. After that first incident I don't think I got involved again and my wife took over the discipline of the kids which I think included back hander's and don't forget the bi polar moments.

My parents came out and stayed in the new place but the atmosphere was toxic. My wife was crucifying them to the extent I had to removed them to a place in Hillbrow where I would try and see them as much as I could after work. Eventually, they returned to Scotland.

Job wise things had progressed and as a Director of the Transvaal Region I was now responsible for retaining, servicing of blue chip/public companies and new business. A Profit Centre Head with 10 support staff, ongoing supervision, training of staff and account executives.

With the house repayments and everyday costs of living creating more debt, I decided to take on a part time job in the evenings at Fidelity Guards. They specialized in money matters and had a warehouse near our offices in New Doornfontien, Jhb. The boxes of money arrived with pay packets inside for their client's employees. One had to arrange the money on a table in front of you from metal boxes containing hard cash. Then the appropriate cash was placed into employee's pay packets. Hopefully with all the money on the table it had then to be dished out according to the pay slip until no cash was left. Then onto the next clients cash box and so on.

This went on between 5 pm till midnight but as you can imagine the hours took their toll and mistakes were made. Some employees were getting more and some less. This only appeared when all the packets were finished and you ended up with extra money in front of you or a shortfall.

It became very time consuming and frustrating having to recheck all the pay packets to find your mistake. This warehouse had around 100 part-timers, mainly women. I had to bribe some of the ladies, a few from Minets' office, with chocolates, to come and assist me to find my mistakes. Thank God for their help. Months of this got to me and I was knackered running two jobs. Eventually packed it in as the money was pittance but helped a little.

With all the pressure of work, house building, debt, burning the candle at both ends something had to give. If I think back God was sending me a message and maybe to teach me something as I kept coming off the rails. If I stayed on the straight and narrow all was well but not to be.

One day I was having a pee and felt this lump the size of a marble in my testicle. Went to the doctor who sent me to a specialist, Dr Cohen. He did a few tests and within days I was booked into hospital.

When I told my boss David Harper, I had cancer he thought I was joking. I was 43.

My family were shocked and my wife assisted and cared for me during this time, even shaving me the day before the operation in the you know where area. Deep down this was her chance to get rid of my crown jewels. Anyway, appreciated all what she did for me under the circumstances and caring for me.

I tried to keep calm in the build up to the operation with a lot of praying that I would get through the process. In those days surgeons used to cut near the tumour and months later patients died due to a spread of the disease.

Dr Cohen explained that he would cut well away and extract accordingly. He said that my remaining testicle would take over the extra work load and would grow into a cannon ball. So in that case I said "while you are at it snip an inch off my willie". I wanted to be the eighth wonder of the world but it never materialized. He did show me the extracted tumour in a jar.

Everything went well but I did not sleep and was in hospital for around a week. The Guys from the office smuggled in a Castle Lager.

Eventually I went back to work and my checkups were fine but the doctor dropped a clanger to play on my mind. In those days they could not check if the disease had spread elsewhere in the body. Another operation was required, a biopsy, to scrape samples from my inner organs. Like a butcher's shop, just pull out all the innards from my chest/stomach and scrap some tissue off each organ, NO PROBLEM.!!! A nine inch/25 cm cut would be made. This happened a few months after the first operation and was a much bigger op. The shaving this time was done by a nurse, razor in the one hand and a pencil in the other for you know what.

When I awoke in intensive care, I had tubes coming out of every orifice in my body with machines bleeping away. Another wonder of the world is how they get a particularly large diameter tube up that wee hole in the willie. Then you think how is it going to come out and where it has been, the pain! All learning curves as they say.

I could not talk and every time I had a visitor the machines went racing as my excitement showed that I was alive and well.

Couple of days later I was back in the ward and did not sleep for 3 days. I had picked up a cough/tickle in my throat that would not go away. Every time the cough would send shock waves through my body and I held a pillow over my stomach/chest area where the stitches and wound were.

You know lying in bed with the cough repeating 24 hours was like a sort of payback time. I prayed myself stupid for this irritation to go away so I could have my first sleep without pain. Three days later I was out for the count. It made me think of the time when my dad was in the Glasgow Infirmity when I was a lad and he spent a couple of months in a serious condition following an articulated truck jack-knifing, crushing his car at a set of traffic lights. Did a lot of praying then too.

I eventually went home to recuperate and had checkups every year for yonks even to this day. This would include a finger up the arse, whilst in the fetal position, to rub the prostate gland to see if firm or soggy. Firm was a healthy sign. This was a turn on I used to look forward to every year especially the scratch marks embedded on the wall paper as I lay sideways on his surgery bed.

New talent as a Project Manager juggling life and credit cards,
Mission Impossible to Mission Accomplished,
A Man's home is his Castle,
Forget a Ship in a bottle -
How does a Testicle in a bottle grab you?

CHAPTER 19

Initiation or drunken orgy, I can fly, My team players, 2 Main board directors killed. Married 13/5/1972 Divorced 13/4/1989 17 years. Bought another home and renovated. Morning grooming in Chief Executives Penthouse. A new lady or two, Selling keys to hotel room, Psychologist but no straight jacket.

After my cancer operations, my team at Minets, had held the fort and visited me at home to discuss any problems and keep me up to date. Bruce Wilmore did a sterling job looking after Dorbyl. Debbie Coetzee, a Rhodesian girl was a star.

All new employees who joined had to go through an initiation. It was a drunken orgy event. So my mate Kinsley Fourie and I took Bruce to lunch to a Portuguese Restaurant with lots to drink, finishing off with umpteen Tequilas and cigars. We were almost walking on air and I remember Kingsley at the bottom of exit stairs, say 10 steps down, jump he said and there was I free falling down these steps into his waiting arms, a circus trick of note. We all survived and wondered how we ever got home.

Down the years Bruce formed his own insurance facility for 4 X 4 vehicles and later sold his business and became a Rand millionaire. Bully for him and well deserved. He became a heavy drinker but I think eventually came right. At one stage he looked like Wild Bill Hicock. Lost track of him and one day hope to visit Jhb and try and meet him and the old brigade.

Andy Coughtrie was another team player. Vic Field and I had an initiation pub lunch with him. We mocked him because he wore brown shoes and had a few buttons missing on his suit jacket. He poured his beer over my head so I did likewise with him. Bonding moments.

Andy also broke away from Minets and opened up his own broking firm. He moved to Durban and bought a share in a broking house.

Visited him now and again and he took me along to see the new home he was building in Durban. He has done very well and will try and visit next time in Durban.

Debbie wanted equal pay and opportunities as the guys for work done. She was not rewarded and left for the opposition, Price Forbes/Alexander Forbes. However, she wanted to come back to Minets on condition she worked for me. This happened and she eventually became the first lady director in the Tvl Region and deservingly so. She got divorced and married Frans Campher a main board director. Eventually both of them went to the UK. My last position in Minets was working for Frans, the story to follow later.

Around this time three directors were travelling by car to Sun City and were hit on the crest of a hill, John Buckley, Oliver Catley, died instantly. David Brunt survived but it took months for him to recover with very serious injuries. John and Oliver were great guys as well as David whom I correspond with from time to time to this day.

I was a loose cannon again, jolling and matters at home were sliding. I don't blame my wife for thinking the worst of me. We were in 2 different worlds and the threat of divorce was there.

Phone calls were made to my boss about my behaviour at home but no one realized I was provoked at times, it was a tit for tat scenario. Divorce proceedings were put into motion. We were married 17 years of the good, the bad, and the ugly and I insisted on the date being 13th. Turns out 13 was my lucky number.

The ex-wife got the custody of our 3 kids, I had reasonable visitation rights and paid R500 per month per child maintenance, plus I was responsible for all medical expenses. She received a flat R25.000 cash payment, 50% share of the sale of the house, car, furniture etc shared as agreed. I had to cede 3 assurance policies to kids until they became self supporting. My passport was held by attorneys and my 3 kids had to be deleted from my passport. Separate UK passports were eventually arranged for the kids, with all legal costs for my account.

I cannot quite remember where we moved to separately but it became evident that for the kids it be seen that we try and make a family life, although we were divorced. I remember repainting a flat near Rosettenville. It was awful and the walls covered in dirty marks. This all had to be cleaned and was repainted by me. My ex-wife and the kids moved in and later I think they moved to a flat in Glenanda.

I bought a house in Glenanda for around R60.000, It was the worst house in the street and had been occupied by Chinese who did all their cooking in the house for a take away shop they ran. The house was well built and I decided to renovate getting hold of sub-contractors to do this and that.

The driveway had single concrete lanes a foot wide for the car wheels to run on. It had a double garage, large pool, cottage pane windows, 3 bedrooms, 2 bathrooms, patio and outside washing room. The garden was alright after I had redone it.

I had trouble with the contractors who never turned up and some did poor workmanship. Somehow I managed to redo the driveway in brick, also the surrounds of the pool area and outside patio area from the lounge. In areas changed old slasto to bricks. Added a brick braai area with a tall chimney. Created flower beds built with bricks to a few feet high.

Inside was full of dark wood on the ceilings, a fireplace where I laid black slate around it. The kitchen and bathrooms were all retiled, new taps and sinks plus new shower added in bathrooms and at the end I repainted inside and out and then had new carpets laid.

I probably spent R25.000 on all of this but it ended up not too bad and years later I think I sold it for round R180.000.

The water was switched off when some new plumbing was done and as I was staying in the house it was awkward and for a couple of weeks I secretly drove in very early to Minets' office and showered/shaved/shitted in the Chief Executive's bathroom facilities in the penthouse suite on the top floor of the office. Did this very discreetly.

We then all got back together as a family and tried to keep the peace for the sake of the kids and life went on for a few more years.

I remember buying boxes of frozen chickens and brought them home. I unloaded from the sliding door side of the Kombi. When finished I jumped into the driver's seat and without closing the sliding door on left hand side drove into the garage. The sliding door got mangled as I entered the garage. I came to a halt and reversed but the damaged was done.

Next day with the sliding door hanging on its hinges I drove to the panel beaters to get it fixed. Yes, I had a few drinks in me at the time. Stuff up.

I remember I had guests once and was showing off the crystal whiskey glasses I had won at golf. They were in a special wooden box and as they were being examined a glass slipped out of the person's hand and shattered on the slate fireplace. Say no more.

In the office I had a team of employees that I was responsible for. One of the ladies worked on claims her name was Linda. She had a young child but her husband gave her a hard time. She confided in me and eventually she parted from her husband after he beat her up. She was from Port Elizabeth. I got familiar with her and one thing led to another. On some Fridays I would ring her from the pub and visit her later in the evening for my rations. I was now involved and after months I decided to leave home and stay with her, which only lasted a short period. Linda did not take it well and tried to overdose and ended up in hospital for a few days. I guess some people in the office found out. One can never hide an affair, people talk.

Around this time, I had a session and the next day I was in no fit state to slot in at a Dorbyl mini conference on Insurance. While I was doing my bit a question was asked and I briefly gave an answer but more was expected and I froze, could not talk, just stood there while people next to me said, talk John, but nothing would come out. These minutes felt like hours. I just sat down and could not find a place to crawl into. Eish!!! Punishment for something I did with a capital P.

I was always on a high which made decisions easier and after 3 days away from home I decided to return. Luckily, I was accepted back. I really did not want to create another relationship and was happy to flirt around without commitments.

I continued to ride the wave and another sexy girl, Ria, joined Minets. I was out to lunch at the New Library Hotel Jhb, on a Friday, with the lads and in orbit. I then asked one of them to phone the office and speak to her, I told him to say that I had just been knocked over by a car and was presently lying in the foyer of the hotel calling out her name.

She took the bait and left the office for the hotel and on arrival was greeted by me and the lads, she was upset but eventually saw the funny side. We met a couple of times for drinks. She then became the office bit, being chased by all and sundry. A sultry girl.

I was dedicated to my work and came in on Saturdays before golf at the Wanderers and even some Sundays, if need be, and kept my work up to date. Senior management did not notice this because 90% of them were never seen over the weekends.

On the golf side I was still winning prizes and anyone, especially the non drinkers that won a bottle of whiskey, I would buy their bottle from them at a good price. Everyone was happy.

At home I make an unforgivable mind lapse and missed seeing Karin dressed up and leaving for her Matric Dance, a very special event in her life. I only remembered the morning after a drinking session the evening before. Karin was very upset, but the damage was done and could not be reversed.

Once on holiday to the Natal South Coast, I met a few of the Minet guys i.e. Bruce, Andy Ian Georgson at Shelly Beach and we went fishing in a small boat. I was prone to sea sickness, bought the medicine and ear balancers. This did not help and within minutes of leaving the shore emptied my stomach on a number of occasions and lost my Roy Orbison Raybans. All I did was to hold onto a chrome pole for the next 2 hours, no turning back for me. When I did return a lady on the beach gave me a Coke and within minutes of being on firm ground, I was ok. Never again, said Captain Cook.

As I wanted to be a reborn rock singer, I started by buying a Casio Keyboard. At lunch time I used to travel home to Glenanda for lessons with my piano teacher. It was painful and just could not read the music so the teacher started to number my keyboard to help. We had a burglary and when the teacher arrived for my lesson and I told him the Casio had been stolen - he burst into laughter. He said John that's the best thing that could have happened as I was going nowhere.

Another beauty before the roof caves in. At a Minets cocktail party, let's call him Dave and I got chatting to 2 ladies, whom we had not met before. At end of the evening, I suggested the 4 of us go to a nearby hotel. We booked a room but the ladies got cold feet to our advances and we all called it a day.

A waste of money for the room, no way Hosea. As Dave and I walked to our cars I discovered I still had the room keys in my pocket. Believe this or not but out the corner of my eye I see this Toyota Taxi with music blaring, jammed packed with at least 10 people and the roof rack stacked with mattresses, blankets, suit cases, chickens in wire mesh cages.

Quick as a flash I ran over and spoke with the head Honcho along the following lines. Guys we have these keys and a room in the hotel opposite and for R200, you can occupy the room. No problem boss and they duly paid up and drove their vehicle to the front entrance of the hotel. From a distance we watched the commotion unfold as they started to unload and enter the hotel. Picture it, a Laurel and Harvey movie. We were in hysterics but decided to vamoose before we got pointed out.

With all the goings on I was finally reprimanded by management and pulled into an office in front of Directors and got the tenth degree, this that, my affair with Linda, the jolling and so on.

I told them the affair was over and I would cool down things. They insisted I see a psychologist and went on weekly visits where they discussed me in depth and did their reports on me and reported back to Minets. I got a clean bill of health so to speak, no strait jackets necessary.

I did not mind and probably helped my frustration that I was not getting the attention of my superiors regarding my work load and over 10 years of dedication while others were getting credo by being up the bosses' arses.

I watched my P's and Q's but did not lose my personality and continued to work hard and give service second to none. Whatever work I did was the way I would like to receive information, clear and concise. A beginning, a middle and a conclusion.

Minets went from strength to strength and was in the top 3 insurance brokers in SA with branches in all the major cities as well as all the surrounding African countries.

I guess 17 years married not bad I suppose under the circumstances, with all the building alterations maybe Project Management should have been my profession, the bubble finally bursts.

CHAPTER 20

Port Alfred, Eastern Cape, Bitten by small fish, Manna from Heaven
but not for John, Resign from Minets after 13 years service, Move to
Durban as Branch Manager of American insurers - Cigna Ins Co Ltd,
Moved to new home in Amanzimtoti Kwa Zulu Natal,
Cops stop me with illegal registration plates.

Sun City, the biggest entertainment resort in Africa for holidaying, 2 golf courses – Million Dollar Nedbank Golf tournament held there every December and still to this day, theatre, gambling, restaurants, swimming pools. Enjoyed Elton John and Rod Stewart perform there.

Took my parents for a visit and my dad fell asleep in the heat next to the ninth green and was woken by the water from the sprinklers that got switched on.

Reminds me of a dreadful motor accident. Driving back from Sun City, John Buckley and Oliver Catley (a Welshman) died instantly and David Brunt was seriously injured as well. It took months for him to recover. Played against Oliver in the Insurance football league. We were all employed by Minets at the time.

I kept in touch with David and visited him decades later at his home on the Evinrad Golf Resort in the Cape. Bernice and I stayed with him and his wife Angela who I had known for yonks from Enthoven days. Brunty was a clever lad and every time you went to discuss strategy on insurance accounts one would come out of his office and say, what the fuck was he talking about, space age stuff. He was a doyen of the industry and a good man.

I don't know if I mentioned earlier but my working buddy, Kinsley Fourie and I played in the very first Million Dollar Amateur 4 round golf competition at Sun City organized by Gary Player.

Certificates were dished out for our scores. I had 2 in the late nineties and 2 over a hundred. Played in winter on same layout as the big event but the ground in winter was like concrete and our shots kept running into the ravines edging the fairways. That's my excuse.

There was entertainment every night and got drunk as skunks which did not bode well for our golf. Those were the days.

Kit Keey, our chief executive at Minets, had a home in Port Alfred on the Cape East Coast and I managed to get the nod for a few days staying next to the river Kowie which flowed into the sea.

I hired a small boat and went up the Kowie river getting stuck on sand banks from time to time. Did fish and when my catch was unhooked from the rod the little blighter bit me and hung onto my finger. First and last time this Captain Cook sailed a boat.

We enjoyed the stay but the kids caught measles.

Kit Keey was a great guy and a statue should have been erected. I don't think he was involved in slavery, his employees were well looked after.

Did go to his home in London with another Minet employee Colin Shewring our surveyor on a short visit. Remember peeing in his garden after a heavy night. I visited him at his office in London on some other business trip. Also played golf with him at River Club in Johannesburg with fellow employees, Tim Tucker and Chris Step. He was a member and they and the wealthy members financed the costs of running the club between themselves and billed members annually for all the running costs.

Minets UK decided to buy a bigger shareholding in Minets SA. Shares were issued and directors were offered shares valued at R4.50 per share as quoted on the SA Stock market exchange in Hollard Street Jhb but offered to Minets' directors at next to nothing.

This was manna from heaven and bundles of these share allocations were offered, the higher up the ladder you were the more you got.

Even when they were listed on the SA stock exchange you could buy more and some staff borrowed money on their homes and took loans as greed set in. Just human nature I guess and the sheep followed.

Others sold their allocations the same day before the shares hit the stock market and made a killing. These were the guys who made an instant fortune while the other greedy ones paid the price in years to come as the price dropped to around R1 per share.

The great thing was the dividends were large and paid yearly tax free. At my level the yearly dividends were well over R100.000 tax free. Now that was big, big money in these days and this bonsella went on for years.

Alas, I was the ONLY director countrywide who did not receive my entitlement. David Harper our MD sat me down in his office, pushed the share envelope towards me then withdrew it. This was followed by a lecture and I was told that if I behaved myself over the next 6 months, they may consider giving me my share allotment. This really hurt me badly. One cannot understand the feelings I went through and what was to follow.

13 years down the track and this is how I get treated. Even as I write I am getting flashbacks and terrible down feelings as I had problems handling this over the years thereafter.

My whole life was about to change and still wonder if I had done my sentence of 6 months 'good' behaviour and received the share offer where the wealthy life style would have taken me. Maybe on a self destruct route, who knows where I would be today.

There were other characters that criticized the main board directors, were two faced and, I could go on. They were looked after.

I was not a bad person and had given my lot through the years, cancer and all. Not a rocket scientist but as steady as a rock and looked after the clients, kept them on the books and was very popular. As Kingsley Fourie wrote recently, the clients loved me. Why me as they say.

On top of this, new structures were formed and I was kept at the same level, moved sideways, demoted in other words and to work for someone new. I objected and eventually sat down with the new guy, explained my exasperation. In the end I accepted and worked with him, Frans Campher. I had known him a long time, respected him and we were friends.

The insurance fraternity heard about this that I was hard done by but nobody really worried. I'm alright Jack attitude. It was the principle of what had happened that gave me sleepless nights.

Out of the blue, Patrick Healy, Managing Director of Cigna Ins Co SA, a clever man and Rottweiler of note (his bark was worse than his bite) got hold of me and offered me the Branch Manager job of their Durban office. I had known Patrick for many years and to this day we keep in touch. The current manager was being transferred to the Johannesburg office.

This would be a change from broking to a manager position for insurers who were American named Cigna Ins Co Ltd. A profit share was offered if the underwriting results were good. I am afraid insurers never seemed to get the results due to competition, climate/weather conditions. These always appeared each year and caused untold damage with dire motor accident claims, all affecting the bottom line.

Maybe I should have held back, hung in with Minets for another 6 months and been an angel, yes sir, no sir. However, an olive branch was on offer and life offering me a whole new beginning away from the fast lane of Johannesburg.

I eventually decided to accept but beforehand I went to an employment lawyer and put together a case for constructive dismissal against Minets. You know the principal thing, bee in the bonnet, felt sorry for myself. To no avail as I had no money to pursue the matter and after arriving in Durban the lawyer gave up or was persuaded too.

In all honesty I think Minets got to him. The deal with the lawyer was that he would take a percentage of any damages I received, if I was successful. I still have a copy of that letter that was sent to Minets. I honestly thought I had a good case but I was at arm's length in Durban and it just petered out.

Another 10 years down the track and the courts were more accommodating to this sort of treatment. This prepared me for 2 more court cases in later years. It's the principal thing, what you believe is right and wrong, David versus Goliath. Guess what, I won both cases and received judgment in my favour.

I headed off to Durban on my own and the first job was to find a home. As usual I looked around south of the railway line in the town of Amanzimtoti, I think Zulu for little river/water. This was half an hour from the Durban City Centre where the Cigna offices were, corner West and Smith streets.

The coastal towns south of Durban were many and had been around for decades with lovely beaches. The beaches north of Durban were fewer and pretty rocky. Amanzimtoti has approx 60.000 residents and was cosmopolitan. Mainly Afrikaans speaking with English, Portuguese, African mix of people. Right on main southern freeway and next to the Indian ocean with many lovely beaches. I found temporary accommodation in a furnished flat; in a tall skyscraper block called Sarie Marie and commuted back and forth to Durban for a good 6 months until I found a permanent home.

The beach front had around 10 skyscraper blocks of flats built in the early sixties and was a real eyesore but, it was the in thing at the time and had beautiful views. The town had all the amenities such as garages, pubs, restaurants, police station, schools, golf course, craft markets, rugby, cricket, soccer grounds gym and Hutchison Park where the Highland gathering was held each year, pipe bands and all. Beaches had life guards so all in all a nice place to bring up the kids in the next stage of their lives with good schools nearby.

By the way I have now spent 21 years in Scotland, 23 years in Johannesburg and about 27 years in KwaZulu-Natal to the age of 71. I retired two months later then headed back to the UK.

I have worked since the age of 17, 54 years in the insurance industry and 10 jobs later, now that is something. Almost perfect attendance in each job but for my cancer/hernia ops and long lunches.

You have heard of the expression a Double Whammy. In the last few years I had 2 operations for cancer, got divorced, lost my job, had to sell my beautiful home, establish a new job, move lock stock and barrel to another part of SA with my VW Kombi and trailer, buy another home which I eventually I had to sell to finance my 3 kids at University. Get to know new people, build up new business relationships, the mental side of it all, hold family life together, and handle the evil drink.

All these seen on their own individually, are the most pressured and stressful times in a person's life.

I guess it was will power that got me through and making it happen. Don't forget my Guardian Angel because someone else was looking after me in many ways.

Don't know what sort of whammy you would call what I endured but it certainly over shadows Mel Gibson, as the new Braveheart on the block.

A new life ahead, maybe, exciting and challenging at least, as I continued on the treadmill of life.

Found a house to suit my budget, Nyala Place, Amanzimtoti next to the Japanese Gardens with a back wall of the house facing the Gardens. I always tried for a corner house or in a cul de sac. This home was in a fairly quiet area and I had already worked out where I was going to extend on a subcontract basis.

Kingsway High schools were near, next to each other and shared the same grounds. The English and Afrikaans schools had a good name in the area with sports' field facilities on hand. The competition between the 2 schools in sports was very competitive, especially in rugby. The English speaking against the Afrikaans speaking. The Afrikaans school always seemed to win the rugby.

After discussions, the family decided to move to Toti and at the end of the day enjoyed their new environment with all the local facilities, beach, pools, golf courses, supermarkets, close to Durban and sub-tropical weather on hand. The children formed friendships at school, some became life-long friendships.

Moving furniture in dribs and drabs was done at the weekends from Jhb to Toti, a drive of 8 hours. I would pack the Kombi and trailer for a number of weeks to complete the move.

On one journey Karin, my daughter came with me and just outside Jhb on the motorway I was pulled over by the police. They had checked out the registration plate on my trailer and it belonged to a Mercedes Benz saloon car.

A couple of weeks earlier I had lost my trailer plate but found another one on the edge of the road and decided to attach it to my trailer as opposed to going through the torture of applying for a new licence. This involved lengthy periods standing in long queues at the Licensing Department and one always had to return for this or that. This of course was illegal and they were going to lock me up but for Karin being there. I explained I was taking her back to Pietermaritzburg University.

I got off with a warning then out of the blue they noticed I had 2 registration plates stuck together on my VW Kombi. Already suspicious they insisted that I show the hidden plate which lucky for me, was the old Transvaal plate which had been replaced with one for the Natal area where I was now residing. Phew nice let off but the police checked it all out before letting us drive on.

Well, nothing like a change and who knows I may have ended up scribbling myself or ending up in some dark place with all the money from the Share Deal at Minets, which of course I did not get. So, who knows, I grabbed a straw so let the games begin. Hallelujah!

CHAPTER 21

*Natalians' clique and pee'd Eau du Cologne environment, Royal Natal
and Point Yacht clubs, Durban Insurance Golf Society, Trials and
Tribulations in office,Lady murdered 2 floors above our office, Thrown
out Durban Country Club - 2 prestigious clubs so far, Trouble with a
capital T, Office broken into and blue films found,
5 years of feeling sorry for myself comes to an end.*

Switched to the new job now which had a different environment and
the Durban insurance fraternity were very clicky. As Branch Manager,
I was responsible for retaining/ servicing/new business in the KwaZulu-Natal area. I managed 14 support staff for Cigna which was represented World Wide.

The insurance market consisted of corporate brokers and many smaller
broking firms that ruled the roost. A cocktail party was arranged for me
to meet all the main players - 50 plus people at the Royal Natal Yacht
Club where I was introduced by Patrick Healy our MD from Jhb.

All mainly new faces to me and a lot of meetings/marketing/lunches
in the pipeline, more pounding but I guess I enjoyed the socializing. I
used my Kombi as my company transport, petrol paid off course and I
had underground parking near the office. I attended insurance meetings
and got invited to lots of golf days, cocktail parties and lunch time get
togethers. I received a lot of exposure, including the players and got on
well with the insurance crowd.

We had a boardroom with a drinks cabinet and used to entertain every
Friday for staff and invitees. I occasionally had a snifter with my colleague, Jimmy Smart, every other second day, due to the heat of the day
of course.

I joined DIGS, Durban Insurance Golf Society, purely for those in the
industry. We played at a different course every month. It was great. They
played for a Short Spade, about 3 feet high, finished off in stainless steel
and brass.

If you won, one would take the spade to the jewellers and have a little brass plaque made with your name and date on it. This was stuck onto the blade of the spade. Over the years I won it over 20 times, took a photo once showing all my winning plaques.

Years later some idiot lost the spade with all the history on it. It is still played for to this with and Dennis Tuttle and Tony Beardwell, who were the organizers every month. I played with DIGS until I left SA in 2017 - a total of 25 years. They always held a year end braai after the last game of the season in December at Beachwood Country Club.

I was also a member of the Point Yacht Club which overlooked the Durban Harbour Bay and many yachts berthed there. Beautiful views and great homemade pie and chips were on the menu.

Pace became a little slower but the socializing was immense with any excuse for a pub lunch or drinks and a chin wag. Most of this was on the house, as people used their expense accounts.

It was difficult breaking into the various cliques as the Durbanites were very uppity, but I called a spade a spade. Nice people upfront but I did not wish to turn my back. There were spies in the market place reporting back to head office. As the saying goes "in life, never trust anyone". I called a certain individual "snake eyes" to all and sundry at a lunch one day and there was a hush at the table. Probably not the thing to do but you know who you are.

Before my arrival, the ethic was to slice premium prices to gain market share. However, Head Office in Jhb insisted on a minimum increase of 10% without question on all renewals. going forward. Guess what, all that business went out the front door because of this unreasonable attitude. I was glad I put everything in writing as down the track, when the figures were dwindling and answers were needed. Head Office received them, in writing, per their decisions. Loved it - as I was about to be drawn and quartered.

Cigna, the Americans, were very figure conscience and lots of reports had to be done on a regular basis. In the office we had Leila and Joy, two more spies who had photos of their previous bosses inside the doors of their office cupboards. Two faced they were.

We had to alter the office with new computers arriving with different seating arrangements. I drew up a new seating and desk arrangement.

Leila and Joy wanted to sit together but I split them up. One was a secretary and the other handled the accounts' department. I just knew behind the scenes they were chatting to their previous boss at Head Office to override me.

I finalized the plan that had to go to head office, which was in a rolled up form and I put an elastic band round it. I put a mark in pencil so I would notice if it had been interfered with. I went out to lunch and placed the plan in full view of the ladies. Sure enough, when I returned, they had had a look-see and noted where they were sitting. In due course they would have spoken to head office. Sure enough, I received a telephone call from head office re the new plans telling me these ladies had to sit together. I refused and gave my reasons and the fact that they must have looked at the plan to know where they were sitting. You get my drift. I won the day.

Maureen Pillay was another employee who did not enjoy the changes. After all the cabling for the computers had been rerouted through the channels on the office desks, she decided to undo hers on her desk as she did not like facing the entrance to the office. We hardly had many visitors.

I lost it and in full voice made her reverse her actions and I said if she wanted to complain to ring the MD in Jhb who at that time was a Hollander called Ton Broeders. After my altercation with her I went into my office and phoned him. I told him the story and to expect a call from her which happened within minutes of me putting the phone down. She had to rectify.

Our offices were in the Durban city centre on the corner of Smith and West streets and the building was a good 20 floors in height. A couple of floors above us were the offices of the local Insurance Institute, administered by a lady, her name has gone for a moment, her face glaring at me, oh how the mind goes.

Part of her duties was to mark papers on exams set by the Institute. One day she was found dead, she had been murdered. The culprit was never caught but the story goes that one of the pupils in the insurance industry was unhappy with his results and did her in. The police could not prove it but they had their suspicions. A sad, shocking and sobering day.

Many of my drinking holes were within a 10 minute walk. The Union Club was on the third floor across the road and on Fridays, in the pub area, we had a strip show on the house. Another place called Smugglers' Inn, based in the older dock area, was well renowned for its shows, curry and rice meals and was popular for tourists to Durban. Nearby was a pub called the Victoria that served good fish dishes, curries etc, run by a Portuguese guy.

Then there was the Revolving Roma restaurant on the 10th floor, overlooking Durban Harbour Bay with 360 degree views. The restaurant actually moved slowly around in the circular built building and was run by Italian chefs/owner. Still there and has been for decades. To first time visitors it was a shock especially when you told them there were people in the basement pushing the restaurant around and around as per a Galley ship.

We had the golf country clubs to frequent such as Durban Country, Beachwood, Royal Durban in the city centre and the beautiful Mount Edgecombe, consisting of two courses up the North Coast of Durban.

Earlier mentioned being thrown out of 3 prestigious clubs - Wanderers Golf Club, another I can't remember and the Durban Country Club.

I had been lunching and heard that Eagle Star Ins Co were having a big do and many dignitaries' from Jhb were attending. I came out to SA with Eagle Star and Brian Wilkinson met me and put me up for a few days. He was 10 years older than me and made it to the top. When I heard he was going to be there I decided to gate crash the event. I had no invite and when I arrived at the reception there was no name card. I grabbed one with a lady's name and strode off to the main dining area. I got nabbed just before going through the last set of doors, gave security my story but was escorted out pulling and tugging.

However, I spoke with them and asked if they would go back and speak to Brian and mention my name to get in. This would do the trick I thought but Brian told them to throw me out, I guess in jest. That was sad and never got to meet Brian ever again. That's life.

James Petrie Smart, who I mentioned before, was an underwriter at Cigna and around 10 years older than me. We became drinking buddies when need be. Jimmy loved his Cane, a white spirit (made from sugar cane), especially with coke (called Spook & Diesel). On many occasions, especially Fridays we would head for the Point or Royal Natal Yacht clubs.

For blotting paper, we would have the club special of pie and chips. These clubs still poured Imperial tots, which were like a double, but at club prices. We would talk the biggest load of codswallop under the sun while sharing a can of coke over 2 drinks each, loaded with ice and drink as if there was no tomorrow.

Cane had its magic affect but was a time bomb that would get you later. Anyway, that was our tipple all afternoon, sometimes ending up outside on the bench at the club that faced the bay. We would sit and watch the tide ebb in, six feet away looking out onto the bay. Who needed a yacht? We would always scrape together our remaining pennies for that final drink.

Eventually we made our way back to the office, a 10-minute walk, for around 4 o'clock. That was the time we opened the office pub for the staff and started all over again in high spirit. We were still there after the staff had left at 4.30 and, we remained until the traffic had quietened down at around 5.30 p.m.

Here is something different. A claim's assessor specialist, George - a Greek, occupied offices above us for many years. However, he was moving out and offered me his collection of blue films. Why not? On occasions, we viewed them after office hours for whoever was there, with the films secretly hidden away, under lock and key. Believe this or not, a year later our offices were burgled, the thieves broke into our bar, found the blue films, had a party and ransacked the office. It was a mess leaving everything all over the place.

Fortunately, I was first in at 7am and as I arrived the office door was wide open. The caretaker said the police were on their way. I was in a serious predicament and quickly gathered all the films before staff began to arrive. The caretaker came to me and knew my predicament but decided not to mention the blue film aspect as he had to do a report which would have gone to head office and the police and I would have been in deep shit and maybe loss of job. Lucky, lucky me again.

I had a go a Jimmy once, on a Monday morning, and the whole office heard. There was a big cricket event at Kingsmead Dbn, SA versus India. Jimmy promised to get there early and reserve some space on the grassy area with good views, put fold up chairs and blankets down. He would then meet me at Castle Corner, an area in the ground where beers were served, at a certain time. He was not there and we ended up sitting in the open concrete stands well away from the action. I kept searching for him in the crowd and spotted him sitting in his fold out chairs with family and great view point. I attracted his attention, as he had reserved a spot for Bernice and me. He took us to a grassy patch where he had put down a small blanket, a meter by a meter that you could not swing a cat on with spectators packed in like sardines and no fold out chairs that he had promised to arrange. It was awful and he returned to his view point. We were not happy and went back to the concrete seating area and had taken a picnic basket thank goodness. On Monday, I let rip in the office as after all the prearrangements he had agreed he had not adhered to. The whole office heard John in full voice. Days later we smoked the peace pipe or drunk the drink.

Once over a festive season after a few drinks at lunch time Jimmy and I bought some bubbly and decided to visit a broker. They specialized in Body Corporate/Buildings/Flats so we marched into the offices but it backfired as everyone was on a different planet from us so we turned tails and scarpered.

Any profit share bonus to Cigna branch or country wide never materialized as the Motor and Fire/Accident segment of the business always ended up in a loss situation. Natal was in the storm/flood belts and sure as God made little green apples we, had a couple of biggies every year. One cannot prevent natural losses in the insurance game. A good year would be great but alas.

This added to my bouts of depression - did I make a mistake leaving Minets and moving to Durban? Thinking back there were pros and cons and at the end of the day the pros won. However, it took 5 years to get my mind right and shake off the demons.

All I heard was how successful Minets were, huge tax-free dividends paid out, guys buying fancy cars, new homes. News reports on their successes and that they were now the second biggest broker in the land. Receiving calls now and again from Minet employees saying you should have hung in and when visiting the local Minets office for business had to hear of the Group's success.

Every night at home, sitting out on the patio, I had a few drinks to mummify myself but the mind kept going back to what if scenarios. However, after 5 years I shrugged off the guilt and feeling sorry for myself or whatever and enjoyed life going forward. Maybe if I had remained in Jhb and had the money I would have gone into the fast lane and written myself off. The release was magic, my Guardian Angel to the rescue again.

Just to recap on the enjoyable holidays we had over the years. I remember my time share units at Bakubung, next to Sun City, the unit in Margate South Coast called La Cote D'Azur and Kruger Lodge right next to one of the entry gates at the Kruger National Park Game Reserve. All were self catering and Bakubung had a hop on, hop off on bus service to Sun City. We had game drives available every morning and were taken into the game park called Pilanesberg Game Reserve plus golf at Sun City and Lost City which had crocs in the water hazard next to the green of a par 3 hole. The evenings were great and one could hear the calls of many animals at night. It was special. Bakubang overlooked a Hippo pool beyond a fence for easy viewing, plus swimming pool within Bakubung resort.

The La Cote D'Azur room had a balcony overlooking Margate Beach and the Indian Ocean which was far warmer than the Atlantic. It also had pools and restaurants on hand with a 5-minute walk along the beach to Margate Town Centre which was popular. Plenty of golf courses were nearby, which I played many times including the Wild Coast Sun. It was so relaxavous in this sub-tropical area.

The Kruger Park Lodge had a pool, a mini golf course and a hippo pool. This bordered the Kruger Park and was 5 minutes down a dusty road to an entrance gate. We visited the Park many times and enjoyed the environment.

On one trip, driving around in Kruger, when the kids were small, our Opel Kadet was almost flattened with the 5 of us on board. Down one of the side roads we startled a giraffe as he came out of the bush. He was on a slide in front of us about to fall on the car but managed to get his footing and righted himself. It was very close. We picked up a baby tortoise on the side road, next to my door. Robert wanted to keep it but it pissed on his lap – he did not want it anymore.

All these Resorts had their own style of buildings/units, private and up market. A pleasure.

We enjoyed 5 star accommodation at these timeshare units through the years but the levies escalated and eventually had to trade them off into a Flexi Club point system, unfortunately. I managed to trade off against points at Flexiclub Leisure Holidays, who were holiday specialists with their head office based in Pinetown, Durban. This was a new adventure and ended up holidaying throughout SA for years at self-catering units, which was ideal.

One would use up the points gained each year, as a member. However, I always had to pay an annual fee for the facility but not as expensive as the other 3 units mentioned above that I had through Stocks and Stocks.

Flexiclub had opening dates for the various seasons and one had to book as soon as possible for the best locations before other members beat you to it. Ideally, I would visit their Head Office in Pinetown first thing in the morning and get in the queue. The popular venues would go that same morning and what I used to do is book the best ones. Christmas year end and school holiday peak periods which I would rent out at much higher 'peak' fees which in turn paid my annual fee. When I secured my booking, I used to put cash in an envelope which I quietly handed to the booking lady. Did this year in year out, which paid dividends. Sometimes it was better using renting agents as they had more exposure to customers looking for a holiday unit. They took a hefty commission of 20% but it put money in my back pocket. I still had points left over to book other places at Flexiclub elsewhere in SA and Mauritius. I kept most of my bookings in a folder on my lap top so will not bore you with these fabulous holiday resorts, or should I?

I remember a trip to Knysna with the family. I decided to visit Knysna which had beautiful views of the sea entrance to Knysna Bay. Getting there through the beautiful homes on the hills, one had to travel up a one in ten road incline which put a strain on the engine of VW Kombi. Thereafter, I decided to visit Plettenberg Bay and on the way there the engine blew. I managed to free wheel to a Shell garage in the distance. The engine had gone as I did not manage to switch off the car when I heard the engine rumbling. I had a few seconds to recognize the engine was about to go to save it by switching it off. At the garage the head mechanic, who had won an award for the best in the area, gave me the bad news. The engine was non repairable and he suggested a reconditioned engine. Seemingly in the Western Cape, a factory produced reconditioned engines for the VW group in general. This was going to take a good month so we had to hire a car for the rest of our holiday and to get home. Money money, money. I had to fly back when vehicle ready and whilst there took the opportunity to visit Paul Fouche, who had retired in Sedgefield as I used to work with him at Enthoven's, for a chin wag.

I love travelling, even with the hiccups, seeing new places, surrounds and was sure the family did as well. I think people who go year in year out to the same place must be bored stiff. It was not my cup of tea. Variety is the spice of life.

The move to the tropical environment in Natal worked out well for the whole family. Life was pretty well laid back and I loved the humidity, the sea, beach walks and the abundance of golf courses nearby. It certainly beat the heavy traffic of Joburg, a concrete jungle and mine dumps, Cook's Tours/Holidays.

CHAPTER 22

*Extend home at Nyala Place, B P Garage, My Accountant Piet Pienaar,
ANC changes 100 street names in Durban, Corset for my back. Karin,
Robert, Gordon at University and the costs thereof. Finances in dire
straits and sell home at Nyala Place, Rent townhouse at Richfield Park.
Fights with Chairman of Body Corporate,
Kids fly the nest to Wimbledon, London. A cheeky offer on repossessed
Townhouse through my bank plus loan to support.*

Like all my previous homes, time for an alteration to the home in
Amanzimtoti, next to the Japanese Gardens. It was a small family room
extension with walk through from existing and doors out to the garden.
It was a flat roofed effort and got involved with an Indian fellow who
worked for the local Municipality.

It was mainly done at weekends and took a while. At the end I felt I
was overcharged for this and that with surprise costs to be paid and was
done on a subcontract basis. However, it served the purpose in the end.

The garden had large trees, bougainvilleas and crotons. With the back
wall facing the Japanese Gardens which one could view. The lawn was
patchy and sandy with ants. Every time I mowed the lawn it was like a
dust bowl. I used to tie a rope to my Flymo mower to cut the slopes at
side of house facing the road which were like 1 in 10 radius.

The area was sub tropical and from the water features in the Japanese
Gardens mosquitoes were in abundance. The occasional green garden
snake appeared and never knew if harmless or a green Mamba which
is dominate in the Natal area. Plenty of monkeys pinched one's fruit
through the kitchen windows with dogs barking loudly in the background when they saw and heard the invading monkeys. This home had
cottage type windows/doors in wood which, with the heat, I had to varnish almost every year.

In Toti I got to know John Hutton who ran the BP garage where I
bought my petrol. He had a little frozen fish outlet which I bought from

now and again. He had a friend called Johan and we went for drinks nearby on occasions.

John eventually got divorced which was sad as he had a lovely little girl. Later he set up a business letting out trailers and I need to try and see him some day.

The guy who installed our curtains was a friend and I used to pop into his shop and have a few beers, forget his name.

Piet Pienaar of accountant's company Senfin was the man who handled my tax returns and did a good job. He worked from his home on the hill behind the schools in Amanzimtoti. A decade later he bought an old house at 268 Che Guevara Rd, Berea Durban, as an additional office and he still looks after my tax affairs from there.

To piss off the whities the ANC government changed a good 100 street names from old British colonial to revolutionaries and into Zulu etc. Not great for visitors/locals to Durban who got lost with all the changes.

I had lower back problems for decades and wore a corset. It became chronic whilst in Natal. I visited 2 chiropractors in Toti, 2 in Durban, plus masseurs. I even went for acupuncture. On occasions I buckled up and needed pain injections. I used one lady for a long time who was near the office I worked in, as she was a 2 minute walk away. Eventually I consulted with surgeons but I had heard of too many failed operations so put up with the pain and discomfort.

I started going to the public, open air swimming pools in Durban. It was not the one on the beach front for the holiday makers but was an Olympic size used for competitions. The large one was under shade with seating for the public and the other was in the sun. It was a 5 minute drive from the office. This was great relaxation at lunch time and helped my back.

Next stage was to join Virgin Active Gym/Pool facilities in Toti and also a Yoga class for beginners. The yoga lady had red hair was good and both forms of exercise helped greatly with my back. Sitting as an office Johnny all these decades had not helped.

Today, in Gillingham UK, I swim and go to gym 3 times a week and seldom have problems but now and again get a little twitch. Since Covid, I do my exercises from home with a daily walk which saves me £40 p.m.

at the gym. These days I stand in front of my lap top that sits on a box on my desk at chest level. I should have done so decades ago.

At this time Karin was attending Pietermaritzburg University and shared a flat in a high rise block of flats near the University. I visited now and again. I think she had a waitress job part time. She obtained her degree as a Dietician with flying colours over the 4year course and this was good news.

Bought Karin a Yellow 2 door Toyota, which was old with rust but was reliable. She used the car to get around and visited Toti from time to time over her 4 year period at varsity. Besides this, one had to give a little pocket money, pay for the car R10.000 and the 4 year course which amounted to R100.000. It was all worth it in the end as she has put her degree to good use over the years.

After qualification she managed to get a job at the prestigious Brook-dale Health Hydro Balgowan, Pietermaritzburg, which included in-house board. From there she would visit at weekends but had a horrible and dangerous road trip home in very heavy fog to and from Brook-dale which was in a mountain belt. I did the drive once which was very scary with only 10 feet visibility.

Near Karin's little sleepover house at Brookdale someone had a litter of kittens. She selected d a beauty and named it Champers because of its colouring. Champers eventually came to our home in Toti and became part of the household. I did not really like cats and Champers was difficult to get to know. She loved licking water from taps, outside or in the bathrooms. She would beckon you to the taps for her daily drinks. She lived 19 years and we eventually got to know each other.

Karin moved back to Toti from Brookdale and decided to open a practice in a complex in the centre of Toti. She bought a new red VW Chico 1300. Things changed when the complex was sold and she decided to go to the UK to work for a Health food company in marketing.

I took over her car and paid the balance owing for the red VW Chico. I drove it for 430.000 kilometres before it was stolen from the driving range in Hillcrest many years later but that's another story.

Karin met Brad Stransky, brother of the famous Joel Stransky who won the World Rugby Tournament at Ellis Park in Johannesburg in 1995 with the last drop kick of the game against the All Blacks, never to be forgotten. On a number of occasions, I met old man Stransky at his home in Scottburgh on South Coast. It was a 15 minute drive from Toti and the home was right on the border of the Scottburgh Golf Course. Brad was a rugby referee. They got on well and courted for a number of years travelling in a Kombi through Europe. They travelled around the famous Monaco racetrack. Brad was Jewish and Karin Christian and a marriage seemed impossible so the relationship came to an end. Brad passed away in 2021 from cancer.

Robert was the next to attend Pietermaritzburg Uni on a Computer Science Degree which he eventually got after having to resit one year as he had asked one of his classmates to take the notes. The Professor found out and he was reprimanded and it cost me money for another year at the Uni. Just over R100.000 in total for all his years, plus a R10.000 Mazda, another rust bucket, fuel, insurance and pocket money. Robert got his degree which was a blessing.

Robert assisted his friend on Toti beach as the friend was about to be attacked by 5 guys. Robert stepped in front of his mate and said that he might lose the fight against the pack but the first guy who comes forward is going to get his wrath big time. They backed off. VC for Robert's bravery.

He once wrestled me onto a couch when his mum and I were having a go at each other and deservedly so.

Robert went into the computer world with jobs here and there. He ended up in Jhb with Price Waterhouse.

Gordon was next in line for Uni and went to Durban University, nearer home. His degree was Project Engineering, Civil Works and it was, I think, a 5 year course. I ended up buying him a second hand Datsun bakkie, in his favourite colour, blue. It was another bad buy by me and this vehicle gave a lot of trouble but at the end of the day was cheaper than paying off a vehicle in instalments. He sold the vehicle on his way to the Durban airport at the side of the road with cash being handed over by this Indian fellow before leaving for the UK. Another R100.000 for fees, plus insurance, pocket money etc.

The kids I think enjoyed Toti with the beach on their doorstep and friends they had at school. Robert and Gordon played school rugby for Kingsway High School.

Gordon wanted to play tennis and I took him for Saturday morning lessons in Pinetown. With a little bit more dedication and practice he could have moved on.

In a rugby game between Kingsway and Toti High, one of the highlights of the year, Robert got Vaseline or something rubbed into his eyes in the scrum and he was side-lined until he recovered. That's how intense it was.

The Afrikaans school at Kingsway always beat the local English lads. It is in their blood, no matter how loud the parents screamed their support. Year end dinners were held for the rugby school boys with their fathers present.

The rugby boys were great friends and even to this day they keep in contact and have get togethers as grown men with their families. They meet in SA or the UK to catch up now and then.

The Church was also very important and they congregated with their friends there and built their lives around strong beliefs.

Fortunately, I arranged UK Citizenship for my 3 children at a young age which was a blessing in disguise. As twenty plus year olds they all ended up in Wimbledon where a large South African/Aussie contingency lived. What a great experience with lots to do and having jolls/parties/get togethers.

Funny how I left my parents in Scotland at 21 and hardly saw them and now I was getting the same treatment. At the moment, 2020, Karin is in Perth, Australia, Robert in Cobham, Surrey area and Gordon just moved from Johannesburg to Farnborough in UK.

Karin was the first to leave after closing her business and settling in Wimbledon and on the road as a Marketing lady for health foods.

Gordon started work with Group Five Civil engineering and was involved in a new road bridge in Pietermaritzburg which we named Gordon's Bridge, near the new shopping mall erected next to the main Johannesburg/Durban highway.

Gordon enjoyed his rugby and joined Amanzimtoti Rugby Club which had good facilities and played for a couple of years enjoying his time there and winning man of the match awards, which meant you had to down down a loaded drink. They played away games which I travelled to.

I never played rugby as a schoolboy, reserved only for private schools in my day and the weather did not help. I always thought it was an unfair game unless you were six foot six and built like a rhino. There was a tendency to keep your eye on the player as opposed to the ball and a set up for injury which always worried me when watching Gordon and Robert. However, they got through it, although Robert ended up with neck injury when playing in the UK.

Gordon decided to go to the UK with his girlfriend now wife, Sylvia who joined him and they had good times. They came back to SA and married at a Castle near Pietermaritzburg, plus bagpipes and the wedding party men in kilts. The whisky flowed and we had a few drams on the turret with the customary cigar. In the UK Gordon and Sylvia bought a 2 bedroomed council home and did it up. I visited once and they now rent the place out which has been a good investment with growth in its value.

They moved back to SA and have 2 girls Sadie and Peyton, and lived in Randburg Johannesburg. By that time everyone ended up with British Citizenship. The family moved to Farnborough in January 2021.

For the tertiary education of my children, the purchase of cars and more, I had to arrange loans through Nedbank and pay them off. I even approached my employer at the time, Cigna Insurance, for a loan but was refused. All these loans/repayments were adding up and more money was going out than coming in. Eventually I had to sell our home and scaled down to renting a townhouse, to cope financially and that took some doing.

As mentioned earlier, the house at Nyala Place, Amanzimtoti was sold and we literally moved 500 yards to a block of single storied townhouse flats. There were about 16 units built of face brick and all in a row. The place was gated and fenced and I think called Richfield Park.

We rented a 3 bedroom unit with a little enclosure and back garden facing an embankment. The dining room was ideal and stepped down to the living room. This was all open plan from the kitchen through to sliding doors to a shaded patio including a double garage. The garden was small and there was an underground stream passing by all the units.

I was always very conscious of security and had large gates installed on the covered patio leading through glass sliding doors to our lounge. Easy entrance but no more and could sleep well at night.

The place was clean and it was a good area to live. However, when we had severe rain storms all the water would run down the main driveway and flood the 2 bottom units on a regular basis. They had serious problems. I used the balance of monies from the sale of Nyala Place to reduce some of my debt and was just keeping my head above water.

We met an Afrikaans couple next door to us, who were teachers at Kingsway High School. The guy was a PT instructor and looked after the school's rugby team. However, the complex was run strictly by the Chairman of the Body Corporate who lived in the complex. We had a couple of clashes. One where his son continually kicked his rugby ball into our garden. When I eventually refused to release the ball, I got visits from his father, the Chairman, yakity yak and I used a bit of French. Say no more.

Some of the units were still held by the builders of the complex and were financed by Absa Bank. The builders went into liquidation and a few of the units were being sold off at below market price.

I called on Absa and made an offer of R80.000 on one of the units that needed some work. No go. I later upped the price to R90.000 then R105.000 a price agreed to. I was now a property owner once again and arranged a mortgage.

I repainted the inside of the unit, put new light fittings in and re-carpeted. The garden had 2 large storm water concrete pipes sticking up about 3 feet out of the ground with concrete lids, half a meter wide. They were real eyesores to the garden.

At the bird park nearby, I noticed they were draining a water section, removing the silted earth and replacing with new fresh ground. Faster than the speed of light I fetched my trailer, old faithful, and shovelled the old silted earth into the trailer. I went back and forth unloading the earth into the garden of the unit and managed to gather enough to level the garden and concealed the concrete storm water drains. The change was like night and day.

I planted lots of hardy plants using break offs from surrounding bushes etc and stuck them in the ground. Many of these took root. So far no cost and with some hard work I created a new garden. The family had a new home. Karin had 2 little dogs, brought her cat Champers, champagne in colour, who lived the life of Reilly. I had my Kombi/Chico and Merle had her green/blue Honda and the kids, when they were around, parked in open bays within the complex.

The units had a passage way between them, about 2 metres apart and not really in the public's view. We were in a sort of valley and it got stinking hot and very humid, plus we were in a subtropical area. I decided we needed some air conditioning units and required the Body Corporate's approval. However, I went ahead and installed the air con. The external side of the air conditioning extraction fan needed to be in the middle of the passage way outside between each unit as there was no other place for it to be fitted. This particular area was out of sight and one would have needed to stand, stop on the driveway and look down the passage to see the extraction unit. In addition, I planted a bushy tree which would, after a few months, obscure any sighting of the extraction unit. Now the war began.

The Body Corporate insisted that this spoiled the ambiance of the complex and arranged for contractors to remove the unit. Meantime I had contact a specialist lawyer in Johannesburg who confirmed my right to install. I had to fly this guy down and be present when the Contractor and the Chairmen arrived to remove the unit. Threats were flying but we won the day and the Chairman headed off with his tail between his legs.

Funny, months later the chairman put an air con in with an extraction unit facing out from his wall onto a much more exposed area for all to see as he had an end unit. Great how that works.

There was another incident where I sent a letter to all units in the complex singling out a peeping tom. This caused a real stir and had all the occupants congregating on the driveway.

I played golf at Amanzimtoti Golf Club which had a good vibe with a number of Scots around. The course was right on the beach of the Indian Ocean which lapped against some of the holes.

It was a links course and very pretty. However, the fairways were a bit sandy and the club did not have money to spend on improving the course. The clubhouse ticked and the drink flowed. It was ten minutes from home. They had a muster of peacocks on the course, plus a cricket ground.

There was another course, built in 1930 by a corporate Group, AE&CI with a Country Club in Umbogintwini. Great meals were served, with beautiful open verandas, very quaint and Victorian. It had a lot of history and would have been great in its heyday but as things became more expensive these clubs just could not exist financially. It was eventually sold off for a low cost housing development by the Municipality. New shopping malls were also erected.

Down the South Coast there were towns named Scottsburgh, Umkomas, Selborne and Umdoni all with views of the golf course with views/holes facing the Indian Ocean, plus quaint old golf club pubs built in the thirties. Natal had wonderful courses and plenty of them in Durban City - Royal Golf Club, Durban Country Club and Beachwood. We also had Zimbali and Maidstone, further up the North Coast etc.

How it feels to be rock bottom financially, having to sell one's home to make ends meet, and maintain 3 children attending University, having to rent, then a break of note with repossessed unit on the market at a discounted price, reborn property owner again, how things change.
Geronimo!

CHAPTER 23

Cigna close up shop, Another fight, Take matter to CCMA, Joined another American Insurer, The St Paul's Ins Co Ltd, working from home under the banner of Stonehouse Ins Consultants.
Put on Minet's wanted list Dead or Alive, Forget the Great Fire of London. St Paul's withdraw from SA. Lucky me another job with CorporateSure and then an additional job with Admiral - now wearing 2 hats, isn't that something?
Retirement approaching 65 but another issue with contract conditions, Take on Santam Insurers, biggest in SA and win my case.

Cigna were a Worldwide short-term insurer and I was their Branch Manager in Durban between 1992 to 1999 with 14 support staff. SA became independent in 1994. Cigna were American and business ran on figures and bottom-line results. Our premium was good but our loss ratio was poor due to high incidents of motor losses and the seasonal floods and storms in Natal.

In addition, we had a large book of Body Corporates, in essence residential flat complexes and the like. These were vulnerable to storms, flooding, water damage due to burst pipes and poor maintenance leading to water type losses. The competition for this class of business was fierce and eventually had to give notice of cancellation to brokers due to poor loss history most of which was inevitable.

Cigna decided to reduce staff, then followed the culling of staff which was a sad affair, we eventually ended up with 4 employees. I remember taking the last 3 employees for a Christmas treat on a helicopter trip around Durban Harbour, up the north coast to Umhlanga and passed over Harry Oppenheimer's holiday home right on the beach. I am scared of heights, with vertigo big time, but managed to sit in this helicopter with surrounding glass which helped me through the fear.

Ace Insurers in America had taken over Cigna and closure was in the pipeline. I fought hard to keep the office open and went to the CCMA,

Commission for Conciliation Mediation & Arbitration----for fair practice in the work place to avoid closure.

My consolation was a R60.000 payout but "keep it quiet John" and eventually a retrenchment package was the minimum. All these monies went to reduce my overdraft and mortgage.

I was around 54 and missed out in getting my medical aid paid for by a year for the rest of my life. That would have been a real help financially.

An employee in the branch office received the long-term medical aid deal but years later Cigna/Ace decided to buy themselves out of the deal with a lump sum payment of R500.000 to the individual, which seemed good at the time. This person started piling money into one of these pyramid schemes in Mossel Bay where interest returns were mind boggling. Initially the monthly returns were double and too good to be real and monies flowed into the individual's bank account. This scheme was set up by a Pastor fellow in the Cape. The tax authorities found out/SARS/Police and all investors lost their money having to repay everything they had made and invested into this illegal set up. He is still paying back to this day and is in a dire fiancial state. Too good to be true? A lesson for us all.

Anyway, another chapter in my insurance career ends.

My guardian angel came to my rescue with another job. A fellow who I played soccer with way back in the late sixties for S A Eagle. Pat Cochrane, who played for Ibis, contacted me. Pat also stayed round the corner where we lived in Kurt Ave, Glenvista Extension 3, Jhb. He wore a toupee for decades and then came out of the cupboard baring all as smooth as a baby's bum, another Kojak.

He was boss of an American Insurer based in South Africa. Pat was clever and shrewd. The insurer was called "The St Paul" and he wanted me to be the Regional Manager in Durban for the Natal region, I was working from home in Amanzimtoti with Policy Documents/Claims processed by the Head Office in Johannesburg. I looked after the broking fraternity and was responsible for retaining existing business in the area and developing new business in KwaZulu-Natal province.

Besides working from home, I was able to form my own Closed Corporation and called my company Stonehouse CC, after the village I lived in until 21 years of age before heading to SA. This had its benefits and I could write off expenses, food, drink, petrol etc to the Tax man. I was remunerated on a commission basis of 2% on new business premium and 1% on renewal premiums going forward.

The St Paul company had huge dollar capacities to accept business on large corporate accounts, which was very important to the major broking houses. I knew all the brokers and received good support on my visits to their offices. Premium growth over 3 years, R3.2m, R7.5m to R13.1m so, financially things were picking up.

There was a hiccup with my old employers, J H Minet Brokers, that caused huge animosity against me. The story is as follows. A longstanding broker, in his twilight years, left Minets, Durban to form his own little broking agency and work from home. Close clients of his at Minets wanted to support him for the good service he had given them over the years and they wanted to move their business to him. Mike Eccles was very close to the owners of a company called Beier Industries. The chairman, Hans Beier, a German, liked Mike and appointed him as broker to their business, which was a colossal account.

Minets knew the account was under attack and closed the market by getting quotations from all insurers. However, they forgot about The St Paul and me. I had put together a deal, with Head Office approval, that was special and won the business for Mike. Minets had made a huge mistake by not contacting me and I did not disclose that Mike Eccles had approached me, which was fine.

However, when they lost this large prestigious account, they gunned for me and I got phone calls telling me not to come into their offices with a "Wanted Dead or Alive" attitude. Once the dust had settled and after some time, I started revisiting their offices.

Beier had their premises in Pinetown, a large industrial complex in Durban. Their buildings were tiered and had steps from one manufacturing point to the other making components for the motor industry. Risk Management meetings were held every week to ensure loss control was observed with exceptional care in the work place and manufacturing processes.

Years later when welding was being carried out by a subcontractor to fix a pipe somewhere in the building, a spark caught a gas leak. An enormous fire occurred and inflammable oils caught fire and spread throughout the premises. Unfortunately, the fire brigade used water instead of foam to fight the fore. The water flowed down the various tiers taking the fire with it and we had a catastrophic loss of premises and loss of profits for the business – a Great Fire of London so to speak. It took years to rectify and return to profit. The monetary loss was around R300 million.

Of course, people were checking this and that, looking for heads to roll, as someone has to get the blame. Thank goodness my house was in order but when I visited St Paul's Jhb office weeks later in the company of American executives, Pat Cochrane, our Chief Executive turned and pointed his finger at me and said that's the gentleman who put the business on the books.

Funny how people change, even although Pat signed off the initial deal, he was ducking the flak. I did not lose any sleep as my house was in order. The claim dragged on for years with interim payments made on account.

Working from the townhouse in Toti was great. Based in a sort of tropical valley and in summer got very very humid. Between 12 and 2 pm on some days I would have my siesta and lie down as the heat was excruciating. Just lie on the bed and try to sleep until it got a little cooler. That was the way it was.

During this time, I decided to have my eye lids operated on. My eyes were fast becoming pee holes in the snow. I went to a Dr Cook believe it or not who was a specialist. I was in and out the same day. Merely cut away the loose skin, easy peasy but for 2 black eyes for a few days. After returning to work some people said "you look different, John" but nobody knew and I never let on.

I was with St Paul from 1999 to 2002, after which St Paul USA sold their interests in South Africa, Lesotho and Botswana and withdrew. The staff countrywide was hoping that a local consortium would buy the book of business but it never came about, I guess due to over pricing.

We found out that a new Chief Executive had been appointed in the States and he was not an insurance man as such. He was merely out to cut costs and in his first year removed the company's operations worldwide even although they were making a profit. Of course, the bottom line immediately came right and he was on a huge bonus. I guess he made his millions in his first year of operation. Who the hell cares after that, he had made his killing. For me it was good while it lasted for 3 years and received some retrenchment payment. I missed running my own consultancy with the tax advantages. Anyway, that's the way the 'Cookie' crumbles.

Around this time Paul Travers of Minets, who I worked with for many years, passed away in a retirement home. He was in his mid seventies. I travelled to Jhb for his funeral and wake which was held at a well-known German Beer Hall in Randburg. Met many of the old Minets' staff for the first time since departing all those years ago.

I had my hate list of the guys who bombed me, but still their shook hands, walked on and drank with my friends and it was great to reminisce, catch up and laugh with them. It was good. Friends Kingsley and David Brunt were there. Paul was a good man but had suffered with Parkinson's/Alzheimer's. At work he was known as Shakin Stevens, as later in life he used two hands to hold his drink but after 2 stiff ones it was easy peasy to hold his glass in one hand. Loved by all.

The insurance industry in South Africa was long established throughout the land and was very professional. Underwriting agencies were formed where they wrote business for major Insurers for an agreed commission and managed the book for the major insurer on specialised risks. These were popping up in Durban and CorporateSure Insurers offered me a job, specialising in Body Corporate type of business i.e. blocks of flats, holiday complexes, residential and gated estates,.

Due to the province of Natal having magic weather all the year round it was a Mecca for holiday resorts and retirement homes. CorporateSure wrote business on behalf of Santam Ins Co Ltd, who became the largest insurer in SA.

At CorporateSure I was responsible for retaining/servicing/new business and other specifics such as corrective action, implementing a reconstruction of C-Sure client's loss ratios. I compiled a guideline booklet showing processes for management and staff to follow via the networking system in place. It worked well and I was proud of what I had designed and set up going forward.

CorporateSure's whole client base was overhauled over a period of six months, enabling General Management to review the loss ratios of their clients to a respectable level and adjust their premiums and excesses at each renewal for every client on the books.

I had to travel from Amanzimtoti to Umhlanga Rocks, the new jewel, which had been developed over the last few years into a business hub just north of Durban. The motorway was nearby from the south coast up to Richards Bay where SA exported their coal reserves and had huge plants making billets of aluminium at Alusaf. The farm land around Umhlanga was owned by Huletts Sugar who sold off land to developers for the Umhlanga business/Retail Centre and land for the new airport to be named, U-Shaka,

At all my jobs through the decades I was an early starter at my work place and was normally first to arrive and opened up the offices. It took around an hour to get to CorporateSure's offices.

In the evenings though, I always hung around and had a drink in the offices or met guys at pubs for a blether whilst the traffic eased.

I still received invites to golf days and was now in the slow lane and life was more laid back. Even business associates from Johannesburg would ring me when coming to Natal and we would get together. Lunches and drinks were always on the house so to speak and one or another would pick the tab up on their expense account.

Due to my exposure to the marketplace, I was asked by Admiral Insurance, a satellite underwriter of Santam, who specialised in Liability Insurance exposures to represent them in Natal. I was asked to come on board and now had two jobs!

I am, at this stage, over 60 and was well known in the insurance industry with lots of experience. I took on the job which basically meant the wearing of 2 hats and I visited brokers to drum up business in Durban, Pietermaritzburg, Pinetown, South Coast and Port Shepstone, plus north to Richards Bay areas.

Things went well with 2 contracts on the go. Out of the blue, just before I was about to go overseas on holiday to Scotland, my fucking old nemesis appeared, whom I had report to in Jhb. A new contract had been drawn up and I had to sign the day before I went on holiday. I was pressured, under duress, to do so otherwise no job. I found out later that my retirement age was 65 where my previous contract was 70. Sure enough, the Santam policy was to get rid of staff at the age 65 and I was 64 at that time.

My local boss, Gordon Campbell and an Executive at head office, my nemesis, were in cahoots in this regard. I took the matter to the CCMA and won an award of R110.000 in compensation, less tax of course. Not quite what I deserve after 5 years and would have preferred to stay in work. However, I was soon head hunted for another job. As they say you cannot keep a good man down.

Around 2002, my ex-wife and I parted ways from Richfield Park in Toti. Many reasons but she had a heated argument with our daughter and her Aussie friend Claire, just for the sake of causing friction and I decided to end the toxic environment. I sold the townhouse, moved out and rented a small flat next to the motorway, storing most of my stuff in a single garage in that block of flats.

I joined Virgin Active Gym which was a 10 minute walk away, did basic yoga classes and used the swimming pool.

My ex-wife moved into a mobile home park where the units were looked after. A unit was bought by me but in her name. I repainted and renovated the unit. It was not great but it was neat and adequate. It had a little garden and parking and many of the people were retired who lived there. It was secure and people were around to converse with and a swimming pool. She later sold the unit and moved into a block of flats nearby.

She eventually moved in with her son Gordon and his wife in Johannesburg. Gordon had bought a roomy house which had an annex with plenty of space from a German who had kept the house in very good condition. Gordon, Sylvia you were very brave and did a great job under the circumstances.

Lucky me with wealth of jobs appearing and keeping me afloat.
However, retirement approaching at 65 and this did not suit me.
I was still fit and raring to go on till the cows came home and most
important of all I had lots of experience on offer
and was still riding high in the saddle.

CHAPTER 24

The following chapters cover a period while still working up to when I retired from insurance at the age of 71, two months prior to departing to the UK. Dressed to the hilt in my Kilt, Rugby Tickets, Absa Park, Sibaya Casino, New build for John in a development called Plantations in Hillcrest, Arrival of Bernice, my new partner, Trip to UK to see my dad/sister, Anthea, Bernice loves Pipe Bands, KZN, Hernia op, Heart problem, Vehicles stolen, and pets pass away.

I had been travelling up and down to see Bernice in Jhb but on one occasion I asked her to fly down on 7 June 2003 and join me to watch Scotland play the Boks at the Kingspark Rugby Stadium, Durban. I think the Boks just beat Scotland 29-25 with a touchdown in last minute. Eish!

I picked her up at the airport dressed in a kilt, my red-haired jimmy bonnet, St Andrews flag, my cheeks painted with the cross as well. I had converted pantyhose into a one-legged giant Willie, stuffed with balloons, tied round my waist that automatically shot up when I lifted my kilt. It was the eighth wonder of the world. As I walked through the airport, I occasionally lifted the skirt, this huge wallaper sprung out. Well, the Africans went into hysterics with photos being the order of the day. Got to the rugby stadium, got seven out of ten for my dress code from the masses as I walked past the supporters but, as soon as I lifted my kilt, it was 12 out of 10. After the game we went to the revolving Roma Restaurant which overlooked Durban Harbour. This was on the tenth floor which revolved 360 degrees, all to do with guys pushing the mechanism in the basement I told Bernice!

Bernice also joined me for the Durban July horse race at Greyville. I had tickets from a broker who also was a breeder of horses. We were in the posh area with food a plenty and great view point. Won some money, Mickey Mouse stuff, but the thrill and atmosphere were great.

I had 2 permanent Rugby tickets for Natal's home games right in the middle terrace with good views of the rugby pitch at Kingspark/Absa Park rugby ground - Home of the Natal Sharks, compliments of Cigna Insurers. When Bernice joined me at Plantations, we used to go and watch the Sharks play.

When Cigna closed up shop, I held onto the rugby tickets for years until I left SA. Right behind our seats were corporate suites for their guests and on occasion we received nibbles and drinks on the house as we got to know the people. Bernice was an ardent Sharks supporter, their supporters are very biased by the way, and I was for Transvaal/ Lions. After games we joined insurers' braai areas on the parking areas for drinks and food. All in all, a good day's outing with beers in the grounds before kickoff.

The tickets came with R200 of betting vouchers with each ticket/game for the Sibya Casino, Entertainment complex half an hour away over-looking the Indian Ocean which we ventured to after the rugby. Lots of restaurants and, if we won, would treat ourselves to a special meal at the variety of eateries. One could sit and have a quiet drink, listen to the cling cling of the one-armed bandits which Bernice enjoyed or even see a live show. I always played roulette on red colour and did well, the bonus being it paid for meal afterwards. The long journey home late at night took about an hour to Plantations.

I started a new stage in my life and decided to buy a plot of land on a new development in Hillcrest. It was half an hour's journey from Durban near the main highway to Pietermaritzburg and Johannesburg around the end 2003 to build my house. Eventually 400 homes plus 300 townhouses La Piazza/Plantations, 47 Shongweni Rd, house 92 Siena Rd, Hillcrest, Kwa Zulu Natal. Maybe you can Google and get aerial view of the estate.

The weather in Hillcrest was ideal and not too humid. The estate was called Plantations and the buildings had to comply to a Tuscany style. I purchased a corner stand on one of their opening sale days, a bottom of the range price. Phoned my son Robert and we visited it together for a look see then went to Keg pub nearby.

Picked a simple design, 3 bed roomed, double garage, outside shower, bathroom and shower room plus toilet. It was the third house built on the development. It was badly built, piss poor, forgot to make one of the kitchen walls in face brick, would not change, gaps in window frames which were of wood, plumbing about face, breaking concrete floors open to add piping and spoiling the cement finish, forgetting a kitchen sky light - I had to check constantly. Ran out of funds and could not afford screed on the floors and left with bare concrete. The house was set out not as I wanted, the stand was sloped and they cut and filled to level the ground which spoilt the piece of ground I had originally purchased. I could go on.

I was one of the very first owners to occupy a house and all the roads were still not tarred. In the beginning I used black bin bags as curtains taped to the windows. The dust was created by moving plant and equipment. There were +- 2.000 builders on site and until the complex had more houses. The cement trucks etc passed my home and caused a crack to appear on the concrete kitchen floor, which I had to live with and accept. It was there for all to see when I sold the place.

Plantations was a gated complex with a peripheral security fence, dog patrols at nights and had restricted and monitored entry. Huge homes were built and the complex became one of the in places to reside in. Being close to the motorway it was popular with a village centre nearby, which was growing steadily.

To save money I had the concrete floors painted and oxidized. The home had a white paint inside a sort of hospital feel about it. We changed this years later by sponge painting in loud yellow blended colours. It gave a Mediterranean feel to the whole house. The kitchen wall was supposed to be brick with no plaster but the builders stuffed it up, like a lot of other things and plastered it.

I put in grass all around and eventually added bushes, bougainvilleas, and exotic plants. 130 small hedgelings, 3 inches high were planted around the house, which grew to 6 feet in a few years, providing screening and privacy.

Visited umpteen nurseries over the years, something to do on a Sunday and added trees, fig, flamboyant (dug out years later as roots were disturbing the foundations), Quinine tree removed later as dropped 100's of leaves. A large silver leaf Gratisimus Maximus was our pride and joy, 33 Natal Lavender trees 20 foot high eventually, plus Magnolia, etc.

However, this whole estate was once cane fields where moles made their homes and loved eating the bulbs one planted which ruined the garden. We re-did and put chicken mesh around all bulbs and plants which helped but was arduous work. We even tried egg shells. garlic, oil, old cigarettes down their tunnels, to no avail.

The garden changed through the years and decided to take out all the grass and bougainvilleas. We used wood bark, some stone chips for pathways and with the Natal Lavender Trees created a little Forrest like area.

Added a roman type pond but it attracted frogs who, when in chorus gave us sleepless nights. Later removed the water from the pond and replaced the central piece with rocks/stones and lion heads with water piped out of their mouths. An outside courtyard, surrounded with 3 stand alone walls, Tuscany style which required a special builder for that. It gave a secluded area where I concreted a floor and added oxide to give it the right look, plus a Thorn tree, concrete planters with Clivias and rambling roses that spread all over the walls, great area to sit out for drinks, meals, etc.

Built a lean-to pergola and a brick braai-leaning tower of Piza, all my own work at a sun spot outside kitchen.

The veranda/patio outside the lounge/study was enclosed with wooden-framed sliding doors and surrounding floor length doors/windows, great for sitting in during winter months and to view the garden. Years later termites burrowed into some of the wood in the foundations and had to be replaced, which was very costly.

The land was previously cane fields with rats and in the first 6 months of being in the house, started roaming from the temporary rubbish/dump area/builders' rubble area onto the properties. At one stage we had one in the house and could hear it in the evenings nibbling the bottom of the bedroom door. Immediately we set traps with poison pellets and found it was living in our garage where it fed itself nightly and eventually turning to stone. In addition, in the garden we spotted little tunnels on the banks and had to trap with poison again but eventually there were no more cane rats. Other neighbour's homes nearer the rubbish areas got hit worse with the managing agents having to sort out the rubbish dump.

I visited Bernice many times in Johannesburg. Bernice had a 2 bedroom unit in Lone Rock, Lone Hill, Sandton. Built in face brick in a secure complex in a milk and manure belt with parks and shopping malls nearby. Lone Rock was the very first concept of a gated complex and built in the 1980's. The complex had tennis courts and two swimming pools. Pathways were available for walking, doggie walks and was safe and secure.

At the weekends I used to drive up, a journey of around 7 hours each way in my 1300cc VW Chico. We made good memories at Lone Rock, had an African dress theme for Christmas with Claudia and Duncan one year. Bernice had a new lawn and sprinklers fitted to the garden, and eventually a 30 foot Palm tree had to be cut down. Just before she sold it, she had an internal wall between the kitchen and dining room removed for additional light with an open plan design. I cut a little gate in the security door for Bernice's black Scotties so they could venture out to the garden and in again and/or to lie under the shady patio area on hot summer days while she was at work.

It was a magic unit and Bernice trebled her money when she sold her unit to join me in Natal at Plantations. With my VW Kombi and my lifelong trailer, I ferried her down from Jhb with lots of stuff. Bernice and Sue, her step mum, drove behind me in her gun metal grey VW 1600. Later a removal truck arrived with more stuff. 9 years later we became engaged on 12/12/2012 - this being 12 minutes past 12 on the 12th month of 2012 - and married on the 19/4/2013.

Bernice joined me in Plantations in May 2004. I had an assortment of silk flowers years before, to add instant colour and brighten up the place. Bernice washed the dusty flowers and decided to make a smaller arrangement by cutting the stems which I objected to, she then stuffed a silk flower into her mouth and chewed away. I was not amused.

Around 2005 we flew to the UK and visited Jack and Janet in Dorchester. Jack was Bernice's cousin. Then on to my sister Janice's place in Stonehouse to introduce Bernice. All these years, decades that I was divorced, I never told my parents nor my sister Janice that I was divorced in 1989. It was not the done thing so it came as a big shock to them. My mum had passed away years before. Anyway, thick skinned as I was, I took it on the chin, lump it or like it attitude. My sister acted very prim and proper. We were not allowed to share a bedroom. Hilarious at our age of 56 and 57.

From there we visited friends who stayed a short while in SA, Ian and Irene Ferguson in Kirkcaldy for a few days. Visited the local market and had a meal out. We travelled up the east coast to Aberdeen and Inverness. Took a bus tour around the granite city of Aberdeen.

We stayed with Anthea Duigan, Robert Enthoven's ex secretary in bygone days, who was in a village called Beauly in a rented cottage. She was a chef for the Laird for his various functions/meals. Anthea was like a Princess Margaret very larney, smart and elegant but down to earth. Also enjoyed her drinks. We slept at her place and toured around eating at hidden away restaurants in the nearby costal inlets. One evening the pipe band was playing in the main street of the village. It was pouring with rain but most people ventured out, dressed accordingly. Bernice had a thing about the fellows who banged the big drum and would get as close as possible so she could count the hairs in his nostrils. I should have been a drummer!

One evening after a few drinks, Anthea let out about her lover at Minets in Jhb years ago, who visited her in the mornings for breakfast then onto Minets. I was an early bird and Jim used to arrive early as well at the Minet's office. She thought the world of him but he was married. Was this a case of catching the early worm, so to speak?

We then travelled down the west coast of Scotland and headed home to SA. Anthea developed a stomach problem a few years later and after an operation, sadly passed away. She was a jolly person and we enjoyed her company and hospitality.

Plantations had been a sugar cane farm and was still a fairly wild area. Within the estate, they had an area called Mamba Valley with walks, but never ventured there. They also had buck which roamed around and enjoyed visiting people's gardens and eating mainly roses, namely our white Icebergs.

Snakes! We had 2 night adders and a green grass snake over the years. We phoned security who were used to such calls and they came along with their snake catching poles and a bucket with a lid to remove them. Snakes scare the shits out of one.

Many years later when we were having a drought, we had to use washing machine rinse water to water our garden and monkeys started to jump on house roofs searching for open windows to steal from the kitchen. They cause a mess, get all the dogs barking and become a nuisance.

We had large Woolley storks, Giant, Open-billed Mandible storks with pitch black, large glossy feathers, Fish Eagles with their shrill call and Ibis with long beaks, Hadeda birds would wake people up in the morning with their loud calls whilst feeding for worms in the gardens.

Our geyser burst which could have damaged our ceiling but quick thinking by Bernice, switched off the water mains and climbed into the ceiling and mopped up the water.

Our water bills were climbing monthly but could not trace any damp in the outside areas. Our German plumber, Klaus, came with a gadget and he traced the source. Burst, perforated, small copper pipes of poor quality were found. They were replaced and found a catchment area in the foundations - a foot below ground level where the water had gathered. This had to be pumped out. Cost R4 000 to fix. Our water bills had reach R2.500 p.m. This was an expensive exercise overall to rectify.

Although we were in a gated complex with very good security, building activities went on for years and always had the worry of a break in by rogue burglars. We had no window bars and no burglar alarm as the complex seemed safe. However, as a precaution, Mike, a blacksmith by trade, installed Tuscan styled internal gates at appropriate places and a couple of windows, just to give us peace of mind.

Oh yes, there was a mini tornado that ran through Plantations ripping tiles from homes and throwing garden furniture 100's of yards away. I was at work but Bernice said that at around 2 in the afternoon the sky turned to night then 10 minutes of havoc. The house was in a slight dip and avoided the brunt of the storm. Merely had to find our plastic garden furniture, which has been tossed into the street and neighbour's property.

The complex had underground parking for those people living in the townhouse area, which also had a restaurant, pub, hairdresser and a ladies clothing boutique. Had a great New Year's party at the restaurant one year.

One could walk around the roads of the complex which was vast. Enjoy seeing new homes being built, new gardens appearing. It was like being in an Italian village, very tranquil.

Our neighbours consisted of a Chinese lady, who played beautiful piano music and taught Mandarin at nearby private school. Her husband was an Englishman who seemingly spoke some 5 languages. Had a huge home for 2 plus a Husky dog that was never exercised properly. They were a prickly twosome

A young couple, the woman had her colours for SA in wrestling and her parents were very wealthy in that they had factories that made vegan food. Her husband was admired by all the housewives, with his chiselled body that was exposed on a regular basis when he mowed the lawn and rode his skate board. They both worked for her parents who eventually decided to sell up and move to Brisbane and opened their business there.

A new couple arrived and the guy had a habit of reversing into our driveway which soon came to a stop when Bernice kindly put him in his place. Nice thing was that this couple always decorated the outside of their home/trees with lots of Christmas lights over the festive season.

Other side was Ineka, of Dutch origin, and Neville. Neville played squash, was a runner and company secretary at Toyota car plant. He retired and within weeks had strokes then skin disorder, more strokes and became bedridden for good. It was dreadful the change that happened.

Another neighbour, where the grandmother's grandchild had leukaemia. At the same time, the gran through stress, I guess, had to have both her breasts removed. Bernice donated two of her oil paintings for an auction held to raise money towards the costs of the transfusions for the young girl. The paintings raised R2.000.

Had a cobbled stone driveway and due to the mist, damp and rain periods one got a blackening of the cobbles which got worse with a main pump station of crude oil nearby from Durban to Jhb. There was always an invisible discharge of fine oily mist at nights when the pump station did its bit.

Could never really smell the oil and the air was clear but showed on the driveway over time. Years later the pipeline burst with spillage to a complex nearby plus farm land. It took 2 years to move the ground, cleaning agents etc were used by the environmental companies contracted to fix. Millions of Rands and some unhappy people as the air had this heavy polluted smell.

Had to buy a pressure cleaner a Karcher using pressurized water to clean off the black coating that would appear each year also from the invisible fumes in the air. What a difference this made and the cobbles became new again. Took a whole day to do this plus the pavers.

In 2015 I had to have a hernia operation as a lump the size of a tennis ball popped out in my groin, at the same time I ended up with Pleurisy in Hillcrest Hospital. I can still feel the implant gauze and get twitches now and again when I exercise.

Then a few months later, whilst walking, I came to a standstill and had to take baby steps to get home. This happened on a regular basis and my fix was some Coke/sugar. I normally had a brisk walk each evening for about half an hour and this slow down appeared every now and then, got this tightening around the neck area as well. I went to have tests at a heart specialist hospital and they picked up a problem after running on their treadmill, a spike.

I went into hospital for an angiogram and I expected the worst. However my heart was in perfect order but no solution to the spiking. It cost Discovery Medical Aid R35.000 for the day but matter never solved nor sorted out, crazy. Did not solve my problem but after talking to my health guru she suggested potassium tablets which have helped.

I was unlucky with my motor vehicles, second hand, never new out the box. All the vehicles I had were long in the tooth but the biggest disappointment was the theft of Karin's red VW Chico from the parking area at the golf driving range in Hillcrest after 430 000Kms on the clock and two reconditioned engines later. Someone must have followed me into the parking area and had a Chico on their hit list. No vagrants around just golfers who came to the range. It was a shock when it was nicked.

My next vehicle was a clapped out 4x4 Isuzu that I bought from a golfing friend Tony. It was a rust bucket but mechanically sound, used for trips, camping stopovers by just throwing an add on tent behind the cab of vehicle and slept in the load area.

One day at Frontline's office, I parked the vehicle at the rear parking which had sloping ground. Later in the day someone looked out the window and my vehicle must have run down the slope backwards, went through a wire fence and tipped at an angle, yards away from the main motorway with front wheels in the air so to speak. Everyone in the office went into hysterics but managed to tow vehicle out of its dilemma.

A year or so later working for Frontline, the Isuzu got stolen from outside a broker's office whilst parked in the main road plus my golf clubs.

Next car was a Hyundai Getz and day after I got it from a broker's son, who has going to UK, the engine blew on an isolated road in Natal Midlands. The car had a service by the previous owner the day before handover to me, however, the radiator cap had not been screwed back on properly and the engine blew. It cost an arm and a leg to fix but will tell the story later.

We had two animals at Plantations. Jenna, Bernice's black pedigree Scotty, a champion winner many times who had puppies with her male Scottie Jamie. Jenna spent 4 years with us and sadly passed away. Bernice was very upset and it took a long time for her to accept it. Jenna was the last of 3 Scotties she had for more than a decade.

Champers, my daughter's cat, stayed with us for many years having disappeared/got lost for a day and a bit, searching with torches during the night. She loved getting the drips from any tap in or out of the home and a ritual had to be carried out most days. She was a prickly cat but once we got to know each other she would follow me about especially when I cut the lawn.

She lived a long life - 18 years and it was sad when she had to go after not being able to eat and withering away, and when the Vet he took her away she gave me that last look which was devastating. I was very sad.

The Final break, new home in Plantations with years of pleasure developing it, with Bernice at the helm, a safe haven and Bernice, the new lady in my life who I married after 9 happy years together.

CHAPTER 25

Long distance truck stops - a dream, Get arrested for Drunk and Reckless Driving - 4 times over the legal limit, 7 visits to court on my own, Robert and Isaac visit from UK, 2 Jobs once more - Frontline Underwriting Agencies & J Cook t/a Motor Fleet Consultants. Rough seas at Frontline, Alcohol poisoning - Bernice thought I was a goner. Correspondence on retirement procedures, Christmas parties at Frontline.

The following episode was the one that capped them all and I am lucky to be around to tell the story.

When I worked for Corporate-Sure in Umhlanga, Durban, I used to frequent the George Inn in the village square in Umhlanga at lunch times. I bumped into a fellow who worked for General Accident Ins Co, named Jonathan Hatton. I did not know him that well.

We got chatting which led to an idea he had. We started to meet at lunch time at least once a week. The more he talked about his idea the more interested I became.

In essence, he was planning to gather a consortium of investors to be part of long- distance truck stops throughout SA, starting a satellite depot on land at Cato Ridge, next to the main motorway between Jhb and Durban. The land was reasonably priced.

This stopover would cater for the parking of trucks, rest/sleepover, eateries, toilets, petrol/diesel, entertainment, etc. All that was needed was interested parties with lots of money to develop.

He set up contracts and his own company named Ice Breaker, later offering me an interest. There was a catch, I needed to finance him a little. I took the bait, thinking that if this all happened, me, my family would be very well off.

He went off and did his bit trying to get financial backers and we met at the George Inn on a more regular basis. Consortiums were interested but nothing materialized.

To cut a long story short, months later, I told him I was no longer financing him, which at the end of the day was a tidy sum. As they say you learn the hard way through your pocket.

I made the move and we still met but the dream fell away, no backers. Jonathan went to the UK with his family and shortly thereafter he died of a heart attack.

During one of our lunch-time get togethers at the George, Jonathan, and I got into it and went on a pub crawl until 10 in the evening. Bernice phoned and asked that I rather stay over at Jonathans as driving would be risky. But I was stubborn and ran away from Jonathan to my car. He had just fallen down some stairs near the last pub. We had drunk enough to sink a battleship and I should have stayed with him.

I jumped into my VW Chico in the humidity of Durban and headed off to Hillcrest, a good hour away. There is a very steep and curvy hill just outside Hillcrest, called Botha's Hill when the drink hit me. I was all over the road, swerving from side to side and how I didn't hit any oncoming car is beyond me or go off the road - it was a miracle. My eyes were closing and I was in a really bad state as drowsiness set in. I did not realize there was a police lady/dog unit in a car behind me who had phoned the police ahead in Hillcrest to stop me.

When I eventually reached the main road through Hillcrest, I was greeted by blazing lights and beepers from police cars ahead, behind and to the side of me. It was straight out of a Hollywood film. I pulled over to the grass verge and when I opened the door, fell out and had to be assisted. I was taken to the police station where a doctor was called to take blood samples. Bernice was phoned, and the lady from the dog unit said "Does this belong to you?" She was a police officer and was after my blood. I asked where she stayed and if she had any dogs, pointing fingers at her in my drunken state. I was ballistic and when the doctor asked me to stand on one foot, I fell forward through the desk in front of me. My blood was taken which eventually showed I was 4 times over the legal limit.

Bernice had to draw R500 bail money for me at 3.00 am from an ATM on the high street to avoid me being removed to the Pinetown police cells where I would have been thrown into a cell with who knows who, with the threat of rape/aids looming.

When I thought back about the strong chance of writing off/killing innocent people, besides myself, it was nightmarish. A real shock wave and a big wake up call.

My Guardian angel to the rescue again!!!

Bernice was not happy but gave me support going forward.

I was charged with drunk and reckless driving and my alcohol count was off the page.

I decided to take on the judicial system on my own and went to court. I sat there for hours waiting for my case to come up. My court visits were adjourned 7 times. The judge of the day eventually advised me to appoint an attorney, as I could end up with a judge throwing the book at me and suspending my driving license for years, which would seriously have affected my job. In the 7 visits to court I managed to avoid the Drunk Driving charge as the blood results were not processed within the legal time limit. However, the Reckless Driving charge held the same stigma, no pay R200 and get out of jail card free either as per Monopoly.

I appointed an attorney, recommended by one of my insurance friends who knew the ropes. I paid R10.000 in cash for his fees and a plea was put forward. I paid another R10.000 fine plus suspended sentence of 5 years. All through these say 11 times in court, that lady police dog handler sat in court ensuring I got my dues.

I have kept the paper judgment and wanted to frame it. It's now on family memory stick. For a while I did not drink, then did the 2 beers restriction which I abided by, eventually breaking the rules now and again.

Robert, Leona (his partner) and their baby Isaac visited from UK. Leona's son, Jonah aged 11 came as well. They stayed with us for about a week. Then onto the Oyster Box Hotel, Umhlanga, Durban right on the beach front. A really beautiful hotel. Jonah and I counted 21 odd ships in the bay waiting for entry to Durban Harbour to unload their cargo.

We went to U-Shaka Water World in Durban with many activities. I went on the water slide and just before the end of the chute, my foot hit a dry patch. I went head over heels for a few seconds. I bumped my head but I was really lucky not to be seriously injured.

Years later at Sun City Water World the same thing happened. I swore never to repeat this. I got jammed/stuck on the down run due to lack of water. Gordon behind me nearly rammed me at speed but for his swerve at the last moment passing me on the bank of the slide with millimetres to spare. I managed to catch some water and finish my nightmare trip. This could also have been a serious accident.

Robert, Leona and the children had to delay their return trip to the UK due to the volcanic eruption in Iceland and ash in the atmosphere. After 10 days delay, I dropped them off at the Durban airport for their flight home. I stopped in no drop off zone for a few seconds and got nabbed by a police officer. He issued a fine which I fought, many letters later I think I got off or received a reduced fine.

On 2 January 2011, I joined Frontline Underwriting Agency and 6 years later retired on 28 February 2017 having reached 71 years of age. I had been planning to head to the UK after retirement. If I had remained in SA, I would have found an office Johnny position somewhere in the insurance industry to tide me over. A tea serving lad pushing a trolley around an office and chatting to everybody as a last resort.

Frontline wrote business for the New National/India Ins Co Ltd which were formed way back in the 1950's and was based in Durban. Being a Muslin owned company, they received their main support from the Muslim business community.

Outside of India, Durban, KZN, seemingly have the biggest Indian community and their companies supported Frontline. The business was established under the name of Frontline Underwriters Pty Ltd and in the 6 years I was with them they opened satellite offices in Jhb, Cape Town, East London and Bloemfontein. Their Head Office was in Port Elizabeth, Eastern Cape.

Whilst at Frontline, and to their knowledge, Pat Healy, my ex boss at Cigna, whom I had known for decades, gave me the opportunity to earn extra money and I formed J Cook t/a Motor Fleet Consultants. This was for large truck insurance - a facility that Frontline did not provide. Using my broker base in Durban and surrounds i.e. Pietermaritzburg and the South Coast, I managed to bring in additional earnings.

During this time, I used to get up early to be first in line at Virgin Active

Gym in Kloof which opened at 5 am as there were only 5 swimming lanes. It was a sprint once through the doors to get down the stairs to the pool and grab a lane. After swimming I did some weights as well.

Much later I decided to get up early at 4.30 do exercises in the garage at our home in Plantations, Hillcrest then be gone by 5.45 to beat the heavy traffic on the motorways from Hillcrest to Umhlanga, arriving first to open the Frontline offices at 6.30. The main roads were always busy and, if any motor accident/breakdown happened, the traffic came to a stand-still and it was another hour before getting to the office. The trouble was there were insufficient off ramps. At lunch times I went swimming at the Virgin Active Gym at Umhlanga.

At Frontline I was responsible for developing new agencies and new business for the company. This included regular visits to the broking fra-ternity, preparation of quotations on Commercial/Personal Lines and renewals. The work involved travelling to brokers in Richards Bay on the North Coast and inland to Pietermaritzburg/Pinetown, Durban and surround plus the South Coast, which was 2 hours away. This was great for me as I was always on the go seeing people which I did for most of my life, throw in the pub lunches, golf days and I was in seventh heaven. My sweet tooth drove me to buying cake when I visited the brokers and I always had goodies under my arm.

The downside was that New India was bottom of the league when it came to settling insurance claims and had a bad reputation for decades. I was intentionally given specific brokers to look after but they were dead-wood when it came to getting support. I found out they placed their business with more blue-chip insurers so getting growth from them was difficult.

Budgets were never discussed and when Frontline struggled, they were quick to jump on me if new business figures were inadequate. As losses increased on the Motor book plus seasonal storms or floods that hap-pened on a regular basis thereby affecting the bottom-line year and in year out even to this day.

Frontline had a book of business that were loss leaders and to throw it out would deplete income which they needed to keep the business afloat.

I was pressurised by the Chief Executive who instructed me to get more new business or else I would lose my job. It was a whisper in my ear. As I said, budgets were never set nor discussed with a plan of action. Even after phoning the book of brokers telling them my job was in jeopardy, nothing meaningful was forthcoming. Then at the eleventh hour, a major broker down the South Coast asked us to do a deal on a very large account and bingo we got the business.

Another whisper in my ear from the hierarchy was not "well done" by getting the account - it was a "get out of jail" remark to me. I never blew my own trumpet but I had a smirk on my face and this win kept me on board. Later, I felt let down by the management as when going through the initial retrenchment/ retirement exercise based on agreements we had made, it became clear I was being squeezed out. To avoid this, I had to fight my own battle and deserved what I received in the end.

I had good years at Frontline especially the Christmas parties where a great effort was made by all to make the Christmas lunch a great success. The 6 odd years I worked there, snacks/treats were provided on Fridays, with braais held on the veranda once a month. On a regular basis I used to surprise the staff with cakes/samoosas, a rose on their desks every Valentine's Day paid out of my pocket. A Christmas party was organized each year, with a theme/songs /fancy dress, with a secret venue and how we get there left to the very day.

Zelda, a founding member of Frontline made it happen so to speak. Most times we were put into teams of 5 with 20 odd people in the office. We would secretly practice our theme and improvise on dress code. She arranged a mini wedding reception in the Frontline offices in the boardroom after Bernice and I were married, which is detailed in a later chapter. It was beautifully done, lunch/snacks petals, photos, drink, and music with everyone joining in on the occasion. This was a big surprise for both of us.

I retired February 2017, and left 2 months later for the UK.

Zelda and the staff arranged a farewell for me, prepared a photo of all the staff with farewell wishes, lots of beautiful cards with love, thanks for the memories, nice knowing you etc. In my farewell speech I mentioned my life history in about 10 minutes, which was surprise of all and sundry. Paul Meyers, the boss, phoned me and wished me well. His business partner, a second- hand car dealer of note, did not have the guts to do likewise. No lost sleep.

Well, there you are 51 years in the insurance industry and in twilight years managing two jobs at once, on two occasions.
Ten jobs later and still in the saddle, a "legend" in his own time as can be seen with more to come.

CHAPTER 26

Bernice joins me in Plantations Hillcrest Kwa Zulu Natal, Engagement message in a bottle, Batchelors do at Golf Resort with usual fight thrown in, Bernice's Hen party, Wedding 19 April 2013, I sing to Bernice and from beneath my Kilt a bare bum, exposed to all and sundry, Wedding night disaster, Mauritius here we come.

Bernice, the new lady in my life, was divorced. She joined me in 2004 and we spent many happy years redesigning the garden at Plantations, back and forward to the nurseries with my trailer. We called in a tree feller to remove the 11 bougainvillea which had grown huge on front bank of the property. We replanted with 32 Natal Lavender trees, removing the grass and replacing with bark an stone walkways. This only the tip of the iceberg as we spent years changing and caring for our oasis.

Her husband passed away with stomach cancer in 2011

We had lived together for 9 years and I thought it time to get engaged. Why not and long overdue. The engagement was intriguing and wanted to surprise Bernice in a special and unforgettable way. Initially thought of getting a small plane to fly low over the house in Plantations with a banner "Will you marry me?" but the authorities banned fights over residential areas.

Then I decided to use the date, now wait for it, 12/12/2012 at 12:12 o'clock.

I visited a flight club at Virginia Airport, Natal and spoke to some pilots and they suggested speaking to a person at a Micro Light club near Ballito, up the north coast past King Shaka Airport. The plan was that he would fly over the beach at precisely 12 o clock and drop a message in a bottle next to where we were standing.

Before hand I had mentioned to Bernice that the firm I worked for, Frontline were having a secret lunch somewhere up the north coast and we had to rendezvous there. Also, to take a film of the journey and a prize given for the most interesting video.

With video in hand, recording from the time we left Plantations, Bernice looking gorgeous, we set off and I had to go to Nedbank in Umhlanga to hand in something and she filmed us arriving at the office with beautiful views across the Indian Ocean from Nedbank car park.

More footage as we journeyed to the little beach town of Tinley Manor Beach and parked facing the beach. There was hardly anyone around. It all had to be timed to perfection. Whilst parked I took a mock call from my boss saying that a message would be delivered and spoke out loud so Bernice could hear. I said to Bernice that at 12 o clock we will get a message to tell us where to go for lunch. Then as we stood outside the car next to the beach this micro light came buzzing along dead on time and flew low above us.

It drew Bernice's attention and I said "look the pilot is waving and dropping what looks like a bottle. I guess there are instructions on where to go for our secret lunch". The bottle was dropped within yards and I asked Bernice to fetch as I was filming all this action. As the micro light flew past, I asked her to get the message out the bottle but she battled so I extracted it and handed to her to read out. Of course, this was my letter proposing to her and she was flabbergasted and absolutely delighted. Hugs and kisses were the order of the day and we made our way to the car. I opened the boot where I had chilled champagne and glasses to start the celebrations. She said to me "So this isn't a company do?" I said no special company lunch, it was all made up, we are heading back to a Durban restaurant for lunch.

On the way there I said to her I had not bought an engagement ring and would she mind sharing the cost and choose one later. I think she was a bit taken aback and did not realize I was pulling her leg. When we arrived, a reserved table was on hand with a dozen beautiful red roses on the table. The food was excellent.

I said to Bernice we are going somewhere else for dessert so please take a visit to the toilet before we go. However, when she returned, dessert was brought to the table and on the plate was her engagement ring.

Four months previously when we were in a shopping mall I casually asked if we ever get engaged what sort of ring would you like. She pointed it out. I had a good idea and that was the ring I bought on the quiet with which she was very happy.

After lunch, we headed off to the cinema to see the latest James Bond Film, Skyfall, that had just gone on circuit.

It was a great and unforgettable day, can't really express fully but very special.

Four months later we got married on the 19 April 2013 in Johannesburg at a venue called Da Vincenzo. This was an Italian set up in huge grounds, great food, designed for weddings with reception rooms of all sizes, beautiful gardens and a little church/chapel on the grounds, it was ideal. We used to go for meals when in Jhb and the food was excellent. We had a first date dinner in this restaurant. We decided to restrict the numbers to close family, 24, with no children as it was an evening do.

Bernice had an old friend Dina Schamm, a neighbour from bygone years, as her maid of honour. My best man was Kingsley Fourie, with whom I worked and played golf for many decades at the Wanderers Golf Club in Jhb. Kingsley was like champagne, bubbled all the time, a person who if I went into the desert would not drink all the water. A friend for many decades, to this day.

For my bachelor do I hired some units at a golf resort near Jhb. We all brought a bottle of whiskey and a few enjoyable days were had. However as usual too much drink got the better of some. My kids, Karin and Robert had a verbal go at each other with screaming and shouting that filled the valley up just after midnight. It was awful and lead to tearing of clothes and my other son Gordon intervening to calm the waters. He had a wrestling match with his much bigger brother and did well to restrain Robert. In a fit of temper, Robert broke one of the wooden loungers. I was worried that a serious accident was about to occur. It was eventually settled but the weekend was ruined. Pity when things get heated and one just cannot walk away. I ended up having to pay for the damage to the patio furniture but better than having someone seriously injured.

Bernice had her hen's party and went out for a dinner with family and a couple of friends.

It rained the day of the wedding and the temperature dropped to 13 degrees centigrade. Bernice was driven to the venue by one of her sons,

Lance in his Mercedes. The little church was perfect and Claudia, her daughter-in-law designed our initials in petals in the church aisle. The wedding ceremony went well with the Minister.

We had hired a Piper and he played while we had cocktails and chatted to one another. From there we went to our dining room with one large rectangle table arrangement, with guests facing one another and the newlyweds at the head of the table.

Speeches started and everyone added their pennies worth but Lance, full of drink, kept interrupting some of the speakers, which dampened things but otherwise got through it all.

I said thank you to all and addressed every one individually. Bernice did likewise. Kingsley elaborated in his speech but thank goodness all the skeletons were not exposed as a long-standing friend could possibly do.

I sang Ho Roe My Nut Brown Maiden to Bernice, then told everyone how the Scots beat the English using the bum brigade, for those who saw Braveheart with Mel Gibson will recall. Dressed in my kilt I duly faced my rear to the guests and exposed my bare bum to all - an encore was called for.

There was a dance area and had asked Lance weeks prior to the wedding to be in charge of the music in the beginning and to play through the system our first dance and 2 other favourites to get things going. He did not get that right and spoiled the dance intros for us. A no care attitude. Proceedings continued and I think everyone had a pleasant evening.

For our 'honeymoon' night we were going to Bernice's other son, Duncan and Claudia's place, which was near Jhb airport for our flight to Mauritius. However, Lance and his wife Lorette had made other plans. We were whisked off to the Protea Hotel outside the airport to a honeymoon suite! This was a shock as we had specifically said to all on our invitations our preference would have been money, if at all, as we had everything we needed for a home. The interference was not welcome. Can you imagine if we had arranged their honeymoon evening? Who does that sort of thing? If that had happened to them, they would have gone ballistic.

It was late at night/early hours and nobody had thought of our cell phones which were at Duncan's place etc. The telephone system did not operate in the Hotel and we had to ask reception to come and wake us early for our flight. We could not sleep worrying about waking up at 5 am to catch our flight. We had received chocolates and a special bottle of wine in the room. We took them to the airport but they removed everything at the check in. This was all becoming a disaster and when we arrived in Mauritius had to buy cell phones and other goodies left behind as our important items were in separate base at Duncan's home in Johannesburg. We were not happy at all that our arrangements had been disregarded by Lorette and Lance. They had convinced Duncan and Claudia that their idea was the good one.

However, we settled into our cabana with a swimming pool right on the beach. We ate at nearby restaurants, walked the beaches and swam in the blue warm water. We went on a speed boat trip down the west side of Mauritius with several other couples/families. We beached on a nearby island for a barbeque, Mauritian style. Bernice smoked a bit of dube [first time ever] and I had my magical island juice. I had hung my Roy Orbison Rayban sunglasses on a branch of a tree amongst everyone else's belongings but they were stolen. I was furious. On the return journey we went into the water to swim with dolphins.

One day we took bus trip to the capital city, Port Louis into the shopping area and bought a few gifts and a Montblanc pen for Duncan as we stayed at his home often. It was an exciting city with different smells, colourful clothing full to the brim with people.

The Mauritian vibe was very relaxing and one day whilst walking, bought a fresh fish from the fishermen on the beach selling their catch, to cook at home. The weather was ideal and not too warm. I really wanted to snorkel but that is still on my bucket list. Would also have loved a game of golf but I guess not on honeymoon. We had a super time.

Second marriage, the wheel reinvented,
happy times and good times to follow.

CHAPTER 27

New wave of travels for John & Bernice, more Cook's Tours in no particular order. A brief travel experience of many trips.

I love holidaying to different places, meeting people, stinky drinkies, throw in a bit of golf, even just visiting any golf club for a meal/pub menu, places of interest and the sun, of course. I do not recall all my holidays. My kids need to fill me in on the early days but here goes the "Cook's Tours" over the years. Thousands of road miles were travelled.

As a General Motors advert in South Africa said, "Braaivleis, Sunny Skies and Chevrolet"

Using my Flexiclub points system I booked into a self-catering unit in Port Owen right up the west coast from Cape Town. Before hand we stayed in a one bedroom unit, one street away from the beach in Cape Town called the Riviera.

We walked across the street to the huge municipal swimming pools, with views out to the Atlantic Ocean for daily morning swims. This was a very wealthy area with a large Jewish fraternity. It had it all, nearby shops, restaurants, cafes and walks up the hill to the milk and manure belt of the very rich, with homes and views to die for.

It was a great base and caught the Hop on/off red bus into the city centre where we visited the Victoria & Albert waterfront complex. Wandered through, watched fishing boats come and go, sat out and had our fish and chips, then window viewing as opposed to shopping. Plus watching all the different peoples/visitors. It was a day well spent.

Also spent a day in and around the Cape Town city centre, went to an off the pavement boutique restaurant, help yourself food with a few drinks. This was opposite the new stadium built for the football World Cup at Green point.

Being on holiday, the weather good, exploring new places and venues, good food, nothing to beat it, but for being on a golf course hopefully playing decent golf. From Green Point we were within walking distance of our unit which was along the sea front esplanade.

We met up with Geoff and Jackie Patterson whom I knew in Durban. He was an insurance broker who had retired to Hout Bay. They picked us up and we had a Pub Lunch at one of his old haunts when he initially lived in Cape Town. He was a tight arsed guy, you know, lots of money but slow on the draw and all his pockets stitched up.

I always made the effort to contact old acquaintances. John Fraser a Scottish fellow who worked as branch manager of Admiral in Cape Town, when I was branch manager for the same company in Durban, we had met many times. He had cancer but got through it.

John was a tour operator and ran his business from home. I paid for petrol etc and he took us to the Spier Wine Estate, owned by Dick Enthoven/Enthoven family for whom I had ferried his voters back and forth when he was an MP in Jhb. The Estate had displays of injured birds, a rehabilitation centre for all types of animals. A little boy, in the audience, handed me a boa constrictor which made its way around my neck. This was a first for me having now broken the ice after all these years of fear. We had a tasty lunch with wine and we enjoyed the day. John arranged a game of golf at his club and he played well but I played better on the day.

Back at the Riviera flat, my wife's niece and all their family came through and we squeezed into the flat for a few drinks. Went out and bought all ingredients for sandwiches, had a chin wag and they headed home a bit later. It was lovely seeing them.

We were supposed to meet with David Brunt nearby but somehow after searching for where they were staying, we could not find them.

After a great week we headed up the Cape West Coast towards Port Owen. Just past Blauwberg Strand we stopped at a little seaside village and I bumped into a Scot I knew from Durban and had a quick chat.

We travelled a little further and had lunch on the beach at the Strandloper [which means beach walker] where 8 seafood dishes were being cooked over open fires. It was a popular venue with thatched shady spots in and around sand dunes and palm trees where one could sit and eat. This was something different. Lest I forget, one always took photos, hundreds which are stored on my PC.

On the on the way up further north, we stayed at Club Mykonos resort with beautiful sea views of the bay. We had a braai on the balcony with red wine. After a few days we headed off to Port Owen. The self-catering unit at Port Owen was right next to the ocean with braai facilities on hand, all clean and tidy. We travelled around from this base. We met another insurance guy from Pietermaritzburg who had retired there and were invited round to his home for langoustines that he said his fridge was full off. We were never offered one but they managed to serve some peanuts and a drink. As time passed we realized they were not doing a thing about food and it was getting late. Such a let down.

They had a beautiful home with sliding doors and views out over wetland/marsh areas and the sea. The bird life was staggering with an abundance of nesting areas close by. It was very special. Later I heard he divorced that wife and headed back to Pietermaritzburg and married for the third time. Another tight arsed person and he wasn't even Scottish.

When we left their place, our stomachs were yearning a fish meal so we found a little restaurant serving langoustines and had an enjoyable meal.

The next day we had a lunch at the hotel in Vredenburg, overlooking the river bridge with salt flats nearby. In the little town we bought fresh herrings from the catch of the day sold from the front veranda of local homes.

Further up the coast we spent a whole day in Paternoster, a picturesque area with stark white painted cottages, peppered all over the place amongst the sand dunes, next to the Atlantic ocean. There were little stopovers, shops where we popped in and browsed around. Bernice bought some opal earrings. There were few good restaurants and the first one we came to we had breakfast. A bit further on there was a little town on the beach with boutique restaurants. It was busy and popular with tourists.

After driving around, we picked a place and spoilt ourselves rotten with the lunch specials of the day and some good wine, expensive but worth it. The setting was great with a relaxed ambiance, our feet in the sand and after a few drinks we were feeling like a million dollars. Geronimo!!!

On another day, we detoured off the highway to visit Darling, home to Pieter Dirk Uys, a well-known SA comedian, who had his own theatre in the town for seasonal shows. We also visited a wine estate/olive farm.

Whilst in that area we drove to the West Coast Fossil Park with a prehistoric dig site and one could walk around and view the dig up close. There were fossils of bears, sabre-toothed cats, short-necked giraffes and many other exotic animals which inhabited the West Coast some 5 million years ago.

On our return journey we were given directions through back roads staying away from the main motorway the N1 to Jhb due to many major road works, long stops between the stop and go lights.

We drove through many small dorpies, wee one horse towns and historically all interesting.

We stopped at Matjiesfontein, a famous mining town, with day trips from Cape Town for the wealthy families and tourists from Europe in the early 1900's on an exclusive train line. The ostrich farms in the area had become an industry as the feathers were treasured and exported to Europe and across the world. The Matjiesfontein Hotel, the train depot and surrounds were preserved and still in pristine condition, all painted white and used for tourists. We went into the hotel and had a lovely walk around the whole area. All very Victorian, a jewel in the arid surrounds.

On our return journey to Durban, we bought Karoo lamb from a butcher and braai'd that evening in the Karoo National Park, just outside Beaufort West. We had set up our camp/tent around the Isuzu 4x4 with other campers nearby. The lamb had a unique taste due to the grass the lambs ate which gave it a unique flavour.

Nearing Bloemfontein, we passed the turn offs to Jagersfontein where Bernice's mum was born and Petrustein where her dad was born. We contemplated visiting these one-horse towns but they were well off the beaten track. We had the chance and should have but didn't.

On to Bloemfontein and the GPS directed us for the second time on our travels into the verges of large African township. It was supposed to have kept us on the main road but as we learned on a few occasions the GPS can go wrong go wrong. Anyway, we got out after scary moments of being lost and headed to Newcastle, Harrismith, Ladysmith and home.

This was Boer War country and whilst travelling through the town centre of Newcastle spotted a grave yard. I have a habit of walking through grave yards when I can, just to see the names and spot the oldest gravestones.

On that note, I once made love on a fallen over tombstone - different.

The grave yard in Newcastle had a section for British soldiers who died in the Boer Wars and they had rows and rows of puny little white crosses, no more than 8 inches high, sad to see. Finally got home safely after another long trek.

Around 2014, we flew to Windhoek [meaning "windy corner"] in Nambia, hired a car and headed off to a private farm just outside Etosha Game Park. It was owned by a German and he had some game, such as Wildebeest and Antelope, in a fenced off area with water where animals arrived at dusk. The owner had married a local lady who was away on training for her job. Herman the German was a tall fellow, he prepared our breakfast and cooked various game for the suppers we had. Very nicely done and where would you be treated to such a variety of game meat. At breakfast we always made some sandwiches for the road/lunch time with leftovers. Cheese, cold meats, jams with homemade bread. Bernice ordered a 'Herman' for Christmas.

He had a cute little boy and a Rhodesian Ridgeback dog. We slept in a small Gite type place. He had a drinking view point high up where we had sundowners looking at the water hole and landscape. No other guests were there so we were spoilt.

One morning, we headed off in our hired VW to the Etosha game park. The entrance had a fort like appearance with view points, a swimming pool which we used later in the day, a tourists' shop and eateries. It was like a shady oasis. The Park was desolate, flat as a pancake but had good viewing on the first day especially at the main watering hole of which there were few and far between. The main viewing of the park was on the far side so we decided not to drive there. We came back the next day, however, the viewing was poor with few animals.

We bought an arty whistle, made by the locals, as Herman was always calling for his son so this gift was ideal and treasured. We had an enjoyable short stay.

Our next stop was a self-catering place, called the Desert Rose Resort at Hentiesbaai, next to the beach. It was cold place and travelled back and forward to Swakopmund along sand made road with beautifully painted little houses used by the fisherman during the seasons, but a ghost village out of season. 70kms there and back. The landscape was very lunar with dunes, eerie silence, dark and grey with a few shipwrecks just off shore and very little traffic.

Travelled to Cape Cross on the Skeleton Coast, a seal reserve further up and it stank to high heaven. Back and forth to Swakopmund which was a beautiful town where the Germans had put their stamp. It was clean, an historic place with beer halls, restaurants, piers on the water front. The Pelicans walked up and down amongst the tourists.

Bernice found out a bit of her ancestry in a Jewish library. Stein was the name she was tracing that appeared in a family bible as opposed to Steyn the family name. All in high Dutch. The name had been altered way back. Bernice sold this bible which was bigger than a large shoe box to a specialist collector later on before going to the UK.

Visited Walvis Bay and joined others on a boat trip around the harbour and a little out to sea to a seal island. Oysters on board, but not enough. The boat had its own resident seal that jumped on board and scared the shit out of everyone but loved being photographed.

Had a game of golf in Swakopmund which was owned and maintained by a local mine. An oasis in the desert with buck etc roaming around, right next to the clubhouse where I had a beer on the veranda. Really special with all this desert sand and a huge area of greenery for the golf course. On the road back to our self catering we stopped next to ship wrecks lying derelict on the beach and took in the silence and desolation. Must say Namibia was beautiful in its various and unique ways.

We headed to Windhoek and stayed in a B&B. Night out in one of the tourist attractions. Pub upon pub, a sort of maze of eateries with music and a great vibe for all. Next day I had a game of golf at a recently built course next to a new village with schools and a resort. Again, a green oasis. The golf club told me to change my shorts to trousers. Thank goodness I had a change in my suit case in the boot. It was odd bearing in mind it was blisteringly hot. The course was enjoyable but there were signs everywhere to watch out for snakes. Not to venture into the long grass as puff adders abound and I did see one. Had a roll to eat at half-way house. Bernice joined me in the golf cart during the round. Once again, we took lots of photos.

We flew back to Durban the next day and must say had a worthwhile holiday in Namibia. Some thing I noticed was whilst at petrol stations and cafes that South African Afrikaans music was blaring away.

Sorry you are getting all these Cook Tours at once but difficult to slot into the book date wise.

In 2015 we decided to travel by road in my beaten-out Isuzu 2.5 Diesel with canopy at the rear end. There was a homemade sponge mattress and curtains made by Bernice for sleepovers. We just managed to stretch out when the rear lid was lowered and used a tent stretched over the vehicle. It gave us a little enclosed area at rear to change, with 2 camping seats and table when having coffee.

We were heading down South Africa's east coast towards the so-called scenic Garden Route/Route 66. On our itinerary was a visit to Chris Moll, an insurance friend at Minets who had retired near Bredaardsdorp in the Eastern Cape. Our first stop was a place/hotel/self catering in the area called the Wild Coast, near Port St John's, in the Transkei - Nelson Mandela's birth place. This place sat right on the rocks facing the Indian Ocean, a fisherman's hot spot

When we came off the main road, we had 30+ kms of hellish dirt track road with gouges, pot holes everywhere. It took over 2 hours to travel along at a very, very slow speed, with the view of the sea in the distance. You know it's there just over the next hill but an illusion. It was a lovely place and fully booked. If you were not a fisherman not much to do except for grand walks and take in the scenery, which we did. I quietly told management it was Bernice's birthday, so the kitchen baked her a cake. That evening the African staff danced and sang her an African song as they brought the cake to our table. I videoed the event and it was special.

The main food treat for the evening was sea food platters which went down well at the time. However, later, Bernice was sick as a dog with food poisoning from a bad mussel. Found out that the mussels were not caught fresh locally but surprisingly had come frozen from inland. To this day Bernice will not eat mussels. The next day we headed to Jeffrey's Bay and Cape St Francis and it was torture for Bernice. We arrived at our cottage, which was great but Bernice lay there for next 2 days recovering.

I knew an insurance broker from Hillcrest, Terry Smith, who moved to Cape St Francis and opened his own set up. While buying some medicine from nearby chemist, I spotted the signage on his office and visited him for a chin wag. He suggested playing the nearby Jack Nicklaus signature golf course at St Francis Bay. All these signature golf courses cost an arm and a leg to play on but was always worth it. I played on my own and snapped lots of photos. It was a Links course.

Bernice recovered, now in Twiggy mode, and we visited a local lighthouse which had a recovery station for penguins/other birds. We had a night out at nearby pub which was popular for bikers and we enjoyed the laid back, casual harry lifestyle.

Off we went to Port Elizabeth to visit the Addo Elephant Park, with many other animals to view, buck, zebra and giraffe. It was just a day visit. Next was crossing Storms River, via a high bridge where we stopped, viewed, had coffee but did not witness any suicide events. It was actually renowned for several suicide incidents.

Onto Knsyna to a Flexiclub booking in the town which was next to the bay. It had wooden cabins and we had an upstairs unit with a veranda looking onto the canopy/wooded area.

Another Minet retiree, Ian Reynolds [Storky], lived in a housing/retreat called Belvedere, 5 minutes away. He and his new lady Ann, invited us to supper and we stayed over. His previous wife had passed away a few years before. We went to a restaurant together in the town. Tried on 2 occasions to play golf at Ian's local club, which sat next to the Knysna Lake on low ground, so when it poured the course got flooded. Anyway, I saw his clubhouse which had burnt down a few years before but was now brand new, nice and shinny.

Bernice and I drove around the local sights and little cafes which were licensed near the beaches, over the hill from the bay. I had been to Knysna before and the busy town centre was unchanged. I played golf at Simola, an Ernie Els signature course, that sat up in the hilly areas overlooking the bay. Nice course but very up and down. One of my previous bosses at Minets in Jhb, also lived in Belvedere, Barry Jenkins. I asked Ian Reynolds to contact him for a quick drink but he had other commitments. He was a bit uppity; you know what I mean. Anyway, he passed away a few years later. Enjoyed Ian/Ann's company and said our farewells.

Off we went for trip on Route 66 and half way along we passed Ronnie's, a so-called sex shop out in the sticks, had a quick look-see visit, in and out, nothing really of interest

Then we stopped at a B&B for a few nights in a little village called Barrydale. It was great and within walking distance of all the village tourist shops/sights/eateries.

There was a large curio shop for African goods including African masks. Decades ago, I had bought 2 African money masks way back in the Eastern Transvaal which were unique from a curio shop on side of road. I showed the owner, a German, the photos on my mobile. He offered me tuppence. We enjoyed the main street which had a vibe and lots of quirky places. Walked into a second-hand shop and started talking to the owner, a Jewish fellow who years ago had lived in Jhb. He was an ex-gambler who had frequented Sun City and other casinos in Jhb. He knew how to read the flow of cards at blackjack and made big money, he said. Eventually he was identified and was banned from casinos. He retired to Barrydale. I did believe his story.

One day we drove 1km inland on the street where we stayed and just over the hill was a township where all the local Coloured workers retired to in the evening. Hidden away in another world.

We headed off and visited George and the Fancourt Golf Courses which I wanted to play at but needed to be signed on by a member. It was over R1.000 for a round which was a no go for me anyway. We looked around the estate with beautiful homes and had a drink in the main bar. All very palatial where the rich spend their money.

Headed onto this historic village of Stanford in the Cape and met Chris Moll and his wife. Managed to find a lovely B&B a stone's throw from their very old 1820 settlers styled home. We had a braai, swam in their pool, walked to the village green for a market/beer fest. All lekker.

Initially Chris had bought a piece of ground facing the Breede River and spoke of building his dream home often in Jhb at Minets. However, at the last moment received an offer he could not refuse for the ground. We actually strolled along the side of this tree lined river which was special and a beautiful place to build one's retirement home.

I did not say but I think he made a mistake as a coloured township was near his new home, On the weekends blaring music belted out from over the hill next to the village plus football on Sundays on the local green opposite his house. A downer and really spoilt one's quiet weekend afternoons. Whilst there we visited Hemanus, which was nearby and played golf at the Hermanus Club and at the Arabella Country Estate.

After Standford we headed onto the Little Karoo, Montague to another Flexiclub unit. Really nice with hot springs to swim in at the complex. Played the local 9 hole course twice. The village was quaint, with a nice pub, open type eatery on the bend next to a river with lovely nooks and crannies.

Visited Robertson and the KWV distillery which handed out free tots. We bought Klipdrift brandy, green label, looked around the gift shop, and had nice snacks for lunch. In Robertson played golf on a new estate complex nearby, flat and open and Bernice joined me in the golf cart. Beautiful views of the surrounding Langeberg Mountains.

Worcester was next. We parked next to Old Dutch reform church, had lunch in a boutique restaurant, walked around the shops and tasted chocolates. We visited a wine estate farm shop, with white lions enclosed by fencing at the rear and the public pay to go through and view them. This was a busy venue, large parking area with security guards. However, on return to our car, it had been broken into through the left back window and items pulled from the car. We thought the guards were in cahoots as they had disappeared. The police were called, and the insurance claim for personal effects stolen was R7053 - 17 April 2011.

Also visited David Brunt a fellow Minet employee in Somerset West. I had kept in touch and 30 years later he and his new wife Angela, who I also knew from way back at Robert Enthoven, invited Bernice and I to stay in their new home at Erinvale Golf Estate outside Cape Town. It was grand, a secure complex with over 200 homes, played golf on the in-house golf course. David bought me a logo shirt, red, Nike a la Tiger Woods. The nearby Helderberg mountain range caught fire whilst we were playing our game and helicopters were dropping water bombs on this conservation area. The copters were zooming in and out over the golf course, like something out of the Vietnam War. The fire lasted 3 days. Watched the veldt burning away from David's veranda while having evening drinks. A few isolated homes were destroyed and lives lost.

We headed home, with a long journey ahead, through Oudtshoorn, ostrich farms and stopped overnight again at Sanpark National Park at Beaufort West. Put up our tent and were surrounded by trees, had a braai, chatted to other campers, videoed giant tortoises humping each other, sound effects thrown in. The park was supposed to have other game, even lion, but on our drives spotted sweet fanny adams.

Headed onto a little cottage, we had booked near Gariep Dam, with views over the dam. Sat back, braai'd with red wine and beers. Could have stayed longer, so nice. Left early next morning and hit a terrible storm. We pulled off the road for a while as it was dark as could be to miss the hail approaching. It seemed the storm followed us as it went on for hours but missed the hail.

That evening stayed just outside Clarens, a camping site with cottages. We took a cottage as the camping area was soaked. The next day we stroked the many horses at Shumba farm, popped into Clarens, an arty village, with lots going on, then headed home to Hillcrest.

The old Isuzu 4x4 never missed a beat. Bernice had nightmares over the vehicle breaking down in isolated areas. All these stops on our travels were over vast distances taking hours and travelling at between 100-120kms per hour. Most journeys were over 5 hours but I did not mind and enjoyed my adventures in the very beautiful country of South Africa.

As mentioned earlier I used to book Flexiclub units and rent out. Had 2 six bed wooden units in a holiday resort in Port Alfred, Kowie River, Eastern Cape. Nobody was interested so decided to use 1 unit, lost out on the other as I could not find a tenant, family or otherwise. However, in 2013 my son, his wife and kids agreed to join us, Gordon, Sylvia, Payton, Sadie. Bernice and I piled into the Isuzu, double cab, with one of the kids and Sylvia/Gordon taking turns in the canopied area in the back which had mattresses to sit/sleep on with great views of traffic behind us. It worked well.

While there we played on the Royal Port Alfred golf course. Gets the Royal title when a member of the Royal family plays at a particular course, i.e. Royal Durban/Royal Jhb.

When I had finished my game and was loading my clubs into the vehicle, I heard this distinctive jolly laugh nearby in the car park. I investigated and discovered Kit Keey. From 1979 to 1992, I was employed at Minets and Kit was the chairman who interviewed me for the job at his home in Bryanston over tea and scones. In these days one was hand-picked and I was very lucky to get on board this prestigious Insurance Broking House. Kit, was getting on, I had not seen him for over 20 years, so we had a quick chinwag. In actual fact back then Kit had a home in Port Alfred, still has and let it out to me and family where we spent 10 days there. Remember hiring a boat and travelling up the Kowie River before the harbour was redeveloped with island homes etc. I fished and this little bugger I caught bit me and would not let go.

Anyway, back to the Port Alfred Resort. It was cool with swimming pools for the kids to enjoy and walks to the harbour. Went on a boat trip around the man-made islands viewing all these palatial homes bordering the river waters, but protected from the sea.

Took drives to Grahamstown, which is a university town with a lot of history of the 1820 settlers from Britain. Bedford was another settlers' town. Bathurst likewise and there we attended the cattle show day with music and Pipe bands.

The water in Port Alfred was of very poor quality and had to be boiled and bought bottled water when we could. We had grand evenings drinking and braaing.

On our journey home to Jhb we stopped at a boarding house in Fouriesberg, just outside Clarens, Free State. It was busy with lots of bikers. The accommodation was typical turn of the century, stone built and may have been farm buildings or council buildings in days gone by. Now renovated for accommodation, with pubs/eateries/hotels. It was old, clean and good food.

Our next visit was another Flexiclub self-catering complex in Mossel Bay, Western Cape. This was a large town with fishing vessels and they also fabricated steel units for offshore oil rigs. Mossgas had a permanent rig offshore in the search of oil/gas over many years. The beaches were plentiful, with many Afrikaans speaking locals. I would have loved to have retired in this place which was off the beaten track so to speak. It had all the amenities required such as butcher, bakeries, fishmonger, big supermarkets, lots of good restaurants, the town centre was clean and we had a unit with sea views.

During one of our walkabouts, we spotted a small piece of land between existing buildings, in the centre of town with views out to sea which would have been ideal to build a retirement home but probably very expensive due to the ideal location. Each evening we would find another drinking spot, with great surrounds, walks around the various inlets. There were magnificent homes on the water's edge to admire, town houses with balconies for relaxing on, the sound of the sea as we walked along the board walks. Nearby were other inland waterways/rivers with little art and craft shops built and in-house eateries. It was quaint and grand.

Played golf on Louis Oosthuizen's club sitting on top of the hill in the town centre. Another signature course called Pinnacle Point Country Club, ran along and above the rocky coast next to the sea. One hole was over the sea, par 3 and you had to land on the green spot on. I decided it was a waste of golf balls, admired it, but moved onto the next hole.

One day, near to Mossel Bay, we went to a sort of Game Park with elephants which Bernice was and still is dead scared of. However, visitors could walk with attendants and a number of elephants. Bernice kept her distance but eventually mellowed seeing how tame they were with their trainers. She ended up feeding apples etc by hand into their trunks. This was a first for both of us and great to experience.

Talking about holidays, Bernice and I visited Karin in Perth, Mandurah. Due to space problems Karin asked if we would stay in one of her friend's cottage/fishing cabins. However, one had to really rough it and when the bugs, spiders, creepies appeared the alarm bells went off and we squeezed into Karin's place. At that time Karin's boyfriend was Rusty who got on well with Aaron, her son and taking him fishing, snorkling, etc and built up a strong bond. Rusty was a Kiwi, back and forth from NZ. He was a carpenter doing flooring decks, etc. After Christchurch, NZ earthquake he got steady work. He was a down to earth fellow and did visit us in Plantations, SA with Karin.

Our plan was to see more of Aussie so flew into Cairns arriving just after midnight, nowhere to stay. Wandered from hotel to hotel but all very expensive. We should have pre booked on line, a lesson learnt. However, we found an online cafe and booked into the oldest hotel in town, Victorian, with a certified plaque, at an affordable price, probably 3 Star. In morning we wandered around the town centre to the beach which was glorious, much like Durban would have been like in the Empire days.

Just sitting watching the early birds come for morning swims in giant pools next to beach. The cleaners in their buggies sweeping up, neat and tidy before it became busier. Did a bit of shopping, nice Opal jewellery and gifts for people.

We booked a trip to a small island on the Barrier Reef on a commercial boat service with a journey of about 1 hour. The night before we had a good evening and went off to sleep as we were pretty exhausted. We had set the alarms for early rise to get to the boat terminus before departure. The alarms did not wake us and luckily, we were woken by cleaning staff. We had 20 minutes to get there. We were exhausted, quickly put on tee shirts, shorts, flip flops, ran like hell through the town, eventually bare feet, no brushed teeth, but made it by the skin of our teeth. The booking was for that day only and the tickets had been expensive. We made it.

Arriving at the island everyone disembarked, with hours to explore. We went on a glass bottomed boat and the variety of fish/colours were exquisite. One could walk around the island, take little boat trips, swim or enjoy the various eateries. Wandered around the island with lots of other tourists and had hamburgers followed by ice creams. Bought a black top for Bernice, Barrier Reef in sequins which was expensive but special.

The time came to go into the water - 4 feet deep, on the shore edge with snorkel which I still had to master. I am doing my bit, all of a sudden, the sand was disturbed and out came this baby stingray. I jump up spluttering and back pedalling, yelling to Bernice as I seriously got a fright. After a special day headed back to Cairns.

The next day we took a short train journey from Cairns through dense jungle with hill climbs to a little mining village from way back. All beautifully preserved with a station and all. There was another stage where a cable car would go further up the mountain above the tree tops which was really high. Beautiful views, water falls, including old mining extractions and with walks right at the top. We really enjoyed Cairns with its calm, sub-tropical weather. Sadly, I never checked the golf courses out.

Next, travelled by train to Brisbane for a stopover and stayed with Muriel and Dick, relatives of Bernice's step mum Sue, we knew them from Joburg days. They met us at the train station, took us to their grand home where Dick worked from. The home was situated amongst beautiful forest-type woodland environment. We spent 3 days enjoying their hospitality. They dropped us off in the city of Brisbane, where we rode on the water taxis to see the Brisbane city sights.

We wanted to see the Gold Coast, but were persuaded by Dick to travel further down the coast by train, which we did and stopped off at a coastal town. We had neighbours in Plantations who had left SA sometime back to start a new life in that area. Their intention was to open a business in Australia that prepared vegan food, packed and ready for distribution, supplying large supermarkets similar to SA such as Woolworths, etc. However, we had no definite contact details and gave up the search to find them.

We left Brisbane and our next train journey was to Sydney to see a Scots friend named Norrie and Fats, his wife. We all worked together at Minets and I had visited them when they were in London and bought a teddy for one of their daughters. We made our way over Sydney Bay by ferry to Manly and was met by Cathy Downs, another fellow employee from Minets. The news was that Norrie and Fats had to go back to Joburg for a Portuguese wedding in La Rochelle, South of City, so ended up staying with Cathy and her Scots husband. They had a large, beautiful home and spent some time reminiscing of Minets' family. Straight into the red wine. Cathy was doing wedding events, including a gift facility. Shown around with so many cosy inlets with restaurants/beaches around. Years later, Cathy passed away at a young age from cancer.

It would have been great to live in this part of the world but very costly. We took a day trip into Sydney with great food places, but expensive. An Aboriginal man was playing his 20 foot Didgeridoo with a microphone on the end, to all the visitors at the quay side. We boarded one of the free red city buses, hop on/off, stopping at the Mint and then onto the Prison where we walked around and scrutinised the books showing long lost inmates. Even a few Cooks were mentioned. Visited the gallows and saw the sleeping quarters of the prisoners, which were hammocks. To think that if you stole an apple in England this is where you could end up. The ANZAC War Memorial was impressive as well as the Sydney Opera House. We viewed this from a distance and walked around but did not go in as it was very expensive for our SA Rands. We visited an old pub for a well needed pint.

Time had come to say goodbye, back to the station and boarded the train to Melbourne.

Train journeys are my favourite form of transport. One can sit back take in the view and the countryside as well as enjoy a drink. However, on this trip an Indian, Hindu went into chanting mode which lasted a good hour. Everyone looked irritated by the continual chanting. I got hold of a train inspector who advised that it was allowed and nothing could be done to prevent passengers from stopping the noise. I got up and sat next to him chanting Beatles and Stones numbers. I'm joking but that went through my mind.

Bernice had arranged to stay with a previous banking colleague who worked at Standard Bank, Northcliff in Jhb. However, on the way to Melbourne we received a message from her telling us that she could no longer accommodate us. This was a huge blow as we had no alternate accommodation, nor was it budgeted for. We arrived in Melbourne City Centre and eventually found a boutique hotel. The receptionist advised us that if we booked online, we would get a better rate. We headed out, found an Internet cafe and did booking online. It was lovely. There was a mini kitchen with cooking facilities. It had a heated swimming pool on the third floor which we could not wait to use. Nice and private as there were no other bathers.

The hotel, being on the Yarrow River, had an entertainment centre within walking distance. This centre contained lounges, eateries, food emporiums, open air bars, etc. It was cold and there were shooting fire flames, heating the whole outside area to an extent. Generally, Melbourne was cold and we wore all the clothes we had, which was not much, as we had packed only onboard luggage for a month's stay.

The following day we visited the huge Melbourne Aquarium, where one could walk in through a glass tunnel with all the fish, sting rays, sharks, etc above our heads. It was the best Aquarium we had ever seen.

Caught a tram to nearby suburbs to get a feel of the environment and jumping on and off, at appropriate places of interest. There were Victorian homes in St Kilda with an old-world charm where I guess young families would commute to the city. We stopped and had a standard drink on the outside veranda of a hotel/bar.

We had planned to visit Adelaide but had run out of money and our credit cards had taken a pounding. We decided to leave and flew back to Perth.

In Perth I had, let's call it a tiff with Bernice, told her to f--- off back to SA. She was set to return and tried to book but could not get through on phone, waters calmed down. We returned to South Africa. In the plane we were told, whilst flying, that the particular plane we were on, should not really have been in the air as the model was basically unofficially out of service. Good ol' SAA. This was terrifying as we only have mostly ocean water between Perth and Durban. Needless to say, we took a few stiff drinks.

Bernice had use of a ten day time share unit every year that she/ex husband enjoyed as part of a consortium in a place called San La Meer, on the South Coast of Natal. It was a gated Estate with very expensive units/ hundreds, owned by the Sanlam Group. Had a magnificent golf course plus a 9 hole chip and putt. Protea Hotels had a place in the Estate where one could use the restaurants, tennis courts and pools. This was built right next to a river with boat rides. The beach was 5 minutes walk with security passes required for the beach that had its own restaurant/eatery/ drinks/icecreams/tea/scones/coffee that over looked a beach pool, under shady palm trees.

There was an access road next to the Estate that came down to the Blue Flag area, called Marina beach. No dogs were allowed in San La Meer but Bernice used to smuggle her Scotty dog Jenna, the last remaining one with Jamie and Megan both gone. We put her in the boot and took her inside the unit. We could not take her for walks on the Estate, so we went to that beach and put her in the boot. We went out of the Estate and used the side road to the Marina beach where she enjoyed runs on the sand and chasing the lapping sea waves. Gave her a shower on return and she was happy.

Down that same road there were a couple of gay guys who ran an exotic garden centre where we bought plants, and from time to time brought my trailer down from Plantations, an hour's journey to buy in bulk. Near San La Meer one could journey up and down the South Coast, visiting market gardens, coffee plantation, a crocodile park. The Wild Coast Holiday Inn for golf, lunch, shows and a casino . Ramsgate, another beautiful area was special for delicious pancakes, salty/sweet etc. I knew this part of the coast well when I spent holidays with my family when they were young to the Marina Beach Hotel right next to San La Meer. Excursions to San La Meer came to an abrupt end when Bernice's husband sold his share to fuel his gambling habit.

One year Bernice and I decided on a week away to Dullstroom, Eastern Transvaal area. We came to a cross roads, asked a local who said go right and then left and you will reach the accommodation we had booked,

Not to be. We drove but found nothing and no places to stop and ask. It was getting dark, and panic setting in. Being lost in desolate places is nerve racking, it was almost 10 o'clock and pitch dark. We stopped, turned left down a sand road and decided to give it a few more minutes. Suddenly, just around a bend, on a dirt road, our head lights caught the name of the place we were looking for and the entrance gate.

Can't explain the relief to get there and were handed a basket with tartan cover/bottle of Chardonnay wine Bernice's favourite, then into our tree house accommodation. We had missed supper and the guest house had kindly prepared this for us. We were so hungry; we tore into the sandwiches prepared for us. There were cheese and biscuits, coffee, and the wine did not last long, but I always carry a bottle of whiskey for emergencies and got pissed. Next few days we travelled around this beautiful scenic area.

I remember a trip from Hillcrest to Johannesburg in the Isuzu 4X4hen we stopped halfway at a place called Harrismith at our usual eatery Wimpy. This was around the time Johannesburg had erected lots of Toll Gates in and around the city. Money had been spent on new interchanges but the public were dead against paying the bills which were expensive and costs added up. Photos were taken of one's vehicle travelling between the cameras and monthly bills posted to the public. The public were up in arms and refused to pay the high fees. The toll gates have now been reinstated but the public still refuse to pay.

So, in my wisdom I had a plan. At our half way stop I smeared my vehicles number plates with Vaseline, threw sand onto the plates which disguised the detail of the registration number. In the car park all the patrons were applauding my effort and I guess copy cats were in the making. We were on our way to a Toll Gate just outside Johannesburg called Heidelberg and had to go through the barrier system. There was a police car parked on the verge and as we drove through, they must have noticed my camouflaged plates. After I had travelled 200 yards they were after me, sirens blaring. I put my foot down and the chase was on. However, with the traffic cops catching up, I said to Bernice I would pull over and we must jump out and wipe the plates with tissues as quickly as possible. Too late and as we were rubbing away the police car arrived and caught us red handed. They got out their charge book but no reference to what we had done. 2 cop cars eventually arrived. The one officer said how can an old man get up to tricks like this. They escorted us to the Heidel-berg police station but on the way, they stopped. I had told them I was picking my son up from the airport. They asked if I could pay the fine of R500 and luckily, I had cash on me and this saved the day. They gave me a receipt and off I went. I had learnt my lesson i.e. only apply Vaseline just before one enters Joburg City where the Toll gates were unmanned and used camera technology.

We certainly had ants in our pants, nice to visit friends throughout SA and vast distances travelled with no breakdowns of vehicles -
a blessing for Bernice.

CHAPTER 28

*Some drinking stories in Natal from 1990 onwards besides
Joburg hey days prior to this.*

A few wake up calls, one wouldn't think so after decades of a certain addiction, so let's call these drunken flings/orgies or I have a weakness for the evil drink. Funny that. I have only thought of this in these late chapeters! Love the Jekyll & Hyde until all fall down time. Anyway, water under the bridge now and cupboards full of skeletons.

On occasions I met some of the insurance fellows after work on my way home at a Keg pub called The Station Arms in Kloof, Natal. It was outdoors next to old train/carriages that were used as drinking booths. Trains ran on Sundays from the station as a tourist attraction from Kloof up to Cato Ridge inland. Once booked a train ride for myself and Bernice, with Gordon, Sylvia and kids, plus Sylvia's parents. At Cato Ridge there were market stalls plus braai and drinks, followed by walk and return ride. It was a great day and the kids enjoyed it immensely.

Right back to the Keg pub where probably about 10 of us were blethering away sitting at the outside benches. As usual the drinks were flowing and I was on the red wine. 2 glasses later, I felt very dizzy and excused myself. Just managed to find my red VW Chico to head home. I drove off, took an early wrong turn left, which landed me in a large empty secluded parking area. It was the only car there so I stopped right in the middle of the parking lot. I was gone, spinning and phoned Bernice. I thought I was in the Casino parking on the North Coast, an hour's drive - that's how delirious I was. I told her I could not drive and she said to sleep it off in the car as she would not drive that distance at night

I was leaning against the car and as I bent down to get into the car, I hit my head on the car window frame, blood gushing everywhere and all over my shirt. I just managed to fall into the driver's seat, blanked out till about 3 in the morning, then drove home. I still have the scar on my head.

I had no excuses and the drinks that night were within my capacity, but, someone spiked my drink. Young students served at the Keg and maybe I pissed one of them off, and perhaps eye drops were added, which can knock you ballistic. It was not a pleasant experience.

On another occasion, there was the DIGS (Durban Insurance Golf Society) monthly golf game held at a course in Pietermaritzburg, an hour inland away from Hillcrest. I got a lift from Simon/Craig Smythe. They lived in Hillcrest, so I had a 'taxi' home with no worry of drink and drive problem.

I partnered Bert Ewing, a fellow Scot, who hit a hole in one and drinks were on him at the club after the game. I was into the whiskies and remember the bar lady sort of not pouring properly from the decanter, so I chirped her. Yes, you got it right, I got the eye drop treatment. By the time we left the lads took me under their arms and poured me into the back seat of their vehicle. It was a bumpy ride home as Simon hit kerbs now and again. They took me to my front door, legless and was dragged along the driveway, knocked on the door, then literally dumped on the lounge floor in front of Bernice. All I could slur was, "lassie bring me a bucket quickly". I survived even with the tongue lashings I received.

Frontline had a visit from Jhb by 2 cowboys to talk about Reinsurance and took Ashwin, the Branch Manager and myself for a slap-up lunch. Ashwin hardly drinks so I ended up the punch bag, matching drink for drink. It was fine as one had food as blotting paper. However, they were staying over in Durban and insisted on drinks after work. A pub crawl of note where I ended up knocking back many whiskies as best I could to cement a good rapport for future business we were about to arrange. I could not drive home and Ashwin was only too happy to assist seeing as how I had filled in to make the evening a jolly one. Again, my legs packed up and with no excuse this time re eye drops.

When we got to my home, Bernice and Ashwin hauled me onto my bed. I was gone. Bernice later put a glass mirror against my mouth to see if I was breathing, as I appeared dead. I honestly think I had alcohol poisoning and seriously may have died but for my Guardian Angel and Bernice getting me right.

Ashwin collected me in the morning and we went for breakfast to recap on the day before. I asked him to keep the matter quiet, but like all human beings he could not resist, told a few brokers, after I had laid my liver on the line and I got the usual mocking phone calls. As the saying goes never trust anyone. I promise, promise, promise they say, "I will never tell a soul".

The following event is the one that caps the lot and frankly, I am lucky to be around to tell the story. When I worked for Corporate-Sure in Umhlanga, I used to frequent the George Inn in the village square in Umhlanga at lunch times. I bumped into a fellow who worked for the General Accident Ins Co, but did not really know him well, named Jonathan Hatton. Got chatting which led to an idea he had up his sleeve. We started to meet at lunch time at least once a week. The more he talked about the idea the more interested I became.

In essence, he was going to broke a consortium of investors to support and be part of long-distance Truck stop-overs throughout SA. Starting a satellite depot on land at Cato Ridge, next to the main motorway between Jhb/Durban where the land was reasonably priced. This stop-over would cater for the parking of the trucks, rest/sleep over, ablutions, eateries, petrol/diesel, entertainment, etc. All that was needed was interested parties with lots of money to develop. He set up contracts and his own company, later offering me an interest. There was a catch - I needed to finance him a little. I bit the bait, thinking that if this all happened, me, my family would be very well off.

He went off and did his bit trying to get financial backers and we met at the George on a regular basis. Consortiums were interested but nothing materialized. To cut a long story short, months later, I told him I was no longer financing him, which at the end of the day was a tidy sum. As they say, you learn the hard way and it's always through your pocket. I made the move and we still met but the dream fell away. Jonathan went to the UK with his family and shortly thereafter he died of a heart attack.

During one of our lunch-time get togethers at the George (as previously mentioned), Jonathan and I got into it and went on a pub crawl until 10pm at night. Bernice phoned to find out where I was as I had said not to cook I would bring home some lovely supper. She then asked that I stay over at Jonathans due to the state I was in. I was stubborn and ran away from Jonathan to my car. He had just fallen down some stairs, and dropped all the food I'd bought, near the last pub chasing me to change my mind regarding home. We had drunk enough to sink a battleship and I should have stayed over at his place.

I jumped into my car in the humidity of Durban and headed off to Hillcrest, a good hour away. There is a very steep and curvy hill just outside Hillcrest, called Botha's Hill. The drink hit me and I was all over the road, swerving from side to side. How I didn't hit any oncoming car, or go off the road was a miracle, the eyes were closing, I was in a really bad state.

I did not realize there was a police car behind me who had phoned the police ahead in Hillcrest. When I eventually reached the main road through Hillcrest, I was greeted by blazing lights/beepers from police cars ahead, behind, to the side of me, straight out of a Hollywood movie. I pulled over onto the grass verge and when I opened the door, I fell out and had to be assisted. I was taken to the police station where a doctor was called to take blood samples. Bernice was phoned, and when she arrived, a police lady from the dog unit, said to her "does this belong to you". She was after my blood and in my drunken state I asked where she stayed and if she had any dogs, pointing fingers at her all the time.

I was paralytic and when the doctor asked me to stand on one foot I fell forward through the desk in front of me. My blood was taken which eventually showed I was 4 times over the limit.

Bernice had to drive to an ATM to draw bail money for me. Luckily I was not moved to Pinetown police cells where I would have been thrown into a cell with who knows who, with the treat of rape/aids looming.

When I thought about the strong chance of writing off vehicles or killing innocent people after sobering up, I was beside myself. It was nightmarish, a real shock and a big wake up call. My Guardian angel to the rescue again!!!

Bernice thought the worst of me but gave me support going forward again. Got charged with Drunk driving/Reckless driving. I decided to take on the judicial system on my own. Went to court, sat there for hours until my case came up, but every time the case was adjourned. This happened 7 times, with the Judge of the day eventually advising me to appoint a lawyer, as I may end up with a judge that throws the book at me, suspends my driving license for years and which would affect my job. In the 7 visits to court I managed to wriggle out of the Drunk

Driving charge as blood results were not processed within the time limit. However, Reckless Driving held the same stigma - no pay R200 and get out of jail free either.

I decided to get a lawyer recommended by one of my insurance friends who knew the ropes, R10.000 paid in cash to the attorney and a plea put forward. In addition, I received a R10.000 fine plus a suspended sentence of 5 years. Through all these appearances in Court, the Police lady/dog handler sat in court ensuring I paid my dues. The paper judgment I have kept and wanted to frame. However, I have recorded a copy on memory sticks handed out to my kids.

For a while I did not drink, then did the 2 beer restriction which I abided by, eventually breaking the rules now and again. Since being in the UK, I have strictly adhered to the drink and drive rules/laws and have never seen road block.

Very, very fortunate to be alive and if I had killed someone where would life have taken me? Really don't want to think about it.

CHAPTER 29

Back on track, Fools rush in where angels fear to tread followed by a nightmare of note, why us. Life membership to Hibiscus Retirement Villages established on the south coast of Natal all next to or near the Indian ocean, Isuzu vehicle stolen, replacement Hyundi engine blows one day after collection.

In 2006 I looked at a magazine and saw this newly formed golf estate called Cotswold Downs and the photos looked good. The estate was between Hillcrest and Waterfall, Durban, KwaZulu-Natal, next to the main road, 5 minutes from Plantations where we lived.

I asked Bernice to join me on a Sunday afternoon drive to the estate. It was paradise, please Google, and see what it turned out to be.

The golf course had been laid out and much of the infrastructure, roads, storm water drains, thousands of new trees on an already dense environment had been planted.

The Estate agents, Wakefield's had a site office with a model of the ground showing all the various sites for sale. On site was the chief executive Keith Wakefield and his son Miles. They had golf buggies on hand to ferry prospective buyers to the stands/ground for sale.

Proclamation to build a home was still a few years away. We collected the sale's pack, while still dribbling from my mouth, we headed home. The prices of the stands varied between R400.000 and R1.300.000, depending on size and views. The place was built in a valley with a river running through it, cliff edge views and forest - it was special, with the prices only going to increase due to supply/demand/exclusiveness.

I was In my early sixties so this would be my perfect retirement for Bernice and I with a home in a beautiful golf gated estate of 400 homes. Exciting!

The money would be raised against my existing home and Bernice's townhouse in Jhb plus savings. This would be manageable and we bought a stand in our joint names, with the intention of selling our existing homes to purchase build a new home on a golf estate.

Right the die was cast and we headed back a week later, stood in a queue. We were ferried out to sale sites and saw remaining stands. We picked one high up on cliff edge overlooking the forest below and green golf holes down in the valley. We selected one at R720.000 just for the ground.

In addition, I had seen a corner site on flat ground with a 360 degree view priced at R520.000 and contacted Geoff Patterson, who had just sold his Insurance broking firm. He had a friend Alan Delport who had a building company that hired out plant and had numerous industrial properties in Pinetown. They had a look see and we agreed to invest with a 3 way split and intended building a home and hopefully make a decent profit. One could build a 3 storey home with great views.

We were waiting for the land to be proclaimed so we could build but then the dream changed into an almighty nightmare. The place was put into liquidation of sorts. Keith Wakefield had fraudulently used the "loan agreements" (our payments) for the flawed and false "sales" agreement. Investec was involved as well. At the end of the day there was a big hush hush and it looked like all the major players had a finger in the pie (scandal). The owners, about 120 affected, had no money to put into a pot and fight the crooks.

There was an immediate huge drop in the prices of the land to extremes. 120 buyers got caught and would have had to enter new contracts with back payments on levies/rates etc that nobody could afford. This went on and on.

Our own piece of land, the R720.000 we managed to sell for R220.000 and lost a bucket load. A young guy bought the stand. He already had a big home in Cotswold but wanted to scale down for his family as he had cancer. He passed away 6 months later.

The other piece of ground, the 3 of us decided to share back payments on certain costs, and ride it through. Bought in 2006 for R520.000 sold in 2016,10 years later for R700.000 net of commission. In between we had to pay for levies and rates and every other cost they could load on you. Cotswold Estates were now charging us monthly on vacant ground for admin costs, cutting grass, security which really should have only applied to an erected home. Nothing like getting screwed again and again.

I wrote, fought the issue, as I always do, but they had us by the short and curlies - moral of the story - read your contract conditions thoroughly, especially the small print. R1.204 per month on a vacant piece of land, Eish! Municipality valued the site at R700.000 but I got estate agents to give me values of around R500.000. I sent these valuations to the Rates Dept and the figures were reduced to R500.000 which cost R1.000 for the processing but saved on the ongoing monthly costs.

At the end of the day we made no money. I ended up managing, being an accountant, paying and recovering monies from the other two. Alan Delport died during this period so lawyers were involved. It was a paper nightmare trying to balance everything but after 10 years the load/ mill stone was off my shoulders when we sold for R700000.

Believe it or not the Wakefield family got off scot free and remained on site to continue selling years later the same sites we had paid and lost our money on. They should have been drawn and quartered. The estate is exquisite now but it ruined many people financially without recourse or money to take on the culprits. That was the sad part as everyone and the powers that be, were covering for each other and knew the man in the street did not have the financial muscle to even rattle their cage. If we had the finances our dream house would have been built. The views are stunning and would have made money long term due to supply and demand of the place. Google Cotswold Downs, Hillcrest, Durban SA to see the layout/photos/homes.

I invested R2.200 for a life time membership to Hibiscus Retirement Villages down the south coast of KwaZulu Natal. This gave me options of choice at Margate, Ramsgate, Pennington and Scottburgh. These are very nice and established retirement developments except for a new one near Scottburgh. All of these comprised of 1, 2 and 3 bedroom homes/ flats, with frail care facilities, swimming pools and plenty of social activities such as bowls, tennis. There were bus trips available, events plus a newsletter every month.

Units ranged from R500.000 to R1.2m. I visited all the retirement villages except the new one under construction in Scottburgh. Most of the people were of the blue rinse brigade and we were never really ready for the last happy hunting ground. We are far too active, with the world still to see. However, it will be available when we are ready. The complexes are fully fenced with gated security. The beaches are 5 minutes away with plenty of golf courses nearby and holiday spots peppered up and down the coast.

My Flexiclub timeshare annual fee for year 2016/17 had increased to R14.000 p.a. and was becoming ridiculously expensive. However, I decided to renew for a further period and use the timeshare in the UK at self-catering units in Cumbria and Ayrshire. Flexiclub had limited selections on this side of the pond and one could arrange a much better deal locally. Decided to cancel the Flexiclub subscription and save the annual fee which we could use locally towards trips around the UK and Ireland. This was another era over but the Flexiclub facility in SA gave us super self-catering holidays throughout SA for decades. With all these bygone property options one may think there was a property baron in the making, tee hee.

On arrival in the UK in 2017 we went to Portugal and 18 documents had to be provided for a Visa for Bernice. This entailed a necessary trip to the Portuguese Embassy in London, with stay over at the Premier Inn close to their offices. It would have had to be done every time we wanted to travel to Europe. A great inconvenience and an expensive exercise. No way Hosea. We decided never again and would wait till Bernice gets her British Passport as it will then be easy peasy except that now, with Covid 19 appearing, it really upsets the apple cart regarding travel and still no British Passport after 6 years.

A year before we left SA my Isuzu 4x4 was stolen from a main road outside a broker I was visiting in Overport, just outside Durban. Pat Smythe a senior partner at Smythe Bros Ins Brokers, whom I visited on a regular basis mentioned that his son was heading off to Manchester, and selling his 2 year old grey Hyundai Getz for R75.000. I had a look and bought it April 2016. We had reserved 10 days at Drakensberg Golf Resort through Flexiclub and collected the vehicle the night before our travels. It had been put through a service at Hyundai garage 2 days prior so all was well and off we went the next morning to the Drakensberg via Bulwer, near our resort. The landscape was pretty hilly and remote. The car overheated, blew the radiator cap with steam coming out bonnet. I cut the engine, but it was too late and came to a stop. The car was damaged with the engine blown. The radiator cap had not been properly fitted after service and was missing.

Having just been through a service I did not check the engine compartment and should have. What followed should never have happened. We rolled to bottom of hill, well out of cell phone range. The road was not busy and tried to wave down the few vehicles that passed but nobody stopped but for an African driver. We asked him to stop at a garage on his way and send a breakdown truck, but it never happened.

It was midday with a scorching sun and panic going through our minds. African men were gathering on the bank across the road from nearby and just looking. Sorry to say but we had all sort of visions going through our minds rightfully or wrongfully. A couple of cars went by, my dancing and waving did not help until a vehicle passed and then reversed. The driver's first words were that "this was not the ideal place to breakdown".

He was a local farmer and we were extremely relieved, but neither of us had a tow rope. The farmer approached the crowd that had gathered. He spoke their language, Zulu, and went searching for some form of rope with which to tow the car. Believe this or not he found, in the shrubs an old worn-out canvas type tow rope which he managed to adapt and towed us to his brother's garage, 20 minutes away. As we got to the entrance to his brother premises the tow rope broke, but we were safe. A sign on the side of the road said, in red letters, Jesus Saves! True as bob. The garage was at his brother's farm specializing in repair of heavy farm implements and big trucks. He said there was a good mechanic in the village and would take the engine there for repair.

We still had another 45-minute journey to our resort and he kindly volunteered to drive us there. I paid for petrol, bought some braai meat for him and his family. On the way there he smoked weed, mentioned farms were in troubled times with break-ins, worries for their families.

He also spoke the local lingo and when we arrived at the entrance gate of the resort there was an altercation in letting us in. They would not allow him to drop us at the unit as he had his doggie in the truck. Just then the manager arrived in his vehicle. Matters were resolved and he drove us to our holiday home. We said our goodbyes, but would keep in contact re engine repair which was going to take weeks and so far from our home in Hillcrest.

We had a few stiff drinks in our cottage but Bernice and I were in a state on what could have happened. We needed someone to come and fetch us at the end of the week. We contacted our friends Sandy and Derek in Hillcrest asking for their help. They kindly agreed to fetch us but we needed to cut short our stay by one day to suit them. We enjoyed the few days we had. They arrived, had lunch. Just managed to get the entire luggage etc into Derek's vehicle. I paid them for the petrol. We thanked them no end.

However, on the way back Derek decided to take a short cut but little did he know we were to travel through the largest township in the Pietermaritzburg area. Within a hundred yards of realizing we were on the wrong road Derek climbed out and asked some local for directions, instead of turning round, which we should have done. He was determined to follow the road. It was a traumatic journey of 1 hour till we reached the rush hour traffic in Pietermaritzburg. Everyone was nipping, quietly praying nothing would happen, safety was the problem. Majority of SA whities just do not venture into townships/locations, just in case one gets stopped, vehicle hijacked, robbed murdered raped — it happens. We eventually got home safely.

Getting the engine fixed was another mountain to climb. The body of the vehicle is at the first port of call i.e. the farm garage for heavy duty machinery/trucks. The engine was moved to a mechanic in a nearby village, which he dismantled as the block had to be rebored and sent to a Pietermaritzburg specialist.

After a few weeks down the track with nothing really progressing, my local garage boys in Hillcrest, Troy and Matthew, suggested we take a breakdown truck and load the car at the farm where it was parked. Then on to the mechanic in a village nearby to collect the engine and drive to Pietermaritzburg for the block and have the job finished in Hillcrest, Durban.

With the decision made, Matthew and I left early one morning, did the 3 stop visit and returned late afternoon. The wheel had to be reinvented again. On the trip I had to pay the various parties for work done, in cash and it was not cheap. Then the final costs, this all came to around R30.000, part of which was covered by insurance but I ended out of pocket for quite a bit.

The lesson was learnt to check one's radiator and water before going on a journey. By the way the radiator cap was never found at the scene of the breakdown. I thanked everyone involved. Within the year I sold the Getz to a local dealer in Hillcrest for a fair price before departure to UK. The engine was still brand new.

A few months before leaving SA, we booked 2 Flexiclub units at the Magaliesberg Resort just outside Johannesburg and invited my son Gordon and his family and Bernice's son Duncan and his family. There was a golf course, swimming pool, lots of entertainment and braais in the evening. I also Invited my friend Kingsley along for the golf. It was a good farewell get together.

At this point I was suffering with a serious hernia problem in my groin area the size of a tennis ball which popped out on occasions and had to be strapped up on an ongoing basis. I had the operation which was carried out at the Hillcrest Hospital and a gauze casing was inserted. Whilst in hospital I caught Pleurisy to add to the misery. Years later I still get twitches when doing exercises etc.

Preparing for Retirement but how things change, Dream home gone with financial loss. The vulnerabilities of travel with consequences, friends to the rescue.

CHAPTER 30

*Sale of house with use of drone, Life's belongings gathered over decades,
sold for next to nothing. Visa application, Bernice's breakdown,
Short stay in Flat before move to the UK.*

In our preparation for going to the UK we had a number of estate
agents plying for the opportunity to sell the house in Plantations, Hillcrest. One estate agent brought a drone to our house, sent it into orbit
and within minutes the security at the complex arrived on our driveway,
saying that neighbours had complained about their privacy.

After 6 months of having people trek through one's home every weekend, plus weekly visits Annette/Ant of Soukop, the home was sold to
an African gentleman who after seeing it, made a cash offer the next
day. I was very fortunate to sell as the housing market was on a free fall.
We had been in the home from 2004 to 2016. Money put into Nedbank
Green Bonds at 10.5% over 5 years and still waiting till expiry 2022 hopefully before SA implodes.

Unfortunately, after we moved the new owner flattened and ripped up
the garden by taking every single bush, plant, tree, all the beautiful rocks,
a brick braai and lean to, the outside patio and walls were destroyed and
merely replaced with stark lawn. Prior to this many people would stop
to take photographs of our landscaping to copy into their gardens. The
shock was awful and had to be seen to be believed. It was like night and
day. People were queueing at the side of the street loading the freebie
plants etc for their gardens. It must have felt like Christmas. The new
owner painted the inside of the house a hospital white, which previously
had pastel Tuscany type colours along with all Bernice's wall artwork
painted out throughout.

Prior to moving out we had to get rid of our household contents which
had built up over decades and was very sad for us. A couple ran a Moving
On business who organized buyers to visit over 2 days at 15 minute inter-
vals. They bought up almost everything at ridiculous prices and took a

week to move all the STUFF. Goods were laid out for inspection in the house, garage and driveway. Losing treasured goods was painful, all my vinyl records, turn table, speakers, furniture, garage stuff, alas no Ming Vases or Picassos appeared. The garage was full of clothes on hangers to buy. This was traumatic, as years of possessions were gone and removed on the spot.

Our next-door neighbours from Eastern Europe bought all our crystal decanters etc, their home was full of crystal goodies - they were avid collectors, I guess. They wanted to buy our place but their bank put a lower value than our asking price so never materialized.

Until our departure, we rented a townhouse for 7 months within Plantations from October 2016 to end of April 2017 with two underground parking spaces. We fell in love with this unit. It was strange acclimatizing to the smaller space but put us in good stead as to what to expect in the UK. The unit had an outside space/mini garden/palm trees and an abundance of birds that visited for their daily feed that we put out for them.

It was upstairs/downstairs with view over a green servitude and other homes/gardens. Used to practice chipping in the servitude area.

During this time, we tried to recover our rates deposit on the Plantations house of around R5.000 from the Municipality office in Hillcrest. I went there almost weekly but this is Africa and they just seem to fob things off especially when it comes to refunding money. The Government is quick to threaten when they want your money, but to give back monies owed to you stand almost no chance. The paper work was in order showing what was owed to us and in the end the Municipality told us to visit the fourth floor of their main building in Durban and speak to a lady who would organize it. Another body swerve and to visit their offices, in the city, stand in long queues is a nightmare, another delaying factor.

The same happened on our telephone account, just could not get a R500 refund due and shown on our account in black and white. It's was like drawing hen's teeth.

While I am at it, the Government's National TV station SABC chased, harassed, appointed their debt collectors/attorneys to threaten me over a period of 10 years for outstanding license fees for TV after I sold it.

Thank God I kept all my paper work which I repeatedly sent to them year in year out. We still have all the data on file on my computer to this day.

However, one evening at friend's home, Hans, he mentioned I should be entitled to a refund of Unemployment Benefits. So, I contacted a lady in the Cape who specialized in this. Over months I received a total refund of R42.000, which came in handy. It was paid on a monthly basis over time but perseverance paid off. Yeah, payback time for me. Geronimo!!!!

Whilst at the unit, Bernice took a bad turn. After the traumas of the breakdown of the vehicle trip via Bulwer, in the Natal Midlands and the rescue, would not go away. She visited her doctor, who recommended a psychologist. There was an accumulation of events around the same time which all added up and she was diagnosed with PTSD. She remained in the flat, pacing up and down. She stayed on the couch most of the day. Her medication consisted of anti-depressants, tranquillizers, sleeping tablets, Rescue tablets and lots Rooi Bos tea, known as Red Bush in the UK. This was a complete breakdown. She was down and out so to say. Not the same person, no driving, no gym, no venturing out.

An accumulation of events that may have caused this were, selling of the homes, all our furniture which had people coming and going for days, a life's collection with memories, a tiff with her son/wife, her brother committing suicide in America after shooting his wife then himself and setting their home on fire. She would take baby steps inside the flat, eventually slow walks with me on my arm and she did not want to go to the UK. I had to attend one of the sessions with the psychologist and went through many issues, ensuring that Bernice would be looked after by me in the UK as she was negative. After 6 months things started to improve but she was still in another world so to speak. We did get to the UK.

Bernice had to organize her Visa to the UK, which involved mountains of paper work and journeys back and forth to Durban's emigration office, with queues on every trip.

Prior to this we contacted a firm in Cape Town specialising in emigration at a price. After our first outlay to them of R4.950 and calculating costing for all the stages it would have cost an arm and a leg, so we did our own thing. I noted somewhere it cost all in all around R60.000 plus R8.000 one way air tickets with Emirates to UK by the time we left on 2nd May 2017.

Regarding Bernice's UK Resident Visa for leave to stay application and appointment was set up which cost £885 [R15.487]. Then a 5 year residency UK fee of National Insurance of £1093 [R19.127]. All this was processed at offices in Overport just outside Durban, back and forth and we felt we were being ripped off. What a relief when this was all finalised and Bernice received her first 2 and half year Visa to stay in the UK. I would probably still be living in SA but for Bernice's UK Citizenship which takes 6 years to obtain. In same breath we still have to travel around Europe etc which I will enjoy as the next part of life, (but for Covid). As they say variety is the spice of life. Hoots Mon.

In 2000, Bernice bought a brand new VW 1600 and used the vehicle until we left. She sold it days before we left for the UK for R40.000 cash, which was a good deal. She found out that the car was still in the name of the finance house, Stannic, when transferring the vehicle to the new owner, even though the car was paid off in 2002. Stannic still had the original documentation after 17 years which was extracted from their archives. A new log book/ownership delayed the transfer to new owner. We were back and forth to the testing/license grounds with long queues. She eventually paid someone to carry out the paper work as flight day was approaching fast. Glad when finalised and 2 days before flying out, all was in order and the new owner happy and paid in cash.

A week before we left for the UK, people were still arriving at our flat in Plantations to view items we were still using but had sold - the fridge, some furniture etc. My son Gordon arrived to take the trailer full of odds and ends for him before heading back to Jhb as he had just been on holiday in Natal. It was fully loaded.

In 1971 bought this trailer from a guy at Enthovens which I kept for 46 years. I passed it to my son before leaving for the UK. Gordon could use this on holiday etc. What a worthwhile buy. At one stage it had new aluminium/galvanized body made as rust damage had set in to the frame work whilst at the coast. A gem indeed.

The TV was sold on the morning we left. We needed proof of a TV License from the buyer which had to be submitted to the SABC otherwise we would have ended up with back payments and being hounded by the them once again.

Finally, everything was sold or given away. We were scheduled to arrive in the UK with 2 suit cases each. Our friends, Sandra and Derek, kindly agreed to ferry us to the King Shaka Airport just outside Durban. We paid them R200 for the petrol and were dropped off at airport entrance doors with quick good bye.

My fulltime working life finally ended - a 53 year career in the insurance industry at the end of February 2017. I had retired. It was a good innings and I was fortunate to have been employed till then. If I recap over all those years of my career, it was dominated by my relationship with people and the balance was my insurance knowledge of the business. I initially wanted to be a draughtsman but there was a shortage of jobs available in Scotland. I was encouraged by my father to take a clerk's job with the Eagle Star Insurance group and the rest is history.

The future plan was to move to the UK at the beginning of May 2017 and we would be staying in Gillingham, Dorset, England, with a lady who had been a neighbour in Plantations, named Alison. This would be for a short while until we could find accommodation within the village.

Last but not least, we needed to arrange transport from Heathrow to Gillingham by National Express bus service. It is pretty easy to get off a flight at Heathrow and board a bus/train outside terminal 3 then on to Gillingham Dorset. There is a railway station in Gillingham but the National Express route by bus was to Salisbury only. Allison and her mom would collect us and take us to her home.

After all this, we arrived in the UK with two suit cases each.

So, UK, here we are, May 2017. Let the games begin on the next stage of life.

Well, a lot of toil and turmoil but eventually we made it happen as two over seventy-year olds head off to begin another life style. This will be recorded in my diary that I've created since July 2020, but that's another story.

APPENDIX

When I attempted my book, it was head down and I merely recorded what came to mind from my childhood until my retirement in March 2017 at the age of 71.

The finished article should have flowed better but my grammar is limited. I am now too agitated to fix it. So, I hope you enjoy it as is.

For ease of reference, for me, I have noted a few highlights missing but, these may have been covered in the book chapters already in one form or another.

To make matters worse, I traced some letters/snippets to and from my dad with dates and found it difficult where to place the detail into the appropriate chapters. After 2 years down the track, I am tired, lazy and want to bring my book to a closure.

Here we go, in no particular order.

GOLF CLUBS/HISTORY PLAYED THROUGHOUT MY LIFE

During my youth until I left Scotland for South Africa at age 21, during my 50 years in Southern Africa, and on my return to Britain.

Between the age of 21 and 71 I lived in South Africa, spending 25 years in the Province of Transvaal (Gauteng) and 25 years in KwaZulu-Natal.

I played 123 courses, shown below, some many times and had 4 holes in one. 450 courses in South Africa overall.

HOLES IN ONE AT 4 COURSES BELOW

Bryanston Tvl,
Mooderfontein, Tvl,
Amanzimtoti, Natal,
Kloof, Natal

SCOTLAND SOUTH WEST

Bellisle
Brunston Castle
Barassie
Loudoun
St Boswells

Prestwich
Troon
Craggan
Rosemount
Cruden Bay
Cardrona

HEARTLAND

Carnoustie (My Sixtieth birthday treat when I flew over to Scotland)
Gleneagles King & Queen
St Andrews

SOUTH EAST

Gullane
North Berwick

CENTRAL SCOTLAND

Bellshill	Lanark
Bothwell Castle	Mount Ellen
Carluke	*Strathaven
Carnwath	Wishaw
Killermont	Brunston
Hamilton/Rikkerton	Castle St Boswells
Hollandbush	

My home course until the age of 21.

ENGLAND

Eskdale
Silloth On Solway
Long Sutton
The K Club/Ireland
Wheathill
Salisbury & South Wilts
Wincanton

Strathaven Golf Club Scotland, twice winner of Kilwuddie Cup 1963 aged 17 & 1965 aged 19 years. Plus, Match Play Champion 1965 aged 19.

A full history of the above two tournaments follows:

THE KILWUDDIE CUP

This, the club's first trophy, was presented by Mr James Hamilton, Aldersyde, Uddingston, at the formal opening of the golf course on Saturday, 13 June 1908, when he handed over the silver bowl "to be competed for annually, as the Kilwuddie Cup"

On 13 July 1908, the committee decided it would be played for on the first Saturdays in September, October and November – the player with the best aggregate score of the three rounds being the winner. The club minutes recorded the detailed scores of the competitors in that first year, when over twenty-six completed the three rounds. The first winner was J.B. Ross with an aggregate of 259 having played off a scratch handicap in the first two rounds and +2 in the final round.

This was the only occasion on which the winner was decided by stroke play, the committee having met on 19 January 1909 and resolved that the Kilwuddie Cup should be competed for by competition by knock – out system. The cup has been competed for each year since then as a hand-icap match play competition, and today attracts an entry of over 160 competitors, the worthy winner having to triumph over several rounds.

MATCH PLAY CHAMPIONSHIP

This competition was inaugurated in 1962 and is played for on a scratch, match play basis. Players with the best 15 scratch scores from certain qualifying round and, the defending champion, are eligible with the final being played over 36 holes.

The Club's history was published 2007 with 120 pages on the Strathaven Golf Club, "A Centenary History" by Willie Park.

SOUTHERN AFRICA

TRANSVAAL

Kempton Park	Huddle Park, Yellow, Blue, White,
Benoni	Irene
Benoni Lake	Jackal Creek
Blue Valley	Kensington
Bryanston	Killarney
Centurian	Krugersdorp
Crown Mines	Kyalami
Jhb [Jhb] & Woodmead	Leeuwkop
Dainfern	Maccauvlei
Durban Deep	Meyerton
Eagle Canyon	Modderfontein
Ebotse	Observatory
Emfuleni	Ohenimuri
ERPM Eye of Africa	Parkview
Germiston	Pretoria
Glendower	Randfontein
Glenvista	Randpark 2 Courses
Goldfields West	
Houghton	

Reading
Royal Jhb
East/West
Ruimsig
Serengeti
Silver Lakes
Southdowns

Springs State Mines
River Club
Wanderers Home Course
Wingate
Pecanwood
Magalies Park

EASTERN CAPE

Fish River
Humewood
St Francis

LIMPOPO

Elements
Hans Merensky
Legends
Zebula

NORTH WEST

Gary Player Sun City
Lost City
Pecanwood

WESTERN CAPE

Arabella
Erinvale
George
Goose Valley
Hermanus 2 Courses
Knysna
Langebaan
Montague
Mossel Bay
Pezulu
Pinnacle Point

Plettenberg
Robertson
Shelly Point
Simola

FREE STATE

Clarins

MPUMALANGA

Graceland
Kruger Park Lodge
Sabie River

KWA ZULU NATAL

Amanzimtoti
Bluff
Bosch Hoek
Cato Ridge
Champagne Sports
Cotswold Downs
Darnall
Drakensberg Gardens
Eshowe
Empangeni
Gowrie Farm
Howick
Kloof
Maidstone
Margate
Maritzburg
Monks Cowl
Mt Edgecombe
Mtunzini
Port Shepstone
Princes Grant
Durban Country Club, Beachwood/Dbn

Royal Dbn
Sakabulu
San Lameer
Scottburgh
Selbourne
Simbithi
Southbroom
Umdoni
Umfolozi
Umhlali
Umkomas
Victoria Pmb
Wild Coast Sun
Windsor
Zimbali
Umbogontwini

NAMIBIA/IRELAND

Omeya, Windhoek
Rossmund, Swakopmund
The K Club, Ireland
2 Others in N Ire

EDUCATION

Stonehouse Primary village schools.
Larkhall Academy Senior Secondary in nearby town where I passed my
9 O Level exams.
Night classes at Insurance College in Glasgow.

STONEHOUSE PRIMARY SCHOOLS

First school photo - Camnethan Street, Stonehouse, Lanarkshire,
Scotland. Second row from top, first left. I always wished I could wave
a magic wand and meet up with the class as they are today – that would
be special.

Second school photo – new school built in Sidehead Road, Stonehouse a few years later. I guess I was around 9, 1946 + 9 = 1955.   The teacher was Mrs Murdoch with 40 children in the class.

AWARDS

- Many book awards for perfect attendance at School, Sunday School
- 9 O'Level Passes
- Queens Medal at Boys Brigade
- Associate Certificate of Insurance Institute UK
- Marriage/Divorce Certificates
- 4 Holes in One Golf Certificates
- Minets Debating Runner Up Award
- Drunk/Reckless Driving Certificate
- Strathaven Golf Club Scotland, twice winner of Kilwuddie Cup 1963 age 17, & 1965 age 19.
- Also Match Play Champion 1965 age 19.
- Wanderers Golf Club Johannesburg SA twice winner of Presidents Cup and Match Play Champion, years 1972/73, age 27.

OPERATIONS

- Strawberry birth mark removed as a child.
- Cancer Op Testicle Removed followed by a biopsy of all major organs i.e. big cut, pull the organs out, take scrapings and shove everything back in. A nightmare of agony.
- Hernia Op with pleurisy thrown in for good measure.
- Sent to a Psychiatrist but no brain damage. Straight jacket not necessary.

WORLD TRAVELS

When I lived in the village of Stonehouse, Scotland until I left for South Africa at 21, I hardly ventured anywhere other than below:

Sunday school trips to Ayr and surrounds, holiday trips to North Berwich, Scarbourgh as a family, golfing days to nearby courses.

Spent September weekend at Blackpool with David Jones, one of the gang and, we also went to Douglas Isle of Man for a week's jolling.

With Boys Brigade on camp to Denmark and spent a day in Sweden. Visited Tivoli gardens, stood on the little mermaid at edge of sea.

Travelled to London for interview with Eagle Star Insurers for move to South Africa.

SOUTH AFRICA

Lived and worked for over 50 years and did a lot of road travel. Spent many holidays throughout SA over the decades and stayed in the larger cities on business trips. I've been around SA many times and the scenery is very beautiful.

SWAZILAND

Took my mum and dad to the Holiday Inn in Mbabane and many golf days were held by Insurers year-in year-out with local casino on hand. I also joined the Irish and Scottish annual golf days.   A three-hour drive from Johannesburg.

MOZAMBIQUE

The South African Railways & Harbours ran tourist bus trips/stays to Maputo in the early days/the seventies. Went on an excursion and enjoyed the free prawns served in the bars overlooking the harbour.

BOTSWANA

A one-day trip to Gaborone to survey a very large retail warehouse for insurance cover.

LESOTHO

On holiday in Natal did a quick road trip, in and out, to visit Lesotho tribal village for the day.

RHODESIA/ZIMBABWE

A fishing invitation with Minets to stay for a week at a lodge on Lake Kariba. Caught a Tiger fish which I had stuffed and hung on my wall at home for many decades. Also stayed at the Hilton in Salisbury/Harare for an evening.

NAMIBIA

Drove to a lodge just outside Etosha Game Park which we visited. Also, Swakopmund, Walvis Bay, Henjies Bay, and Windhoek. Played 2 golf courses. - oases in the desert.

PORTUGAL/ITALY/SPAIN

Prior to marrying Merle in Scotland, we travelled to Lisbon, Italy, Madrid and Seville. We saw all the famous sites and attended a bull fight, which I did not enjoy.

HOMES (19 in total)

- 2 Glen View, Stonehouse, Lanarkshire, Scotland, UK (Born in Lanark) from birth to age 21 when I left for South Africa. A Council house in a housing scheme. Corner home in a cul de sac. Little garden in front, side garden, rear triangle lawn garden with washing line. All other gardens at rear faced each other where the mums could blether and gossip when hanging up the washing.
- In 1967 arrived in SA Johannesburg. One month board paid by Eagle Star Insurance Company at the New Library Hotel in Fox Street, city centre.
- Next a few weeks at Casa Mia Hotel in Hillbrow, Jhb.
- Then moved to more permanent boarding accommodation at the Rondebosch boarding Hotel in Hillbrow where meals were served as part of the monthly bill. Hillbrow was on a hill/koppie and many immigrants lived there. Half an hour's walk down the hill to the office plus return journey in the evening.
- Moved to a little flat and shared with a guy from work named Sandy? Cannot remember and detail other than the few items of furniture I bought.
- Then an Englishman Gordon Farleigh who I worked with at Eagle Star Insurers, mentioned a vacancy at a private house he stayed at 60 Geranium Street, Rosettenville a suburb just half an hour's bus ride from Jhb city centre.

- A few years later moved back to Hillbrow/Joubert Park area to a rent controlled block of flats called High Holborn. Shared this with a Scots friend John Aithon. He was out on a contract basis and knew him from Strathaven Golf Club in Scotland. Stayed in this flat for many years including whilst married.
- Bought a piece of land to build a house on through Corlett Drive Estates. This was south of the city near a major motor intersection called Uncle Charlie's. The developer folded and I lost my down payment.
- My new employer Minets had a connection with Nedbank and arranged a mortgage to buy ground and build a house. Interest rate 2.5% with ground and home built for R23500 at Stand 233, 80 Vista Drive cnr Granville Ave, Glenvista, Johannesburg. This was on the koppies south of the city with beautiful views. Did a lot of work on my own, driveway garden etc.
- Decade later decided to build a palatial home in same area. Again in the koppies with beautiful views, 6 Kurt Avenue, Glenvista Ext 3 Jhb – photos attached. I was the project engineer and handpicked the sub contractors. Ended up in financial difficulties, the stress of it all giving me cancer and sold 4 years down the track - photos attached.
- Then moved 5 minutes away and bought an old house in Van Beek Ave, Glenanda, Jhb. Renovated on sub contract basis and turned out grand.
- Direction in life changed and moved to Natal, a place near Durban - Amanzimtoti. Stayed for months at a block of flats on the beach front called Stella Marie.
- Then bought a home at 1 Nyala Place Amanzimtoti overlooking the towns Japanese Gardens, with more renovations.
- Years later battling with finances and kids at universities had to sell up and moved to a rental place 2 minutes away called Richfield Park - 16 townhouses.
- A couple of years later the developer owed money to Absa Bank and managed to negotiate the purchase of a unit they wanted to sell at a discounted price. So back on the property ladder.
- Years later ex wife and I parted ways and moved to a flat in Amanzimtoti town centre next to highway overlooking Hutchinson Park sports fields.
- Then moved to Hillcrest west of Durban. Saw ground for sale in

gated complex called Plantations. Decided to build per choices on hand -Tuscan style. 92 Plantations, Hillcrest. Lived there for 13 years.

- Prior to leaving for the UK moved into a townhouse in the Piazza village, within Plantations estate for 7 months.
- In 2017 decided to move to the UK. Ended up in a 2 bedroom rental, Gillingham, Dorset, and here to this day August 2022 at age 76.

JOHNS CARS THROUGH THE YEARS – 13 VEHICLES IN TOTAL

- On arrival in Johannesburg used the bus service and then was promised a job as a bar tender at a golf club. I needed transport so in 1969, bought this 1960 Charcoal grey Morris Minor. Used my Barclaycard with seven visits one morning to branches in the Johannesburg area. Drew maximum limit of R50 x 7 = R350 - the cost of the car. I gave up my job at the Roadhouse then, at the last moment, the barman's job fell through.
- I had great fun with the Morris but it was aging and becoming a death trap. Bought a 1962 imported VW 1300 Beetle originally imported from Germany, white in colour. Used to pull trailer up and down the koppies (hills) in Glenvista, Jhb collecting rocks at the weekend to build perimeter wall at first home being built at 80 Vista Drive, Glenvista, Jhb
- Bought second hand light grey Opel Record from Andries Vorster, my wife's dad who was a salesman for L Suzman.
- Then second-hand white Toyota Corolla, long snout from fellow employee at Robert Enthoven, insurance brokers where I worked.
- Eventually got a company car at Enthovens, second-hand white Toyota Cressida, Marie biscuit wheels. Remember having 2 punctures on way home once.
- Next was a burnt orange Ford Cortina 1600 which I had for a month before moving to Minets Brokers.
- Minets gave me a hand-me-down blue General Motors Chevair Automatic.
- Next car from Minets was a cream Opel Kadet 1300 collected from Kroonstad in the Free State. I scaled down and used the money for trip to Scotland. Vehicle got stolen from Cinema complex in Alberton when family went to see Superman.
- My boss, Paul Travers at Minets, was selling his 4-year-old Mercedes Benz 200E Silver Blue with 100.000 kms on the clock. Within a year

the drive shaft went, so much for reliability. My client's wife bought a VW Kombi Caravelle but did not enjoy, too big. I grabbed it and did over 400.000 kms selling it decades later.

- I moved jobs and set up home at the coast, Durban/Amanzimtoti. Karin my daughter, after obtaining her degree as a Dietician, set up her little business. However, decided to head off to the UK and I bought her little red VW Chico 1300 which I used for business. Did over 300.000 kms and was stolen from the golf driving range in Hillcrest Durban. Very disappointed, a great vehicle.

- Bought an old Isuzu 4x4 from golfing friend and drove for many years. Bit of a rust bucket but did the job and travelled/camped for a few years. This vehicle was also stolen outside a broker's office in Pinetown

- Heard from a broker/Pat Smythe that his son was going to the UK. I bought a gun metal Hyundai Getz. The car was put through a roadworthy and the next day I collected. Then the following day went off on holiday and the engine blew as the radiator cap had not been put back properly during its service. Fixed up at cost and sold months later when I left SA to reside in the UK.

SNIPPITS AND LETTERS BETWEEN ME AND MY DAD

14/1/68 Flying to new job in Johannesburg SA. Flight stopped at Frankfort, Las Palmas plus few other places before arriving in Jhb. Everything is beautiful, homes, bungalows, swimming pools. Lots of cars. 2 chaps from Eagle Star met me and showed me around. All my hotel expenses paid for at the New Library Hotel 3 weeks. Chaps think I will have difficulty joining a golf club. Everything is so green. Eagle Star 500 people, gigantic office, near tallest buildings in SA being built, Carlton Hotel and Standard Bank building. Think you would love to stay here.

Then no trace of letters until 1978.

14/6/78 Parcel received - Karin and Rob presents. Karin knows parcel from you. Boots for Karin. Likes nursery school, brings lots of paintings. Rob getting bigger and spitting image of my dad.

Loved cars and his bottle before sleeping. I painted outside of house with a cement-based paint. Was going to visit UK but moved jobs Enthovens to Minets, Dorbyl account, was handpicked. My car a second hand blue Chevair Automatic. Previous car at Enthovens-Opal Kadet. Now getting R1400 as against R900. Sent R50 per month to parents. Got to Match Play Final at Wanderers.

22/1/79 All family to visit UK 23/5/79 to 29/6/79

31/7/79 Letter from Paul Travers main board director at Minets thanking me for work done on Dorbyl. Just joined Minets.

27/10/79 First Pools win third place £25 for my Dad. Holiday Yugoslavia, 5 weeks good weather for our visit. Merle pregnant with Gordon.

1/1/81 Dad and Mum in Minorca. Karin swimming and hair permed. Rob in hospital 7th time in 14 months. Bambi expecting pups. Karin and Rob got bicycles for Xmas. Going to North coast, Umhlanga Rocks Hotel, Natal.

5/2/81 On 26/2/81 parents move council house from 2 Glen View to 2 Sidehead Road, Stonehouse. 33 years of stuff from 5 apartment to 3 apartment. Mum's (Prudence) clothes to Salvation Army. Dad does wallpapering and painting. Merle's dad, Andries, passes away from cancer and his son Andre marries the following week.

10/10/81 More birthday money. Rob bought a robot and clothes, I bought shirts. Karin doing modern dancing, also Miss Piggy at school. Took kids to Sun City. Painted garage doors.

28/4/82 Just returned from 10 days at Port Alfred Eastern Cape, staying at Chairman's holiday home, Kit Keey Minets. Rob caught chicken pox then Karin, Gordon. Cabin cruise up Kowie River, took food spent whole day on river. Took fishing rod caught 2 small ones. Boat had powerful motor and we did a bit of racing. Hit 2 sand banks. Visited Grahamstown, Pig & Whistle. 2 games of golf at Royal Port Alfred, won a gallon of whiskey in sweep after drawing my own number. Next morning spoke into the great white telephone. Drive home was 13 hours. Going to new holiday place Marina Beach, Natal south coast. Won free ticket worth R150 to watch World title opening-fight at Ellis Park Stadium in Jhb. Minets have a private suite at Ellis Park, 22 people. They also bought new office building nearby worth R6M. Went to Sun City, Jonny Miller won R500.000.

2/10/82 More birthday money. Kids opened own savings accounts. We had snow at 80 Vista Drive Glenvista Jhb, photo to parents. Jogging in morning for 10 minutes get to work by 7 am. Planted seeds. Karin had scarlet fever. Rob riding Karin's bike, Karin new bike for Xmas. Liza Minnelli at Sun City. Kids getting spoilt, dog, goldfish, budgie we caught in the garden.

10/10/83 Cannot phone from Minets new office in Doornfontien, Jhb as it has a recording system. New building next to Ellis Park swimming pool, which I use. Drought - using watering cans for garden. Started building new home Kurt Ave Glenvista Ext 3, Jhb. Old home 200 sqm, new one 380 sq meters. Got another car Toyota Cressida R15.000. Rob gets new BMX. Family went to see Elton John at Sun City. Second year at Marina Beach come Xmas.

10/1/84 Mum and Dad been on holiday to Spain. Their Xmas money for the kids arrived and they bought posters for their bedrooms Gordon - Superman, Robert - Porsche, Karin - Ballet Dancer. Also, Karin got a Polaroid instamatic camera, Gordon a remote-controlled car, Rob, a remote-controlled boat. Went to Marina Beach Hotel, Natal South Coast for Xmas and New Year. Merle made fancy dress out of crinkle paper. Gordon Superman, Rob Robin Hood, Karin Fairy, Merle - Bunny Girl, me - Scotsman and I won second prize. Best holiday for years and first time away from home over Xmas - New Year. Played golf at the Wild Coast designed by Bobby Jones Jnr. Rob in hospital new gromits in ears. Swimming a problem. Rob diving for silver coins in hotel pool and did well. Father Xmas arrived aka Peter Chamberlain the owner, sweets, balloons. Expensive taking family of 5 to hotel. First house at 80 Glenvista Drive up for sale and foundations being dug at Kurt Ave Glenvista Ext 3 lots of rock. Gordon learnt to swim on holiday with arm bands. Rob and Karin doing well at school, received certificates for their achievements and Karin did well at her ballet exams. Been jogging and skipping for 10 minutes apiece. Had a beard and shaved it off, look 10 years younger. Told my parents if I got my price on sale of home will fly them over.

2/8/84 Asked Minets if I can trade in 30 days leave for 2 air tickets for my parents to fly over come Xmas/New Year 4/12 – 11/1. Already booked into Cape Town for 5 days. Travel down by train. Two-day bus trip while in C/T. Sightseeing tour around Cape Point plus bus tour around wine farms 8 hours, included lunch and as much wine as you can drink. Also booked into Marina Beach Hotel for Xmas and New Year. Took my dad to Nedbank Million Dollar golf tournament at Sun City. Told Mum lots of new shops since last visit. They will see new home Kurt Ave. Once again like Glenvista no garden established. New home looking good but have leave rented house by Sept. Karin named new puppy Puddles, guess why. Interest rates now 25%. Speed limit 100 to 120klm. Told Mum that I will let her choose something from the Jhb Gold Mine Museum/Jewellery shop when she comes.

11/2/85 James Cowper and wife Margaret in Devon but Mag not happy move back to Scotland. Uncle James having health tests.

19/7/85 Dad and Mum on holiday in Blackpool. Gordon gromets done. Offered to buy my dad's council home, did not agree.

28/3/85 Bus in Jhb went off road 42 kids drowned. Karin 10th in class. Rob good but poor marks for behaviour. Jogging at 5.30 in morning. Rob visits friend on BMX and dog savages his face 7 injections/stitches.

3/11/85 Dad and Mum on holiday again they love the sun. Trouble in SA becoming part of life. Got beaten at 22nd hole quarter final at Wanderers Golf Club. Putted like a blind man. Harold Henning won in USA and Gary Player turned 50. Sean Pieterse dancing at Sun City part of main troupe. Went to Victor Pieterse wedding.

26/2/86 My Dad lost 2 stones in weight. Got usual Xmas money from parents. Sent Dad slippers. Parents off on another holiday. Minets made me full director on Transvaal board got 25% pay increase. Karin gone on school camp and got a small white Maltese Poodle called Clyde. Moving to new house Kurt Ave in June. Joined Glenvista Golf Club. Gordon's birthday, kids coming around from his school class to watch videos, cakes, devour a Mr T ice cream cake – A Team

7/6/87 Visited Gold Reef City Jhb with family. Still doing kids' soccer. Golf at Palaborwa next to Kruger Park with hippos in some of the water holes.

23/10/87 Just returned from UK business trip, brought radio-controlled cars for boys. Karin decided to do a school project on Edinburgh. Gordon won trophy at soccer for most valuable player. Brought some of my dad's homemade jams/jellies home. Merle started part time job.

3/1/88 Dad and Mum returned from Spain. Visited Kimberly hole with family.

20/2/88 Driving second-hand Merc 200 bought from my boss Paul

Travers Minets; 4 years old. Take kids to nearby golf driving range, Karin left-handed.

1/4/88 Dad slipped and broke a few ribs. Dad's golf club subs £200. I am lucky Minets pays subs for Glenvista and Wanderers golf clubs. Went to Parktown hospital for cancer operations re cancer/testicle removed. Rob first in class.

31/5/88 Recovery from cancer operations went to Eastern Transvaal. Karin's drawing of Kippersol tree won prize at school. Dropping kids off at school. Going to Rock and Roll party. Gordon playing good soccer. Bought second hand computer from Minets. Need a loan.

10/7/88 Karin on 5-day trip to Eastern Transvaal with 20 school friends. Other new homes being built near to us.

2/10/88 Require blood tests every 3 months for next 3 years. My Mum had a stroke. Rob's teeth straightened R3675, most under Med Aid. Karin won second prize at flower arrangement competition at school. Also, in final of school's tennis doubles. All kids go for tennis lessons at Glenvista Country Club 5 minutes from home. Photos sent to parents of garden development Kurt Ave. My under 10 soccer team Arsenal played 14 games only lost 2, 4th in league. Mum recovering from stroke.

26/11/88 Won 1st Minets pairs golf 2&1. Karins dog Clyde went down with dysentery recovered at vets after few days. Rob did well at tennis. Fultem Allem won at Sun City. Next year 10th anniversary of Nedbank Million-Dollar Golf Tournament. First prize now 2 million Dollars.

4/2/89 Mum stopped drinking and smoking, taking pills for her heart condition. Runner up at Wanderers Medal final, 82 and 82 less 10 handicap. If I could only putt. Sold home at Kurt Ave Glenvista, Jhb - lost money.

1/5/89 Karin earning pocket money waitering. Bought house at 41 Van Beek Ave Glenanda, Jhb. Rob still first at school. Painting window frames.

2/9/89 Rob into computer games. Spent 8 days at Nedbank holiday flat near Marina Beach Natal South Coast.

26/11/89 Rob/Gordon had crew cuts. Put in garden sprinkler system at new home.EMI Music golf weekend at Wild Coast, Natal on border with Transkei.

1/2/90 Robert at High School.

20/4/90 Sold Merc bought V/W Kombi. Hit South Coast kids now have surf boards. Karin working part time at Steak House. I won most consistent golfer at Wanderers.

1/7/90 Still coaching Arsenal kids league still unbeaten. Minets made me Deputy MD of one of Transvaal Divisions.

5/9/90 Parents always send Birthday/Xmas money for kids. Prudence, my Mum, on heart tablets. Going to Sun City Million Dollar, staying in tents at Pilanesberg Game Park. Sent another cheque home for pools etc. My golf handicap 8. Seeing on TV lots of golf, English football, Natal beat Northern Tvl in rugby Currie Cup final. Visited Elwin his son Lance going for Black belt, Duncan into tennis. At lunch times I swim at Ellis Park pool next to Minets offices.

5/1/91 Another 2 nights at Sun City. Gordon sucks his thumb when going to sleep. Minet management buyout. Rob averaging over 75% at school, received prize, Karin 72% average, Gordon also doing well. Bought table tennis board at Xmas. David Frost wins his second Million Dollar with 2 birdies to finish. Xmas at Elwin's home. Newsreels showing lots of snow storms in UK.

5/2/91 Gulf War on the go. Karin taking extra maths, science lessons. Have a computer at home and kids love it but I cannot adapt. April holiday camp with Elwin, has caravan, hired a tent, 3 people can sleep in Kombi, north of Durban on the Tugela River. Lance called up for army.

7/7/91 £ six to one against SA Rand. Sent some money home. Karin's Matric exams and later going to Germany on a student exchange.

29/8/91 Dad send me details of my small savings accounts. Mum fell out of bed and broke a toe

24/10/91 Rob size 12 shoes. Private tennis lessons for Gordon in Pinetown, lessons every Saturday morning. New job in Durban starts 1/11/91, bought fishing rod.

24/11/91 Karin going to University in Pietermaritzburg SA

22/12/91 Settling down in new job. Karin in Germany till mid-January trip cost around R7000. Gordon made a Prefect. Joined Mt Edgecombe Golf Course 2 eighteen-hole courses, north of Durban.

17/2/92 Karin stayed in Germany with 2 families. 1 family, she was 3 weeks alone, could not get out and about. No snow, no skiing. Went to Berlin wall and broke pieces of wall and brought home.

6/5/92 Attending rugby games at Kingsmead stadium home to Natal Rugby Union, still support Transvaal. Braais after games, very nice times.

9/8/92 Into new offices Concord Insurers, sea views. Staying in Amanzimtoti (Toti) a town half an hour away. Joined Toti running club, trained for Comrades marathon around the rugby fields but picked up a problem with my left knee, even after injections, this put an end to my running. Karin passed exams at Uni.

11/10/92 New Lost City golf course built next to Sun City with crocs in one of the water holes. Played the course once. Found snake in garage, green and I am afraid chopped it to pieces with spade but still wriggled. Concord/Cigna my employers now into mass marketing.

13/12/92 Sent cheque for £476,64 home for pressies Birthdays, Xmas, Fruit Aunt Nancy Janice and kids.

15/3/93 Gordon now 13. My parents send money for a cricket bat. West Indies/Pakistan just had tours to SA. Alain Prost wins SA Grand Prix. Swimming at 6 am before work in Toti tidal pool on the beach, too early for kids. Sea water, filter plant, warm water. Great way to start the day, 47 years of age now. Told my dad to tell guys at Strathaven Golf course that I am coming for a visit.

23/5/93 My dad, Robert, bought a new car Skoda. Rob and I going to Scotland 3/7 to 30/7. Dad redecorating. Asked my dad if he ever wanted to buy council house during Thatcher's reign at discounted price. He being true socialite would want the house to be handed on to next in line for council house. My Mum was a Tory and would have bought but no say in the matter. Drew money from my UK savings account plus what I had for trip. Robert made Captain of school tennis team. Gordon playing rugby for Kingsway school, still to lose and unlikely to beat Kuswag the Afrikaans section of the school. Have been travelling to the school games. Karin sitting more exams at Uni. Baby Jake took world title from Scotsman, a great fight. Teased my dad by saying I will bring SA flag as a gift plus some nice SA Brandy - Klipdrift. Once a year Highland game gathering in Toti, pipe bands, highland dancing judged, stalls, food - a great day and very busy.

1/9/93 Now back in SA, eating like a horse, Janice my sister spoilt us. Told Dad that his jellies/jams enjoyed by everyone. Karin visited over last 2 weekends, doing well and working hard. Thanked my Mum and Dad for spending money whilst with them. Driving to Richards Bay, a large coal terminal up the North coast, 2-hour drive. Quoting on Water Board currently placed with Lloyds. Family going for 1 week to Kruger Park Lodge - 8 hours driving plus natural hot springs. House bond interest rate 16.5%. Still nagging my dad to buy council house and would help him. Dad's garden doing well.

30/11/93 Mums pacemaker to be changed.

12/12/93 Dad attends Captains' Diner at Strathaven Golf Course as a past Captain.

29/1/94 Sent necklace to Mum. Her legs were not strong depressing to hear. Rob and Gordon join Umbogontwini Country Club owned by A.E.C.I. Pool, golf, tennis, restaurant etc in Toti. Family spent time at Kruger Park Lodge Eastern Transvaal right next to entrance gate to Kruger Park. Lodge had hippo pool/river with 9-hole golf course next to course. Also visited Pilgrims' Rest, an old, gold mining town. Kids bought clothes from Xmas money sent by Granny and Grandpa Cook. Holiday at Bakubung Lodge next to Sun City. Played golf at new Lost City Golf course, R100 plus cart/competition R120. At pro shop met Geoff Boycott, shook hands, asked if he wanted to join me but was waiting for his lady friend. Nick Price wins Nedbank Million Dollar. Dad says still got £1500 in UK bank a/c.

Missing letters so jump from 94 to 97.

30/7/96 I'm almost 50, my Mum can't walk, Dad slowing down.

1/11/96 Dad says Strathaven Golf Club rebuilt £1m and now £25 for round of golf. Mum still in wheel chair. She went to pantomime organised by hospital - mum's been in hospital for 3 years following stroke in Spain and tripping in garden to avoid bee, breaking her hip.

7/12/96 Aunt Netta had knee operation.

5/3/97 Spent 2 days in London business trip took Robert

3/6/97 Karin opens business in Toti Dietician before eventually heading to the UK.

27/8/97 Alan my sister Janice's son, gets job working on space helmets and the like.

23/10/97 Dad has prostrate problem on medication for 2 years. £10.000 of stock stolen from golf shop at Strathaven Golf Club

20/2/98 Karin and Brad Stransky went to Edinburgh for New Year

25/10/99. Americans pull out of SA; Cigna close Durban office and I work from home and form Stonehouse Insurance Consultants AKA St Pauls Insurers.

23/5/20 Dad has had his Skoda from 1992 to 2000, 9000 miles. Matt McCrorie professional at Strathaven has cancer.

No further letters traced/found.

MISCELLANOUS

On a number of occasions, watched Glasgow Rangers at Ibrox stadium. Before my 60th birthday took Robert, Karin, Gordon and Bernice to a game against Falkirk, 4-nil to the Gers.

My dad took me on a tour round Ibrox, went through the Trophy Room with all its history, photos, Cups and 2-inch protestant blue piled carpets. Photos were taken and we sat in the dugout next to the playing surface which was concaved to allow the rain water to run to the sides. Almost rose 2 feet to middle of ground. The playing surface was very large and the lining out of the playing surface could vary in size depending on which teams they faced. Under the terrace was an indoor training area/100 yards long, used to kick the ball around etc before a match especially when pouring with rain.

When I was a youngster my uncle Gavin Cowper/news reporter all his life for the Glasgow Herald, took me to a game between Rangers and Celtic on New Year's Day and it was choc a block. The streets were like flowing water of blue and white scarves/tops on the one side and a sea of green and white on the other. It was advisable not to wear any colours but for some reason we ended up in the Celtic end. Very little seating and majority of the crowds crammed behind each other like sardines. I do remember a guy behind me pissing into his empty can of beer and this hot feeling down the back of my trouser legs. These New Year Day games were eventually banned due to the friction between the sects. The same happened to the annual England versus Scotland games held alternatively at Hampden Park and Wembley. Sad but fans were getting out of hand, fights and even killings.

In SA I had a friend, Billy MacIntosh a good Catholic boy, we played together for S A Eagle Insurers. We happened to be both travelling back to Scotland to see family and decided to meet up in Glasgow. Billy invited me to the Celtic social club inside Parkhead, Celtics ground. So, we had lunch and I kept the menu with the Celtic colours and emblem as souvenirs.

My dad took me when I was around 13/14 to watch Hibernian versus Hearts of Midlothian at Hibs ground Easter Road in Edinburgh. I remember it was an opening game of the season and was a bright beautiful day. This around 1959.

Rangers had a great team in the sixties and although I cannot remember my kids' birthdays the team was:- Niven-goalie, Bobby Shearer-right back, Eric Caldow-left back, Harold Davies-right half, Pat McKinnon-centre half, Jim Baxter-left half, Alex Scott-right wing, Ian MacMillian-inside right, Jimmy Millar-centre forward, Ralphy Brand-inside left, Davy Wilson-outside left.

Ibrox established 1887, biggest crowd 1939 against Celtic 118567. Hampden Park largest crowd against England 1937,149415. In the bygone years most of the crowds stood and through the decades, grounds got reduced with seating introduced more safety as they had crowd disasters/panics where supporters were trampled to death.

In 2019 did a guided tour round Liverpool's Anfield, all very interesting with 5/6 European Cup trophies on show. As a youngster I became a Man Utd supporter after their Munich air disaster. They gained a lot of support at that time. United's famous managers were the 2 Scots Matt Busby and Alex Ferguson. Liverpool's Scots managers were Bob Paisley, Bill Shankly, Kenny Dalglish.

Climbed the 246 steps at William Wallace Tower in Stirling.

Attended Sun Cities Nedbank Million Dollar golf tournament many times, got on the heels of Sergia Garcia in his run in on last round to win one year. Saw many star golfers too many to list. On TV watched Jonny Millar beat Seve Ballesteros in a play off after 4 rounds. Millar won at the NINETH extra playoff hole. You don't get it much tenser than that.

The Lexington PGA was held for many years at my home golf club The Wanderers in Johannesburg, followed winners like Lee Trevino, Tom Weiskof, Hale Irwin all Americans.

Visited Durban Country Club during the SA Open, got a young kid to squeeze in and get my Paddington Bear floppy hat signed by Ernie Els.

When I arrived in SA the Chamber of Commerce organised flights to the deepest gold mine in SA in Welkom mine Free State by Douglas DC 10. Very claustrophobic.

During insurance survey stood on top of one of Eskom's Power Stations in SA, Matuba.

Been to the top of Blackpool's sea front Tower.

My dad bought me £25 of Ernie Premium Bonds in 1956, and in 64 years have not won a baw bee.

Been on train, not the Blue train, form Johannesburg to Cape town with my dad Robert and mum Prudence when they visited SA. My way to travel. Never been on a sea cruise.

When I lived in Stonehouse as a youngster had 2 stamp albums plus many envelopes full of extra stamps, got lots of these whilst spending time with my gran at the village post office. I collected from the old British colonial days before many Commonwealth countries became independent and changed their names. This collection was left with my mum/dad and lost trace off. Maybe my sister Janice looked after the collection so when I pass on, my kids must ask Janice if she has. Maybe a few Penny Blacks in that lot.

Played snooker/billiards on Joe Davis tables in village Town Hall facilities as a youngster. Decades later played at the posh Durban Country Club.

Made a tea trolley for my Mum during school wood work classes. Had 4 wheels, push handle, beautifully varnished. Had all the wood joints, mortise etc. A work of art if I may say so. It sat in the room at the council house where all the collection items were placed in glass cabinets etc. in the drawing room where no one ventured.

I need to add email from my mate Kingsley Fourie in Jhb/SA, nothing better than someone else blowing my trumpet for me, dated 17/5/2020.

"Hello Cookie - You never fail to surprise me! A footballer of note (goalie?), golfer (won the scratch knock- out at Wanderers) house and garden designer, great lover (in your youth) well maybe even today, insurance broker of note (clients loved you) and most surprising, to me that is," biographer". WOW !! next surprise, taking a Pilot's licence!!! (I would not be surprised). Obviously, I am pulling your leg a bit, but there is some truth to the above. I am quite envious as I have no outstanding talents – On the bench for the first rugby team, average cricketer (could bowl and bat a bit, but not good enough for the first team) average golfer, never played for first league team, although I was, and am, still a star at playing the nineteenth hole, as for being a great lover, the less said the better. As for being a "pen pal" I am useless at that, as I hate writing on the computer – but I love reading other people's mails (selfish I know).

Well, this is about all I can write at any one time, except to say that I am always thinking about the two of you and hope that you are both doing well. Please keep writing as I value our friendship greatly.

Regards K

P S We are both well."

Some items I wanted to frame and hang on a wall (besides family photos) were the original Prudential Endowment policy my Mum took out when I was born 17/8/1946 for one penny per week, the front page of a 1900 Times paper my dad had kept, and my Drunk/Reckless Driving Summons received in SA. Too old to bother now.

FAMILY TREE

Notes :– * The parents of Elizabeth (Betsy) Dykes were John Dykes (engine driver) and Jane Dykes nee Scott – GREAT - GREAT GRANDPARENTS. Betsy's occupation was given as a domestic servant. Both parents were probably born in Peeblesshire.

4

GAVIN COWPER = ELIZABETH (BETSY) DYKES *
b. 17.07.1859 in Carstairs   b. 04.04.1861 in Broughton, Peeblesshire
d. 09.02.1934 in Eastriggs   d. 19.05.1942 in Carlisle, Cumberland
married 9th December 1881 in Carstairs, Lanarkshire

5

JOHN COWPER b. 03.08.1883
GAVIN COWPER b.1885
JANE SCOTT COWPER b. 1887

JAMES EWING COWPER = JANET PRINGLE WILLIAMSON
b. 02.10.1889 in Caledonian Place, Motherwell   b. 11.02.1888 at 77 Back Street, Dalkeith, Midlothian
d. 12.10.1944 in the Glasgow Royal Infirmary   d. 08.08.1972 in Cleland Hospital, Lanarkshire
married 2nd July 1915 in St Michael's Church, Stanwix, Carlisle, Cumberland

6

GAVIN DYKES = NANCY ISOBEL COWPER GULLIVER
b. 11.06.1916 in   b. 28.02.1918 in
35 Crummock St., Carlisle   Barlestone
d. 22.11.1994   d. 22.01.2001
Teneriffe, Canary Islands   Stonehouse
married 23.06.1945 in Barlestone, Leicestershire
not married

PRUDENCE HATLEY = ROBERT JAMES COWPER   S, W. COOK
b. 14.08.1918 in   b. 29.12.1917 in
Carlisle   Larkhall, Lanarkshire
d. 14.02.1997   d. 11.12.2007
Stonehouse   Hairmyers Hospital
married 04.02.1943 in Blythswood, Glasgow

JAMES DALLING = JANET HILL COWPER BARROWMAN
b. 29.07.1924 in   b. 17.09.1928 in
Cambuslang   Lesmahagow
d. 24.06.1980   d. 07.01.2011
Stonehouse   Stonehouse
married 18.05.1949 in Lesmahagow

7

GAVIN ERIC COWPER
b. 02.09.1947
Bellshill, Lanarkshire
d. 07.01.1973
not married

JOHN EWING COOK
b. 17.08.1946
Stonehouse ?
d. n/a
1st married on 13.05.1972 in St Ninian's Stonehouse to MERLE VORSTER
2nd to BERNICE on 19.04.2013 in Johannesburg

JANICE WILLIAMSON COOK
b. 05.04.1950
Stonehouse
d. n/a
married 04.09.1970 in St Ninian's

JOHN (IAN) BROWNLIE
b. 17.03.1948 in Hamilton

JAMES EWING COWPER
b. 24.12.51
Hamilton
d. n/a
= MARGARET STEWART WATT
b. 11.05.1954
Strathaven
d. n/a
married 07.04. 1973 in St Ninian's Church, Stonehouse Lanarkshire

8

KARIN COOK b. 30.05.1974 in Johannesburg
ROBERT COOK b. 21.09.1976 in Johannesburgh
GORDON COOK b. 09.03.1980 in Johannes burgh

ALAN BROWNLIE b, 17.12.1976 in Lanark
not married
LAUREN BROWNLIE b. 17.07.1979

RICHARD NIEUWENHUYS b. 26.05.1980 in Nottingham
married 25.05.2012 in Santa Barbara, U.S.A.

YVONNE CATHERINE COWPER b. 30.11.1976 Dumfries
1st married in 06.06.98 to MARK WALDIE
2nd in 24.03.2013 to STEPHEN KENNEDY
b. 09.12.69 in Edinburgh

LYNNE MARGARET COWPER b. 18.02.1979 Dumfries
not married

9

ISLA FOX NIEUWENHUYS b. 24.11.2012 in Kirkcaldy, Fife

EMMA MARGARET WALDIE b. 27.12.2000 in Livingstt
LISA IRENE WALDIE b. 21.08.2003 in Livingstt

Compiled from information received from
JAMES EWING COWPER on 22nd February 2016
FRANCESCA BAILLIE on 5th April 2016
by JOHN COWPER on 28th February 2016 ~ rev. 16th April 2016

5

WILLIAM DYKES COWPER = MARY ORR SYME
b. 17.06.1891 in Caledonian Road, Motherwell   b. 1890
d. 1969 in Greenock   d. not known
married 12th June 1915 in Greenock

6

JOHN SYME COWPER
b. 1918
d. 1984
in Greenock age 66
married
ELIZABETH PATON MILLER HOLMES
in Greenock in 1943

LILLEY SINCLAIR COWPER
b. 1920
d. 1985
in Greenock age 64
not married

JOHN RENNIE HOLMES COWPER
b. 1949
Greenock
Renfrewshire
married
ANDREWINA SCOTT
in Greenock in 1971
second marriage to
ANNIE ROBINSON
HILL MARSHAL
in Greenock in 1986
(no children)

ELIZABETH HOLMES COWPER
b. 1947
Gourock
Renfrewshire
married
KEITH HASLAM
in Greenock in 1991

WILLIAM COWPER
b. 1945 (deceased)
in Gourock
Renfrewshire
married
IRENE PORTER b. 1943
in Greenock on 13th January 1967

KEITH HASLAM
b.

CRAIG COWPER
b.

LINDA COWPER
b.
(married)

7

CATHERINE ANNE = WILLIAM RODGER
BARROWMAN COWPER   BLACK
b. 24.06.1953   b. 03.03.1961
Stonehouse, Lanarkshire   Larkhall, Lanarkshire
d. n/a   d. 09.05.2007
married 04.08.1986 in St Ninian's Church, Stonehouse

8

WILLIAM DYKES COWPER
b.06.05.1967 in Greenock
d. 2002 in Greenock age 34
married 27.04.1991 in St John's Church, Greenock
ANASTASIA BERNADETTE AGNES WILLIAMS
b. 22.12.1968 in Greenock

Revised -- 7th April 2016 - information received from FRANCESCA BAILLIE
30th April 2016 - information received from JAMES EWING COWPER

Curriculum Vitae of John Cook

Date of Birth: 17th August 1946

Education
9 O-Level passes UK
ACII UK Certificate

Interests
Keeping fit and healthy by enjoying the gym
Swimming and walking
Playing lots of golf

EXPERIENCE

I had 54 years in the insurance industry and believed in the principles of make it happen/service second to none and the KISS principal, Keep It Simple Stupid.

2010 – 2017 [Current]
Frontline Underwriters (Pty) Ltd
Business Development Consultant

- Responsible for developing new agencies/business for the company, including regular visits and preparation of quotations on Commercial/Personal lines
- The work involved travelling to Brokers in Richards Bay, Durban, Pietermaritzburg, South Coast and Upper Highway

2002 – 2009
Admiral/SHA/Corporate-Sure
Regional Representative/Marketing Manager

- Responsible for retaining/servicing/new business and other specifics such as corrective action, implementing a reconstruction of the company's clients' loss ratios/Corporate-Sure

- Specifically, I compiled a guideline booklet process for management and staff to follow via the networking system in place. The company's whole client base was overhauled over a period of six months, enabling General Management to review the loss ratios of the clients to a respectable level/Corporate-Sure

1999-2002
St Paul Insurers, Durban, RSA
Regional Representative

- Acting as representative, working from home, Policy documents/Claims, were processed by head office in Johannesburg
- Responsible for retaining existing business and developing new business with broking fraternity in KwaZulu-Natal province
- St Paul, USA sold their interests in RSA/Lesotho/Botswana

1992 – 1999
Cigna Insurers, Durban, RSA
Branch Manager

- Responsible for retaining/service/new business in KZN area
- Managed 14 support staff
- Cigna worldwide, short term, was purchased by Ace – closed operations in RSA

1979-1992

J H Minet Brokers, Johannesburg, RSA

Regional Director/Profit Centre Head/Quality Standards Manager

- Responsible for retaining/servicing/new business of blue chip/public companies
- Profit Centre Head with 10 support staff
- Ongoing supervision/training of staff/Account Executives
- Offered Branch Manager position by Cigna Insurers

1971 – 1979

Robert Enthoven/Willis Brokers, Johannesburg, RSA

Account Handler

- Profit Centre, responsible for retaining/servicing commercial accounts.
- Offered a position with International Broker, Minet re blue chip accounts.

1969 - 1971

Stenhouse Brokers, Johannesburg, RSA

Account Handler

- Assistant to Account Handler on commercial accounts
- Offered better prospects/experience with Enthoven/Willis

1967 – 1969

S A Eagle Insurers, Johannesburg. RSA

Clerk

- Various clerical duties in Fire/Accident/Motor Departments
- Decided to venture into broking and joined Stenhouse Brokers

1964 – 1967

Eagle Star Insurers, Hamilton, U.K.

Clerk

- General clerical duties
- Transferred to Johannesburg, RSA

JOHN

75 years ago, today, you were born
Keeping Mum busy, from dusk 'til dawn
Cute, cuddly, a little baby boy
Your family happy & full of joy

Joined Boys Brigade, discipline & rule
100% attendance, Sunday School
Shillings and pennies on a dawn paper round
Peddling in freezing weather, not quite a pound

When the Busby Boys were lost in February '58
You supported Manchester United from that date
Your achievements in insurance, your determination to qualify
You grew wings in your life and chose to fly

The ups, the downs, the errors & choices
The learning curves, the different voices
Perseverance and determination you did not lack
Once going forward, there was no turning back

You built beautiful homes, decorated others too
Providing for your family, as the numbers grew
Rotating credit cards, to stay above water
The university fees for two sons & a daughter

You can take a bow and the accolades
Supporting your family, in buckets and spades
Your fight with cancer, the paralysing fear
Of going through that : clap, clap, 'hear', ' hear'

The beers, the wine, the bottles of whiskey
The crazy drives home, the danger - so risky
Having an escort to bring you back - sooo bad
You must have had a guardian Angel, my lad

You stopped all that until one night for quite a while
But hey they caught you - having been out on the tile
Then followed anxiety and worry, all the fears
A lesson learnt, one would think, "Johnnie" 2 beers

From where you came, to where you are
From family, friends and from afar
Life dealt you a special hand, don't hide
Look back at what you've done with pride

The travels you still hope to do, by His grace
You'll be strong and stay in this space
A great life and good ride's been had
You've earned your stripes, my Scottish lad

17 August 2021

Poem by Bernice Cook

KURT AVENUE

80, Vista Drive, Glenvista, Johannesborg, SA
April 1974

Vista Drive, April 1984

John Ewing Cook

Born 17 August 1946

Photo at the age of 43

Names of Colleagues over my 50 years in the Insurance Industry

Believe it or not, I can look at any name and I get a flash back of that person. I am not listing these names for the sake of it as a filler. I knew these people as friends over many years. When I am in my rocking chair, I will glance at this list and reminisce with memories of bygone times.

Eagle Star Insurance Co Ltd - Hamilton, Scotland

Gordon Patterson, Gordon Clark, Ann Bishop, Margaret Ingils, Alex MacDonald, Mr Dodds, Mr Peebles, Brokers - Solly McNiven, W S Moreland, D W Stedman, Lewis Wotherspoon

Eagle Star Insurance Co Ltd - Johannesburg, South Africa

Fred Haslett, Hugh White, Bill Ferguson, Brian Wilkinson, Woolliscroft, Le Cordia, Basil Clark, Frank Dey, Les Page-Shippe, Mrs Wigsal, Agrippa, Morag Brewer, Jim Murray, Colin Shewring, Joe Hanlon, Billy McIntosh, Pat Cannavan

Stenhouse Insurance Brokers - Johannesburg, South Africa

Adolf James, Bernie James, John McInnes, Mrs Peacock, Renette Lessing, Roger Strickland, Trevor Roshat, Trevor Dissel, Angus Georgeson, Jim Cumming, Dave Bezer , Maureen

Robert Enthoven Brokers - Johannesburg, South Africa

Robert (Bob) Enthoven, Patrick Enthoven, Dick Enthoven, Paul Fauche, Trevor Dissel, Kingsley Fourie, Alan Thomas, David Way, Richard Tot Barberich the 3rd, Trevor Surgeon, Angela Johnston, Leo Neeleman, Peter Needham, Anthea Duigen, Faye, Don Stange, Piere Steiner, Jan De Jong,

J H Minet Brokers - Johannesburg, South Africa

Margie Allison, Rob Ansell, Barbara Ansell, Barbara Antal, Ian Baxter, Lyle Beckett, Jimmy Binos, Rosa Bisschoff, Jacqui Blom, Len Bornman, Ian Boyd-Grey, Val Bruno, David Brunt, Danny Buitendag, Neil Burton, Finlay Campbell, Frans Campher, Ken Catton, Richard Cave, Ian Cessford, Molly Charles, Joan Chernotsky, Roy Cheshire, Lee Clark, Rod Copestake, Allan Crighton, William Croxton, Peter Darke, Ron Davidson, Steve De Bore, Sonja Jones, Mary Dearham,

Murray Dott, Peter Edmunson, Joan Espie, Paul Fauche, Wayne Ford, John Francis, Frank Gardiner, Dennis Geldart, Gavin George, Stuart Gibbs, Jun Gibson, Denis Goodwin, Gail Harmer, David Harpur, Trevor Hebden, Louise Hendrie, Elizabeth Higginson, Dave Hill, Geoff Hitzeroth, Alex Holmes, Jack Huggett, Pat Hunter, Malcolm Hutton, Mary Jack, Jacky Juby, Kit Keey, Sue Kelynack, Kevin Kennedy, Wally Krambeck, Ken Lancaster, Peter Latham, Peter Laurence, Francois Le Roux, Bill Lewis, Pam Lewis, Dave Marais, Ron McCreadie, Bill Melville, Chummy Monks, Eric Oxford, Elaine Payne, Rod Pearson, John Pollitt, Graham Pooley, Tom Rae, Mike Robson, Jim Ross, Jeff Sauls, Guy Scott, Ken Seago, Colin Shewring, Shlom Bazil, Dennis Simmons, Chris Solomon, Ron Sourgen, Shelly Spratt, Chris Stockton, Clive Stone, Linda Stroebel, Jimmy Supra, Jock Sutherland, Denis Ternent, Gavin Thompson, George Thornton, Henry Tours, Paul Travers, Piere Van Blommestein, Tom Van Der Merwe, Betty Van Geelen, Lettie Coetzee, Felicity Vere – Russell, Peter Vermaak, Colin Walton, Tony Weber, Mike Wolstenholm, Nigel Wrench, Debbie Coetzee, Bobby Hunter, Ian Reynolds, Grant Teasdale, Alan Cook, Billy Dewar, Geoff Jones, Tim Tucker.

Cigna Ins Co Ltd - Durban South Africa

Pat Healy, Paddy Murray, Liela Driver, Jimmy Smart, John Merret, Maureen Pillay, Dennis Wilson. Pat Blair

The St Paul Ins Co Ltd - Durban, South Africa

Pat Cochrane, Barbara Du Toit, Jose Fonseca, Julie Fredericks, Jenny Jooste, Peter Muller, Willie Van Aswegen, Chris Wakeham, Jenny Watkins, Kay Wilkinson.

Corporate Sure, Admiral, SHA, Underwriting Managers - Umhlanga Rocks, Durban South Africa

Gordon Campbell, Zoe Todd, Nevash Green, Bruce Gibson, Deena Govender, Brian Govender,

Frontline Underwriters Pty Ltd - Umhlanga Rocks, Durban South Africa

Ashwin Jagnath, Beatrice, Cindy Naidoo/Williams, Maria Van Der Merwe/Williams, Mike Nichols, Pamela Griffiths, Naomi du Plessis, Nelson Nair, Rizwana, Sandra Bramdeo, Taffy Chikanya, Zelda, Paul Meyers, Tarrtn Green, Zelda Aspeling-Botha, Siphiwe, Kuraysha Saib.

Brokers – Kwa Zulu Natal

Bay Union – Dave/Peter Pierce, Chis Treadwell, Hilton Deihl, Ian Zandells. Reid Raetzer – Mike Raetzer, Hylton Reid, Graham Kelly. Schofield – Andy Coughtrie, Graham Day. B Sure – Laurence Chelin, Craig Lithgow, John Cheshire, Nolene, Megan. Nanni – Helen King, Com Risk – Jenny Bishop. HTI – Hamish Thorpe, John Bennett. L A Metcalf – Larry/Glenn. Taylor – Peter Taylor. Absa – Bryant Du Randt, Gary Holland. I J Duncan – Ian Duncan, Peter Borley. Cocks – Mike Cocks. Kimber – Ron/Simon Kimber. Renaissance – Heaton brothers Tom/Mathew/Gale. Cooke Fuller – Matt Gallagher, James Goble, Colleen Saunders, Alan Henderson, Greg Horne. Holburn – Rob Burns, Billy Neethling, George Parker, Sharon Walsh. Leigh – Steven Leigh. Royal – Barry Pringle/Moodley. Scottfin – Garth Reich. Monitor – Murray Wright. RWS – Ray Wright, Marco Passero, Keith Hope, Martin Humphries. Smythe – Rob/Pat/Craig, Rob Jones, Mike Wolstenholme,Ladies.Forbes – Kerry Warick-Oliver. Firstlink – Jan De Wet, oy Orsmond. M R Woollam – Mike. Hawkins – Richard. Indwe – Ynis Moolla, Angela. Deon Schoemann. Alexforbes – Richard Allen, Indian lady. Curnow – Mervin/Craig, Rob Hartley, Andy Chance, Sharon Skeen. Hibiscus – Barry Elliott. Hypersure – Peter Brown. Azure – Gary/Bob Erasmus. Alexforbes – Jeff Jones, Duncan Osborne, Reggie Ganghia, Kogie Moodley, Paul Brand, Selvan Naiker, Geoff Colemann, Jimmy Wilken. Glenrans – Bruce Dixie, Robin Moss, Bert Cheasby, Gill Sutherland, Allan Mc Lean. Aon – Martin Grove, Graham Caulfield. Leading Egge – Craig Simpson. Hawkeye – James Hawksworth. Ibis – Dave Neave. Tuttle – Dennis/Mark Tuttle. Compendium – Rowan Jones, Dave O,Conner, Simon Stockton,Willie Menkies, Dave Pickford, Sharo O,Conner. 4 Square – Gladys Wilford, Paul Lewis, Hugh White. Holland – Dave Holland, Lionel Wybrow, Ian McCullough. Idra – Yvonne Foot, Mike Hubbard, Brian Lowe. Marsh – Peter Van Heerden. McCabe – Colin McCabe, Ingrid DeVillers. Ins Centre – Terry Silver. Some other names that come to mind, Dave Cox, Andrew Packman, Neil Reinecke, Ken Naidoo, Steve Hopcroft, Barry Lemmon, Wayne Griffiths, Hugh Honey, Ian Reekie, Piet Pienaar, Antony Wright, Jim Carmody, Dean Alborough, Malcom Irvine, Rory McDonogh, Dave Tennant, Victor Vaz, Marlene/Dave Powell, Lynn Wicht, Neville Royappen, Blake Shepard, Jim McDonald, Garth

Matthews, Georgie Graham, George Dowling, George Rainair, Norrie McConochie, David Laing, Fred Geyer, Chris Colman, Haig McLaren, Brian Thompson, Jim Strang, Dave Keeling, Carl Van Der Merwe, Denis Watkins, Ian Georgeson, Ian Brown, Bill Sabido, Pushpa Naidoo, Russell Lawson, Dave Deeble, Joel Lauretet, Hans Lind, Darren Harrison, David Karon, Steve Cant, Cal Masterten-Smith, Peter Sherliker.

BV - #0016 - 111223 - C6 - 228/152/15 - PB - 9781913675356 - Matt Lamination